William H.

VOICES FROM
THE WILDERNESS

VOICES
FROM THE
WILDERNESS

THE FRONTIERSMAN'S

OWN STORY

EDITED, WITH INTRODUCTIONS, BY
Thomas Froncek

McGRAW-HILL BOOK COMPANY
New York   St. Louis   San Francisco   Düsseldorf
Mexico   Toronto

Designed by Stanley Drate

VOICES FROM THE WILDERNESS

123456789BPBP79876543

Library of Congress Cataloging in Publication Data

Froncek, Thomas, comp.
  Voices from the wilderness.

    1. Pioneers—United States. 2. Frontier and pioneer
life—United States. I. Title.
E176.F82   973'.0992 [B]   73-9901
ISBN 0-07-022507-9

For Ellen,
who shares
the adventure

Contents

INTRODUCTION:

Between Two Worlds

Americans have been drawn toward wilderness from the start, drawn from the bustle of towns and farm's dull routine, drawn toward something vaguely called "freedom" and "adventure," drawn by a chance for new beginnings. Those that made the journey, the frontiersmen, the men of the wilderness, shaped America's image of itself, providing an ideal and a myth.

The man of the wilderness was the first distinctly American character to evolve outside the European mold. Restless and independent, abhorring the burdens and responsibilities of the settled life—rents, debts, taxes, wages, laws—he had struck out on his own for the wilderness, determined to govern his own life and to live as he pleased. He replaced his settler's coat and breeches, easily torn in the woods and many times patched, with a more practical suit of buckskins; and when his cobbled shoes wore through he adopted the Indian's moccasin. Neither farmer nor herdsman, he ate what the wilderness offered in abun-

dance: roots, herbs, berries, and game. But he learned that
the wilderness could be harsh as well as generous, that it
could destroy him with terrifying suddenness: a blizzard;
an arrow from an unseen foe; the long agony of starvation.
He learned that survival, although it was often enough a
matter of sheer luck, depended also on his own skill and
imagination and resilience. Gradually, more by instinct
than by study, he learned the wildnerness ways: learned
stealth and cunning; learned to see and hear and pick up
scents with the keen awareness of an animal; learned to
read the land and the weather; learned to tell by a broken
stick, or by the turning of the growing grass, who or what
had passed by, and how long ago. He learned, in other
words, what the Indian had always known but what the
European had long forgotten: he learned to live in his body
as well as his mind; he learned to live *with* the wild and not
against it.

Many of the frontiersmen represented in this volume,
sharing with the Indian a way of living so intimately linked
to their natural surroundings, often found that they had
more in common with the red man than with the white.

The frontiersman typically found himself spending
more time in the Indian villages than in the settlements of
his own people—whether as a captive, like James Smith
among the Delaware and John Tanner among the Ottawa,
or voluntarily, like James Beckwourth among the Crows
and Alexander Henry the Younger among the Ojibways.
Adopted, perhaps, by one of the tribes, he may have taken
an Indian name and an Indian wife, raised an Indian family, and soon may have been scarcely distinguished from an
Indian himself. If he was a trader, like Henry or Beckwourth, such an arrangement could be highly profitable,
giving him marked advantages over his competitors. But
even more important was the companionship to be obtained from a people of like habits and understanding.
Hence, the Indian and the frontiersman, though often an-
tagonists, also found themselves bound together by their
common experiences of life in the wilderness.

True, the frontiersman was often coarsened by his
primitive life as a hunter. One veteran of the Rocky Moun-

tain wilderness remarked that "It is easy to make a savage of a civilized man"; and, in the West, those who felt themselves being barbarized by their surroundings comforted themselves with the saying that "God holds no man responsible after he crosses the Missouri River." Yet it was also true that the frontiersman often maintained strong emotional and cultural ties with his own people and traditions, and often those ties seemed to grow stronger the farther he journeyed into the wild. In his dress and habits and way of life he may have been becoming more and more like an Indian; but the frontiersman who didn't carry a Bible in his pack often carried one in his head. Daniel Boone and his companions read *Gulliver's Travels* around their Kentucky campfires and did Swift the honor of naming a stream Lulbegrud's Creek. One old trapper recalled that, while waiting out a winter in the Rockies, he and his friends read from Byron, Shakespeare, and Scott, as well as the Bible, commentaries on the Scriptures, and various "small works in Geology, chemistry, and philosophy." Another Rocky Mountain veteran remembered that at the winter camps "Some of the better educated men, who had once known and loved books . . . recalled their favorite authors, and recited passages once treasured, now growing unfamiliar." Old Jim Bridger had lived in the Western wilderness so long that at one time, he said, he had not tasted bread for seventeen years; yet he loved hearing Shakespeare read aloud, and if he lost the thread of the story he would earnestly ask the reader to go back and start again. (Bridger decided, however, that Shakespeare must have had a "bad heart" and been "as devlish mean as a Sioux, to have written such scoundrelism" as the murder of the two princes in the Tower.)

On the other hand, the frontiersman's attachment to home and civilization could also turn into an arrogrant confidence in his own racial and cultural superiority, even though, or perhaps because, he himself may have been a misfit among his own people. There were may among them, for instance, whose hatred of Indians was pathological. Others, like Jim Beckwourth, were merely smug. Beckwourth spent seven years among the Crows, living as they lived, becoming a war chief, and, by his own account, often excelling them in numbers of enemies killed and scalps taken. Yet he could tell his biographer, without a trace of irony: "I found the Indian would be Indian still, in spite of my efforts to improve him."

But however much of civilization the frontiersman carried with them the wilderness inevitably left its mark upon them. Many found Indian life so congenial that they never returned to their own people. Hugh Glass, Bill Williams, and many others were killed: by Indians, grizzly bears, buffalo stampedes, rattlesnakes, floods, freezing weather, poison water, bad food, thirst, and starvation. Many simply set off from camp and were never heard from again. Others, having survived one disaster after another, were so broken in mind and body that they soon fell victim to madness or disease. John Colter, having saved his skin from the Blackfeet in his naked marathon run across the prairies, finally settled down on a farm only to die a short time later, apparently of jaundice.

Often, too, the frontiersmen discovered that their years in the wilderness made it impossible for them ever to return, as many of them yearned to do, to a more settled way of life. Having fought brilliantly in the wilderness wars of the 1750s, Robert Rogers proved to be ill fit for anything but war; in peacetime his life was a shambles. John Tanner, who had been captured as a child by the Shawnees and raised as an Indian, was in later years tragically unable to find a place for himself either in white or in Indian society. And Jedediah Smith, after roaming and exploring the West for years, decided to make just one more trip into the wilderness before settling down on a farm in Missouri. As he had written earlier: "I returned to the woods, the river, the Camp and the Game with a feeling somewhat that of a prisoner escaped from his chains." But on the way West he was ambushed and killed by Comanches.

Despite the hardships and the dangers, however, a surprising number of these brave and reckless men—the luckiest, the hardiest, the most skillful—survived, lived long lives, and even managed to accommodate themselves more or less to the encroachments of civilization. Daniel Boone, who had helped settle Kentucky, then been driven off his land by debts and legal disputes, found a new home in Missouri, where he lived to be a spry and active eighty-six. George Nidever, who became the first settler in California's Napa Valley, continued hunting and trapping until well into his seventies and was eighty-one when he died. Crusty old Jim Bridger, who lived to be seventy-seven, was still guiding army surveying teams and war parties when he was in his sixties. And Osborne Russell, who had been a member of Bridger's Rocky Mountain fur-trapping brigade, later lead an emigrant party to Oregon, became a prominent figure in local politics and lived to be eighty-one.

The encroachment of civilization upon the wilderness was, in the long run, inevitable. The frontiersmen themselves had made it so. They had come upon the wilderness whole, reveled in it, feared it, been conditioned by its harsh realities. But by their coming they helped to insure that there would not be wilderness long, helped to destroy the very things that they cherished most: the wild, the freedom, the elbow room. Their way of life, like that of the Indians, depended on maintaining the wilderness, which fed and clothed them. But in the midst of plenty, with more wilderness seemingly always ahead, the frontiersmen often indulged in the most reckless destruction of the wild, slaughtering buffalo, bear, and deer wholesale, and leaving the unwanted carcasses to rot. In the 1820s and 1830s, to meet the East's insatiable demand for beaver hats, the mountainmen of the West trapped the beaver almost to extinction. In the process, they helped to destroy not only their own livelihood, but also that of the Indians, whose self-sufficiency had already been undermined by increasing dependence on the white traders' guns, powder, and implements.

Meantime, in their search for peltry and game, the frontiersmen had opened trails, discovered mountain passes, found fertile valleys and rich pasturelands. Their glowing tales, their crude maps drawn on skins with charcoal or in the dust around campfires, tempted others to follow and made the journey seem possible. And follow they did, by the thousands, the traders, the land speculators, the pioneers, and the settlers—over Cumberland Gap, the hunters' trail, into Kentucky; down the Ohio, the traders' path, to Illinois and Missouri; along the Platte River and over South Pass, the trappers' route, to Oregon and California. The newcomer's dream was not far different from the dream of the frontiersman. Both sought a new life, independence, a fresh start. But the newcomer's dream depended not on living with the wild but on conquering it with axes and plows, on clearing spaces in the forests and planting trees on the prairies. Along with the wilderness and the Indians, the frontiersmen were driven relentlessly westward, pursued by the advance of the farms and towns that they abhorred but that they themselves made possible. In effect, the frontiersman inadvertently contributed not only to their own eventual extinction but also to the destruction of the Indians, whose way of life depended on an intimate and undisrupted relationship to the land.

Paradoxically, as the wilderness man moved onward, the more he seemed to fascinate the American public. Settlers and townsmen living far from the frontier were avidly reading autobiographies and memoirs by and about frontiersmen long before the appearance of James Fenimore Cooper's *Leatherstocking Tales*. Robert Rogers' accounts of his adventures in the French and Indian War were immensely popular in London and New York. Daniel Boone, Davy Crockett, and Kit Carson, even in their own day, were becoming as vital a part of the collective imagination of the New World as Ulysses, Siegfried, and King Arthur had been in the mythology of the Old. And in the great cities "Buffalo Bill" Cody capitalized on the country's fascination with its frontier heritage by giving audiences at his Wild West shows a glimpse of a tamed and much romanticized wilderness—even as the last of the real wilderness was fast disappearing.

The fascination remains. For, while few men have been ready to test themselves against true wilderness, many have dreamed of doing so, of finding, as one frontier writer put it, "in a new country, and in new views and combinations of things, something that we crave but have not found."

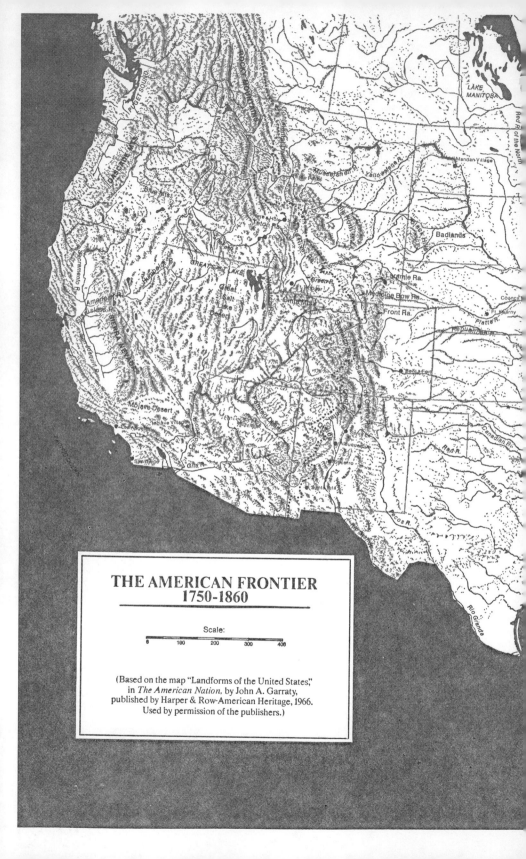

THE AMERICAN FRONTIER
1750-1860

Scale:

0   100   200   300   400

(Based on the map "Landforms of the United States,"
in *The American Nation*, by John A. Garraty,
published by Harper & Row-American Heritage, 1966.
Used by permission of the publishers.)

PART I

The Appalachians and Beyond

1755-1825

1

JAMES SMITH:

Learning the Indian Ways

The settlers who pushed across the Appalachian frontier in the mid-1700s were ill prepared to wage the kind of aggressive campaign against the Indians that was needed to make their homes and families secure. When an attack came, as it did again and again, the settlers made every effort to defend themselves. They built stockades, held off the onslaught as best they could, but when all else failed they fled or submitted to the Indian terror. Nor could they rely on Britain's colonial army for help. Not only was the army usually hundreds of miles away, on the far side of a rugged mountain barrier, but its paradeground maneuvers and rulebook notions of warfare were notoriously ineffective against the guerrilla tactics of the Indians—as became clear in July 1755 when an army of 1500 men under General Edward Braddock was all but annihilated by a force of 300 French and Indians at the Battle of the Wilderness.

Among those who realized the significance of Braddock's defeat was young James Smith (1737–c. 1814), who had been born and raised on Pennsylvania's western frontier and who

*was helping to build a road for Braddock's troops when he was
captured by Indians a few days before the battle. Smith was a
prisoner at Fort Duquesne, on the present site of Pittsburgh,
when the French and Indians set off to attack the approaching
British force, and he was watching from the ramparts when
they returned with their grisly trophies of victory. Adopted by
an Indian family, Smith learned to live, to hunt, and to fight like
an Indian. His experience taught him that the only way the
white settlers would secure their frontiers was if they fought the
Indians in the Indian way: aggressively, with stealth and cunning, and with appropriate wilderness tactics. When, after five
years, he finally escaped from his captors in 1759 and returned
early the next year to his native Conococheague, in what is now
Franklin County, Pennsylvania, he began spreading his
knowledge of Indian ways among his fellow settlers. When
hostilities erupted again in 1763, Smith organized and trained a
band of rangers called the Black Boys, who took it upon themselves to defend the Pennsylvania and Ohio frontier. During the
Revolution Smith—and men trained by him—waged an aggressive wilderness campaign in the West.*

*Woodsman, settler, border commander, and one of the first
Americans to explore the country west of the Cumberlands in
Tennessee, Smith published his reminiscences in 1799. By so
doing, he hoped to enlighten his countrymen about the Indian
art of war, so that "we shall be able to defend ourselves against
them, when defence is necessary." The excerpt printed here
begins just after Smith's capture by the Indians, after he had
been beaten senseless while running the gauntlet.*

The first thing I remember was my being in the fort, amidst
the French and Indians, and a French doctor standing by
me, who had opened a vein in my left arm: after which the
interpreter asked me how I did, I told him I felt much pain;

From *An Account of the Remarkable Occurrences in the Life and Travels of Col. James
Smith, During His Captivity with the Indians, in the Years 1755, '56, '57, '58, and '59*, printed
and published by John Bradford (Lexington, Kentucky, 1799); reprint, with an appen-
dix of illustrative notes by William M. Darlington (Cincinnati, 1907), pp. 9–17, 20–24,
47–48, 107–112, 136–139, 152–153, and 162–163.

the doctor then washed my wounds, and the bruised places of my body, with French brandy. As I felt faint, and the brandy smelt well, I asked for some inwardly, but the doctor told me, by the interpreter, that it did not suit my case.

When they found I could speak, a number of Indians came around me, and examined me with threats of cruel death, if I did not tell the truth. The first question they asked me, was, how many men were there in the party that were coming from Pennsylvania, to join Braddock? I told them the truth, that there were three hundred. The next question was, were they well armed? I told them they were all well armed, (meaning the arm of flesh) for they had only about thirty guns among the whole of them; which, if the Indians had known, they would certainly have gone and cut them all off; therefore I could not in conscience let them know the defenceless situation of these road-cutters. I was then sent to the hospital, and carefully attended by the doctors, and recovered quicker than what I expected.

Some time after I was there, I was visited by the Delaware Indian already mentioned, who was at the taking of me, and could speak some English. Though he spoke but bad English, yet I found him to be a man of considerable understanding. I asked him if I had done any thing that had offended the Indians, which caused them to treat me so unmercifully? He said no, it was only an old custom the Indians had, and it was like how do you do; after that he said I would be well used. I asked him if I should be admitted to remain with the French? He said no—and told me that as soon as I recovered, I must not only go with the Indians, but must be made an Indian myself. I asked him what news from Braddock's army? He said the Indians spied them every day, and he shewed me by making marks on the ground with a stick, that Braddock's army was advancing in very close order, and that the Indians would surround them, take trees, and (as he expressed it) *shoot um down all one pigeon.*

Shortly after this, on the 9th day of July 1755, in the morning I heard a great stir in the fort. As I could then walk with a staff in my hand, I went out of the door which was just by the wall of the fort, and stood upon the wall and viewed the Indians in a huddle before the gate, where were barrels of powder, bullets, flints, &c., and every one taking what suited; I saw the Indians also march off in rank intire—likewise the French Canadians, and some regulars, after viewing the Indians and French in different positions, I computed them to be about four hundred, and wondered that they attempted to go out against Braddock with so small a party. I was then in high hopes that I would soon see them flying before the British troops, and that General Braddock would take the fort and rescue me.

I remained anxious to know the event of this day; and in the afternoon I again observed a great noise and commotion in the fort, and though at that time I could not understand French, yet I found it was the voice of Joy and triumph, and feared that they had received what I called bad news.

I had observed some of the old country soldiers speak Dutch; as I spoke Dutch I went to one of them and asked him what was the news? He told me that a runner had just arrived, who said that Braddock would certainly be defeated; that the Indians and French had surrounded him, and were concealed behind trees and in gullies, and kept a constant fire upon the English, and that they saw the English falling in heaps, and if they did not take the river which was the only gap, and make their escape, there would not be one man left alive before sun down. Some time after this I heard a number of scalp halloos [a yell for every scalp or prisoner taken] and saw a company of Indians and French coming in. I observed they had a great many bloody scalps, grenadiers' caps, British canteens, bayonets, &c., with them. They brought the news that Braddock was defeated. After that another company came in which appeared to be about one hundred, and chiefly Indians, and it seemed to me that almost every one of this company was carrying scalps; after this came another company with a number of waggon-horses, and also a great many scalps. Those that were coming in, and those that had arrived, kept a constant firing of small arms, and also the great guns in the fort, which were accompanied with the most hedeous shouts and yells from all quarters; so that it appeared to me as if the infernal regions had broke loose.

About sun down I beheld a small party coming in with about a dozen prisoners, stripped naked, with their hands tied behind their backs, and their faces, and part of their bodies blacked—these prisoners they burned to death on the bank of Alegheny River opposite to the fort. I stood on the fort wall until I beheld them begin to burn one of these men, they had him tied to a stake and kept touching him with fire-brands, red-hot irons, etc., and he screeming in a most doleful manner,—the Indians in the mean time yelling like infernal spirits. As this scene appeared too shocking for me to behold, I retired to my lodging both sore and sorry.

When I came into my lodgings I saw Ruffel's *Seven Sermons*, which they had brought from the field of battle, which a Frenchman made a present of to me. From the best information I could receive there were only seven Indians and four French killed in this battle, and five hundred British lay dead in the field; besides what were killed in the river on their retreat.

The morning after the battle I saw Braddock's artilery brought into the fort, the same day I also saw several Indians in British-officers' dress with sash, half-moon, laced hats, &c., which the British then wore.

A few days after this the Indians demanded me and I was obliged to go with them. I was not yet well able to march, but they took me in a canoe, up the Alegheny River to an Indian town that was on the north side of the river, about forty miles above Fort DuQuesne. Here I remained about three weeks, and was then taken to an Indian town on the west branch of Muskingum, about twenty miles above the forks, which was called Tullihas, inhabited by Delawares, Caughnewagas and Mohicans.—On our rout betwixt the aforesaid towns, the country was chiefly black-oak and white-oak land, which appeared generally to be good wheat land, chiefly second and third rate, intermixed with some rich bottoms.

The day after my arrival at the aforesaid town, a number of Indians collected about me, and one of them began to pull the hair out of my head. He had some ashes on a piece of bark, in which he frequently diped his fingers in order to take the firmer hold, and so he went on, as if he had been plucking a turkey, until he had all the hair clean out of my head, except a small spot about three or four inches square on my crown; this they cut off with a pair of scissors, excepting three locks, which they dressed up in their own mode. Two of these they wraped round with a narrow beaded garter made by themselves for that purpose, and the other they platted at full length, and then stuck it full of silver broches. After this they bored my nose and ears, and fixed me off with ear rings and nose jewels, then they ordered me to strip off my clothes and put on a breech-clout, which I did; then they painted my head, face and body in various colors. They put a large belt of wampom on my neck, and silver bands on my hands and right arm; and so an old chief led me out in the street and gave the alarm hallo, *coo-wigh,* several times repeated quick, and on this all that were in the town came running and stood round the old chief, who held me by the hand in the midst. As I at that time knew nothing of their mode of adoption, and had seen them put to death all they had taken, and as I never could find that they saved a man alive at Braddock's defeat, I made no doubt but they were about putting me to death in some cruel manner. The old chief holding me by the hand made a long speech very loud, and when he had done he handed me to three young squaws, who led me by the hand down the bank into the river until the water was up to our middle. The squaws then made signs to me to plunge myself into the water, but I did not understand them; I thought that the result of the council was that I should be drowned, and that these young ladies were to be the executioners. They all three laid violent hold of me, and I for some time opposed them with all my might, which occasioned loud laughter by the multitude that were on the bank of the river. At length one of the squaws made out to speak a little English (for I believe they began to be afraid of me) and said, *no hurt you;* on this I gave myself up to their ladyships, who were as good as their word; for though they plunged me under water, and washed and rubbed me severely, yet I could not say they hurt me much.

These young women then led me up to the council house, where some of the tribe were ready with new cloths for me. They gave me a new ruffled shirt, which I put on, also a pair of leggins done off with ribbons and beads, likewise a pair of mockasons, and garters dressed with beads, Porcupine-quills, and red hair—also a tinsel laced cappo. They again painted my head and face with various colors, and tied a bunch of red feathers to one of these locks they had left on the crown of my head, which stood up five or six inches. They seated me on a bear skin, and gave me a pipe, tomahawk, and polecat skin pouch, which had been skined pocket fashion, and contained tobacco, killegenico, or dry sumach leaves, which they mix with their tobacco,—also spunk, flint and steel. When I was thus seated, the Indians came in dressed and painted in their grandest manner. As they came in they took their seats and for a considerable time there was a profound silence, every one was smoking,—but not a word was spoken among them.—At length one of the chiefs made a speech which was delivered to me by an interperter,—and was as followeth:—"My son, you are now flesh of our flesh, and bone of our bone. By the ceremony which was performed this day, every drop of white blood was washed out of your veins; you are taken into the Caughnewago nation, and initiated into a warlike tribe; you are adopted into a great family, and now received with great seriousness and solemnity in the room and place of a great man; after what has passed this day, you are now one of us by an old strong law and custom—My son, you have now nothing to fear, we are now under the same obligations to love, support and defend you, that we are to love and defend one another, therefore you are to consider yourself as one of our people."—At this time I did not believe this fine speech, especially that of the white blood being washed out of me; but since that time I have found that there was much sincerity in said speech,—for from that day I never knew them to make any distinction between me and themselves in any respect whatever until I left them.—If they had plenty of cloathing I had plenty, if we were scarce we all shared one fate. . . .

Shortly after this I went out to hunt, in company with Mohawk Solomon. . . . After some time we came upon some fresh buffaloe tracks. I had observed before this that the Indians were upon their guard, and afraid of an enemy; for, until now they and the southern nations had been at war. As we were following the buffalo tracks, Solomon seemed to be upon his guard, went very slow, and would frequently stand and listen, and appeared to be in suspense. We came to where the tracks were very plain in the sand, and I said it is surely buffaloe tracks; he said *hush, you know nothing, may be buffaloe tracks, may be Catawba.* He went very cautious until we found some fresh buffaloe dung: he then smiled and said *Catawba can not make so.* He then stopped and told me an odd story about the Catawbas. He said that formerly the Catawbas came near one of their hunting camps, and at some distance from the camp lay in ambush, and in order to decoy them out, sent two or three Catawbas in the night, past their camp, with buffaloe hoofs fixed on their feet, so as to make artificial tracks. In the morning those in the camp followed after these tracks, thinking they were Buffaloe, until they were fired on by the Catawbas, and several of them killed; the others fled, collected a party and pursued the Catawbas; but they, in their subtilty brought with them rattle-snake poison, which they had collected from the bladder that lieth at the root of the snakes' teeth; this they had corked up in a short piece of cane-stalk; they had also brought with them small cane or reed, about the size of a rye straw, which they made sharp at the end like a pen, and dipped them in this poison, and stuck them in the ground among the grass, along their own tracks, in such a position that they might stick into the legs of the pursuers, which answered the design; and as the Catawbas had runners behind to watch the motions of the pursuers, when they found that a number of them were lame, being artificially snake bit, and that they were all turning back, the Catawbas turned upon the pursuers, and defeated them, and killed and scalped all those that were lame.—When Solomon had finished this story, and found that I understood him, concluded by saying, *you don't know, Catawba velly bad Indian, Catawba all one Devil Catawba.*

Some time after this, I was told to take the dogs with me and go down the creek, perhaps I might kill a turkey; it being in the afternoon, I was also told not to go far from the creek, and to come up the creek again to the camp, and to take care not to get lost. When I had gone some distance down the creek I came upon fresh buffaloe tracks, and as I had a number of dogs with me to stop the buffaloe, I concluded I would follow after and kill one; and as the grass and weeds were rank, I could readily follow the track. A little before sundown, I despaired of coming up with them: I was then thinking how I might get to camp before night; I concluded as the buffaloe had made several turns, if I took the track back to the creek, it would be dark before I could get to camp; therefore I thought I would take a near way through the hills, and strike the creek a little below the camp; but as it was cloudy weather, and I a very young woodsman, I could find neither creek or camp. When night came on I fired my gun several times, and hallooed, but could have no answer. The next morning early, the Indians were out after me, and as I had with me ten or a dozen dogs, and the grass and weeds rank, they could readily follow my track. When they came up with me, they appeared to be in a very good humor. I asked Solomon if he thought I was running away, he said *no no, you go too much clooked.* On my return to camp they took my gun from me, and for this rash step I was reduced to a bow and arrows, for near two years. . . .

. . . in June, 1756, they were all engaged in preparing to go to war against the frontiers of Virginia; when they were equipped, they went through their ceremonies, sung their war songs, &c. They all marched off, from fifteen to sixty years of age; and some boys only twelve years old, were equipped with their bows and arrows, and went to war; so that none were left in town but squaws and children, except myself, one very old man, and another about fifty years of age, who was lame.

The Indians were then in great hopes that they would drive all the Virginians over the lake, which is all the name they know for the sea. They had some cause for this hope, because at this time, the Americans were altogether unacquainted with war of any kind, and consequently very unfit to stand their hand with such subtil enemies as the Indians were. The two old Indians asked me if I did not think that the Indians and French would subdue all America, except New England, which they said they had tried in old times. I told them I thought not: they said they had already drove them all out of the mountains, and had chiefly laid waste the great valley betwixt the North and South mountain, from Potomack to James River, which is a considerable part of the best land in Virginia, Maryland, and Pennsylvania, and that the white people appeared to them like fools; they could neither guard against surprise, run, or fight. These they said were their reasons for saying that they would subdue the whites. They asked me to offer my reasons for my opinion, and told me to speak my mind freely. I told them that the white people to the East were very numerous, like the trees, and though they appeared to them to be fools, as they were not acquainted with their way of war, yet they were not fools; therefore after some time they will learn your mode of war, and turn upon you, or at least defend themselves. . . .

Early in the year 1760, I came home to Conococheague, and found that my people could never ascertain whether I was killed or taken, until my return. They received me with great joy, but were surprised to see me so much like an Indian, both in my gait and gesture. . . .

Now there was peace with the Indians which lasted until the year 1763. Sometime in May, this year, I married, and about that time the Indians again commenced hostilities, and were busily engaged in killing and scalping the frontier inhabitants in various parts of Pennsylvania. The whole Conococheague Valley, from the North to the South Mountain, had been almost entirely evacuated during Braddock's war. This state was then a Quaker government, and at the first of this war the frontiers received no assistance from the state. As the people were now beginning to live at home again, they thought hard to be drove away a second time, and were determined if possible, to make a stand: therefore they raised as much money by collections and subscriptions, as would pay a company of rifle-men for several months. The subscribers met and elected a committee to manage the business. The committee appointed me captain of this company of rangers, and gave me the appointment of my subalterns. I chose two of the most active young men that I could find, who had also been long in captivity with the Indians. As we enlisted our men, we dressed them uniformly in the Indian manner, with breech-clouts, leggins, mockesons and green shrouds, which we wore in the same manner that the Indians do, and nearly as the Highlanders wear their plaids. In place of hats we wore red handkerchiefs, and painted our faces red and black, like Indian warriors. I taught them the Indian discipline, as I knew of no other at that time, which would answer the purpose much better than British. We succeeded beyond expectation in defending the frontiers, and were extolled by our employers. . . . In the fall (the same year) I went on the Susquehannah campaign, against the Indians, under the command of General Armstrong. In this route we burnt the Delaware and Monsey towns, on the West Branch of the Susquehannah, and destroyed all their corn.

In the year 1764, I received a lieutenant's commission, and went out on General Bouquet's campaign against the Indians on the Muskingum. Here we brought them to terms, and promised to be at peace with them, upon condition that they would give up all our people that they had then in captivity among them. They then delivered unto us three hundred of the prisoners, and said that they could not collect them all at this time, as it was now late in the year, and they were far scattered; but they promised that they would bring them all into Fort Pitt early next spring, and as security that they would do this, they delivered to us six of the chiefs, as hostages. Upon this we settled a cessation of arms for six months, and promised upon their fulfilling the aforesaid condition, to make with them a permanent peace.

A little below Fort Pitt the hostages all made their escape. Shortly after this the Indians stole horses, and killed some people on the frontiers. The king's proclamation was then circulating and set up in various public places, prohibiting any person from trading with the Indians, until further orders.

Notwithstanding all this, about the first of March 1765, a number of waggons loaded with Indian goods, and warlike stores, were sent from Philadelphia to Henry Pollen's, Conococheague, and from thence seventy pack-horses were loaded with these goods, in order to carry them to Fort Pitt. This alarmed the country, and Mr. William Duffield raised about fifty armed men, and met the pack-horses at the place where Mercersburg now stands. Mr. Duffield desired the employers to store up their goods, and not proceed until further orders. They made light of this, and went over the North Mountain, where they lodged in a small valley called the Great Cove. Mr. Duffield and his party followed after, and came to their lodging, and again urged them to store up their goods:—He reasoned with them on the impropriety of their proceedings, and the great danger the frontier inhabitants would be exposed to, if the Indians should now get a supply:—He said as it was well known that they had scarcely any amunition, and were almost naked; to supply them now, would be a kind of murder, and would be illegally trading at the expense of the blood and treasure of the frontiers. Notwithstanding his powerful reasoning, these traders made game of what he said, and would only answer him by ludicrous burlesque.

When I beheld this, and found that Mr. Duffield would not compel them to store up their goods, I collected ten of my old warriors that I had formerly disciplined in the Indian way, went off privately, after night, and encamped in the woods. The next day, as usual, we blacked and painted, and waylayed them near Sidelong Hill. I scattered my men about forty rod along the side of the road, and ordered every two to take a tree, and about eight or ten rod between each couple, with orders to keep a reserve fire, one not to fire until his comrade had loaded his gun—by this means we kept up a constant, slow fire, upon them from front to rear:—We then heard nothing of these trader's merriment or burlesque. When they saw their pack-horses falling close by them, they called out *pray gentlemen, what would you have us to do?* The reply was, *collect all your loads to the front, and unload them in one place; take your private property, and immediately retire.* When they were gone, we burnt what they left, which consisted of blankets, shirts, vermillion, lead, beads, wampum, tomahawks, scalping knives, &c.

The traders went back to Fort Loudon, and applied to the commanding officer there, and got a party of Highland soldiers, and went with them in quest of the robbers, as they called us, and without applying to a magistrate, or obtaining any civil authority, but barely upon suspicion, they took a number of creditable persons prisoners, (who were chiefly not in any way concerned in this action) and confined them in the guardhouse in Fort Loudon. I then raised three hundred riflemen, marched to Fort Loudon, and encamped on a hill in sight of the fort. We were not long there, until we had more than double as many of the British troops prisoners in our camp, as they had of our people in the guard-house. Captain Grant, a Highland officer, who commanded Fort Loudon, then sent a flag of truce to our camp, where we settled a cartel, and gave them above two for one, which enabled us to redeem all our men from the guard-house, without further difficulty. . . .

In the year 1778, I received a colonel's commission, and after my return to Westmoreland, the Indians made an attack upon our frontiers. I then raised men and pursued them, and the second day we overtook and defeated them. We likewise took four scalps, and recovered the horses and plunder which they were carrying off. At the time of this attack, Captain John Hinkston pursued an Indian, both their guns being empty, and after the fray was over he was missing:—While we were enquiring about him, he came walking up, seemingly unconcerned, with a bloody scalp in his hand—he had pursued the Indian about a quarter of a mile, and tomahawked him.

Not long after this I was called upon to command four hundred riflemen, on an expedition against the Indian town on French Creek. It was some time in November before I received orders from General M'Intosh, to march, and then we were poorly equipped, and scarce of provisions. We marched in three columns, forty rod from each other. There were also flankers on the outside of each column, that marched a-breast in the rear, in scattered order—and even in the columns, the men were one rod apart—and in the front, the volunteers marched a-breast, in the same manner of the flankers, scouring the woods. In case of an attack, the officers were immediately to order the men to face out and take trees—in this position the Indians could not avail themselves by surrounding us, or have an opportunity of shooting a man from either side of the tree. If attacked, the center column was to reinforce whatever part appeared to require it the most. When we encamped, our encampment formed a hollow square, including about thirty or forty acres—on the outside of the square there were centinels placed, whose business it was to watch for the enemy, and see that neither horses or bullocks went out:—And when encamped, if any attacks were made by an enemy, each officer was immediately to order the men to face out and take trees, as before mentioned, and in this form they could not take the advantage by surrounding us, as they commonly had done when they fought the whites. . . .

In this manner we proceeded on, to French Creek, where we found the Indian town evacuated. I then went on further than my orders called for, in quest of Indians; but our provisions being nearly exhausted, we were obliged to return. On our way back we met with considerable difficulties on account of high waters and scarcity of provision; yet we never lost one horse, excepting some that gave out.

After peace was made with the Indians, I met with some of them in Pittsburg, and enquired of them in their own tongue, concerning this expedition,—not letting them know I was there. They told me that they watched the movements of this army ever after they had left Fort-Pitt, and as they passed thro the glades or barrens they had a full view of them from the adjacent hills, and computed their number to be about one thousand. They said they also examined their camps, both before and after they were gone, and found, they could not make an advantageous attack, and therefore moved off from their town and hunting ground before we arrived. . . .

ON [THE INDIANS'] DISCIPLINE AND METHOD OF WAR

I have often heard the British officers call the Indians the undisciplined savages, which is a capital mistake—as they have all the essentials of discipline. They are under good command, and punctual in obeying orders: they can act in concert, and when their officers lay a plan and give orders, they will cheerfully unite in putting all their directions into immediate execution; and by each man observing the motion or movement of his right hand companion, they can communicate the motion from right to left, and march abreast in concert, and in scattered order, though the line may be more than a mile long, and continue, if occasion requires, for a considerable distance, without disorder or confusion. They can perform various necessary manoeuvers, either slowly, or as fast as they can run: they can form a circle, or semi-circle: the circle they make use of, in order to surround their enemy, and the semi-circle if the enemy has a river on one side of them. They can also form a large hollow square, face out and take trees: this they do, if their enemies are about surrounding them, to prevent from being shot from either side of the tree. When they go into battle they are not loaded or encumbered with many clothes, as they commonly fight naked, save only breech-clout, leggins and mockesons. There is no such thing as corporeal punishment used, in order to bring them under such good discipline: degrading is the only chastisement, and they are so unanimous in this, that it effectually answers the purpose. Their officers plan, order and conduct matters until they are brought into action, and then each man is to fight as though he was to gain the battle himself. General orders are commonly given in time of battle, either to advance or retreat, and is done by a shout or yell, which is well understood, and then they retreat or advance in concert. They are generally well equipped, and exceeding expert and active in the use of arms. . . .

Why have we not made greater proficiency in the Indian art of war? Is it because we are too proud to imitate them, even though it should be a means of preserving the lives of many of our citizens? No! We are not above borrowing language from them, such as homony, pone, tomahawk, & c. which is little or no use to us. I apprehend that the reasons why we have not improved more in this respect, are as follows: no important acquisition is to be obtained but by attention and diligence; and as it is easier to learn to move and act in concert, in close order, in the open plain, than to act in concert in scattered order, in the woods; so it is easier to learn our discipline, than the Indian manoeuvers. They train up their boys to the art of war from the time they are twelve or fourteen years of age; whereas the principal chance our people had of learning, was by observing their movements when in action against us. I have been long astonished that no one has wrote upon this important subject, as their art of war would not only be of use to us in case of another rupture with them; but were only part of our men taught this art, accompanied with our continental discipline, I think no European power, after trial, would venture to shew its head in the American woods. . . .

2

ROBERT ROGERS:
Wilderness Warrior

When Fenimore Cooper was writing the most famous of his Leatherstocking Tales, The Last of the Mohicans, *he was no doubt inspired, at least in part, by the person and the adventures of Major Robert Rogers (1731–1795), the great scout and wilderness warrior of the French and Indian War. The setting of Cooper's novel—on the shores of Lake George and Lake Champlain in the 1750s—and many of its incidents parallel Rogers' accounts of his adventures on the bloody Northern frontier; and certainly Rogers would have recognized many of his own best qualities in the character of Cooper's mythic woodland hero, Hawkeye. Like Hawkeye, Rogers knew the upper New York woods as well as any Indian. He knew the Indians' language, their customs, and their mode of warfare, and he was as skilled with the bow and the scalping knife as he was with the long rifle. Dressed in buckskins, traveling on foot or by canoe or on snowshoes, Rogers and his band of rangers waged a terrifying guerrilla campaign against their French and Indian enemies—a campaign often marked by appalling cruelty. Rogers himself showed little pity for his enemy, murdering wounded captives when they became a burden and taking scalps without a qualm. But his daring and spectacular exploits made him a romantic figure, famous both in England and the Colonies, and his services to the British cause were of the first importance.*

Six feet tall, with a lean, muscular frame, Rogers had been raised on a frontier farm in New Hampshire, where at an early age he had learned to hunt, to shoot, and to endure the hardships of the Northern wilderness. But he must have learned a few other skills as well, for when, in his mid-twenties, he joined a New Hampshire regiment bound for Canada, it was to escape persecution on charges of counterfeiting. This was late in 1754. Rogers quickly earned himself a reputation as a cunning scout and woodland fighter and was soon leading his own company of rangers. In 1758 he was promoted to major with authority over the entire scouting arm of the British army, and he was present at every major engagement in the North: at Halifax in 1757, at Ticonderoga in 1758, at Crown Point in 1759, and finally at Montreal in 1760, when the French surrendered all of Canada to Great Britain. After the French and Indian War he was sent West to take command of Detroit and other Great Lakes outposts.

Although he was lionized in London in the 1760s as a frontier hero and as the author of his Journals *and of a play,* Ponteach, *Rogers found it impossible to adjust to peaceful society. Various ill-conceived ventures drove him deep into debt, and his dishonesty cost him his employment first as an Indian trader and later as commander of the fort at Michilimackinac, where Lake Michigan and Lake Huron join, and where he was suspected of having treasonable dealings with the French. At every opportunity he returned to what he did best, which was fighting. In 1761 he campaigned against the Cherokee in the Carolinas, and in 1763 against Pontiac at Detroit. He claimed to have served the Bey of Algiers in North Africa in 1774, and he fought for the British during the American Revolution until he lost a skirmish at White Plains and was relieved of his command. Toward the end of the war he fled to England, where he spent the last fifteen years of his life. He died in a cheap lodging house in London in 1795.*

This excerpt from Rogers' Journals, first published in 1765, describes his heady early days as a young ranger captain during the French and Indian War.

Sept. 24, 1755. Pursuant to orders from General Johnson to proceed to Crown Point, and if practicable, to bring from thence a prisoner, I embarked with four men and proceeding down Lake George 25 miles, landed on the west shore, where leaving two men in charge of the boat, I marched with the other two until the 29th, when we obtained a fair view of the Fort at Crown Point; and discovered a large body of Indians about the Fort, from whose irregular firing we supposed they were shooting at marks, a diversion of which, they are very fond. At night, our party crept through the French guards into a small village, south of the Fort, and passed through it to an eminence on the south west, where we ascertained they were erecting a battery, and had already thrown up an entrenchment on that side of the Fort. The next day we gained an eminence a small distance from the former, and discovered an encampment extending from the Fort south east, to a wind mill at thirty yards distance. The troops occupying it, amounted to about 500 men. Having no opportunity for procuring a captive, and finding that our small party was discovered, it was thought best to commence a retreat on the 1st of October. On our rout homeward, we passed within two miles of Ticonderoga, from which a large smoke was observed, and the discharge of a number of small arms heard; but as our provisions were expended, we could not tarry to ascertain the enemy's force. On the 2d, reached the place where we had left the boat, in charge of two men, who to our great surprise had departed, leaving us no provisions. This circumstance hastened our return with all speed to the camp, where we arrived on the 4th, not a little fatigued, and distressed with hunger and cold.

From *Reminiscences of the French War; Containing Rogers Expeditions, With The New England Rangers Under His Command, as Published in London in 1765* . . . (Concord, New Hampshire, 1831), pp. 11–19, 31.

Oct. 7. Orders were received from General Johnson to embark with five men, and reconnoitre the French at Ticonderoga. Accordingly I proceeded at night to a point of land on the west shore of the Lake, where we landed and concealed our canoe leaving two men in charge of it and with the other three, arrived at Ticonderoga point, at noon. Here were about 2000 men, who had thrown up an intrenchment, and prepared a large quantity of hewn timber in the adjacent woods. We remained here the second night, and next morning saw them lay the foundation of a fort, on the point, which commands the pass from Lake George to Champlain, and the entrance to South Bay or Wood Creek. Having made what discoveries we could, and commenced our return, a large advanced guard of the enemy was found posted at the north end of Lake George, near the outlet to Champlain. While viewing these troops, I observed a bark canoe containing nine Indians and a Frenchman, passing up the Lake. We kept in sight of them, until they passed the point where our canoe and men had been left. They gave information that the party had landed on an Island six miles south of us, near the middle of the Lake. In a short time they put off from the Island and steered directly towards us. In order to receive them in the best manner possible, we gave them a salute at 100 yards distance, which reduced their number to four. We then took boat and pursued them down the lake, until they were relieved by two canoes, which compelled us to retreat towards our camp at Lake George, where we arrived on the 10th of October.

Oct. 15. I was ordered to embark with forty men in five boats, with the design of discovering the strength of the enemy's advanced guard, and if possible, to decoy the whole, or part of them into an ambush. To effect this object, our exertions were indefatigable for several days but all to no purpose, and we returned to camp on the 19th.

Oct. 21. I embarked with four men, for Crown Point, in quest of a prisoner. At night, we landed on the west side, twenty five miles from the English camp, marched the remainder of the way and came in sight of the Fort on the

26th. In the evening, we approached nearer, and the next morning found ourselves within 300 yards of it.—My men lay concealed in a thicket of willows, while I crept nearer, and concealed myself behind a large pine log, by holding bushes in my hand. Soon after sunrise, the soldiers issued out in such numbers, that our party could not unite without discovery. About 10 o'clock a man came out alone and advanced towards our ambush. I sprang over the log, and offered him quarter, which he refused, making a pass at me with his dirk. This I avoided, and presented my fusee to his breast. He still pressed forward with resolution, and compelled me to shoot him. This gave alarm to the enemy, and made a retreat to the mountain necessary.* Our party safely arrived at camp, Oct. 30th.

Nov. 4. Embarked for the enemy's advanced guard with thirty men in four batteaux, each mounting two wall pieces; and next morning arrived within half a mile of the guard, where we landed and concealed the boats. Four spies were sent out, who returned next evening, informing that the enemy had no works around them, but lay entirely open to assault. Word was immediately sent to the General, for a sufficient force to attack them, but not withstanding his earnestness and activity, it did not arrive until we were compelled to retreat. On our return, we met the reinforcement, turned again towards the French, and the next evening sent two men to see if their sentinels were on the alert. They were discovered, fired upon, and so hotly pursued by the enemy, that unhappily our whole party was discovered. We obtained the first notice of this, from two canoes with thirty men in them, which we supposed came out at the same time with another party by land, to force us between two fires. To prevent this, Lieutenant McCurdy and myself

---

*Rogers gives a rather different account of this incident in his official report, dated eight days after the event and printed in *The Documentary History of the State of New York*, vol. 4 (Albany, 1851), p. 175: "at length a french man Came out of the Fort Towards us without his Gun & Came within fifteen Rods of where we lay then I with another man Run up to him In order to Captivate him—But he Refused To Take Quarter so we kill'd him and Took of his Scalp in plain sight of the fort then Run and in plain view about Twenty Rods & made our Escape . . ." —ED.

embarked with fourteen men in two boats, leaving the remainder of the party on shore under the command of Captain Putnam.

In order to decoy the French within reach of our wall pieces, we steered as if intending to pass them, which answered our expectations; for they boldly headed us until within an hundred yards, when the guns were discharged which killed several and put the remainder to flight; in which they were pursued, and driven so near to our land party, that they were again galled by the wall pieces. Several of the enemy were thrown overboard, and their canoes rendered very leaky.

At this time, I discovered their land party, and notified my men, who immediately embarked without receiving much injury from the sharp fire which the French kept up for some time in their rear. We pursued the enemy with diligence, and again discharged the wall pieces which obliged them to disperse. They were followed to their landing, where they were received and covered by 200 men, whom a discharge of our pieces compelled to retire; but finding their numbers greatly superior to ours, it was thought most prudent to return to camp, which we reached Nov. 8.

Nov. 12. Proceeded with a party of 10 men, upon a scout, to ascertain the enemy's strength and condition at Ticonderoga, and on the 14th, arrived in sight of the Fort. The enemy had erected three new barracks and four store houses in the Fort, between which and the water, they had eighty batteaux hauled up on the beach. They had fifty tents near the Fort, and appeared to be very busily employed in strengthening their works. Having attained our object, we reached camp on the 19th.

Dec. 19. After a month's repose, I embarked with two men, once more, to reconnoitre the French at Ticonderoga. In our way a fire was discovered upon an Island near the Fort, which we supposed to have been kindled by the enemy. This obliged us to lie by, and act like fishermen, to deceive them, until night came on, when we gained the west shore 15 miles north of our camp. Concealing our boat we pursued our march by land on the 20th, and on the 21st at noon, reached the Fort. The enemy were still engaged in their works, and had mounted four pieces of cannon on the south east bastion, two on the north west, towards the woods, and two on the south bastion. They mustered about 500 men. We made several attempts to take a prisoner by way-laying their paths; but they passed along in too large parties for us. This night we approached near the Fort; and were driven by the severity of the cold, to seek shelter in one of their evacuated huts. Before day, a light snow fell, which obliged us to march homeward with all speed, lest the enemy should perceive our tracks and pursue. We reached the boat in safety, though almost overcome with cold, hunger, and fatigue; and had the good fortune to kill two deer, with which being refreshed, on the 24th we returned to Fort William Henry, a fortress erected this year at the south end of Lake George.

About this time, General Johnson went down to Albany to meet the commissioners from the several governments, whose troops he had commanded, (New-Hampshire excepted). These persons were empowered by their constituents, with the assent of a council of war, to garrison Forts William Henry and Edward, for that winter, with part of the troops then in service.

Accordingly a regiment was organized, to which Massachusetts furnished a Colonel, Connecticut a Lieutenant Colonel, and New York a Major. General Johnson and the Commissioners judged it most prudent to leave one company of woodsmen, or Rangers under my command, to make excursions to the enemy's Forts during the winter; and we remained with the Garrison:

January 14, 1756. Marched with a party of 16 men to reconnoitre the French Forts, and proceeded down the Lake on skates, until we halted for refreshment near the falls between Lakes George and Champlain. At night, we renewed the march, and at day break, on the 16th, formed an ambush at a point of land on the east shore of Champlain, within gunshot of the path, in which the enemy passed from one Fort to the other. At sunrise, two sledges laden with fresh beef, were intercepted, with their drivers. The lading was destroyed and we returned to Fort Wm. Henry in good health, with our prisoners on the 17th.

Jan. 26. Marched by order of Colonel Glasier, with fifty men to discover the strength of the enemy at Crown Point.

Feb. 2. We arrived within a mile of that Fortress, and ascended a steep mountain, the summit of which, afforded a full prospect of the Fort, and an opportunity for taking a plan of the works. In the evening, we retired to a small village half a mile to the south, and formed an ambush on each side of the road, leading from the Fort to the village. Next morning a Frenchman fell into our hands; soon after this, two more men were discovered, but they took alarm before we could seize them, and escaped to the Fort. Finding ourselves discovered by this accident, we set fire to the houses and barns of the village, containing large quantities of grain, and killed fifty head of cattle. We then retired with our prisoner, leaving the whole village in flames, and reached head quarters February 6th.

Feb. 29. Marched by order of Colonel Glasier, with fifty six men down the west side of Lake George, proceeding northward until the 5th of March, when we steered east to Lake Champlain, about six miles north of Crown Point, where from intelligence received of the Indians, we expected to find inhabited villages. We there attempted to cross the lake but the ice was too weak. On the 7th we returned and passing round the bay west of Crown Point, at night entered the cleared land among the houses and barns of the French. Here we lay in ambush, expecting labourers to attend the cattle and clean the grain, of which the barns were full. We remained there that night and the next day until dark, when we set fire to the village and retired. On our return, we took a fresh view of Ticonderoga, reconnoitred that Fort and the advanced guard on Lake George, approaching so near, as to see the sentinels on the ramparts. We obtained all the knowledge we desired, of their works, strength, and situation; and March 14, reached William Henry in safety.

The next day, I received a letter from Mr. William Alexander, Secretary of Governor Shirley. . . . Mr. Shirley requested me to wait upon him at Boston, where he was preparing for the campaign:—leaving to Ensign Noah Johnson, the command of my company, I set out on the 17th for Boston.

On the 23d the General gave me a friendly reception, and the next day a commission to recruit an independent corps of Rangers. It was ordered that the Corps should consist of sixty privates at 3s. (York currency) per day—an Ensign at 5s.—a Lieut. at 7s. and a Captain at 10s. Each man was to be allowed ten Spanish dollars towards providing clothes, arms, and blankets.—The company was to be raised immediately. None were to be enlisted but such as were accustomed to travelling, and hunting, and in whose courage and fidelity, the most implicit confidence could be placed. They were moreover to be subject to military discipline, and the articles of war. The rendezvous was appointed at Albany, whence to proceed in whale boats to Lake George, and "from time to time, to use their best endeavours to distress the French and their allies, by sacking, burning, and destroying their houses, barns, barracks, canoes, batteaux, &c. and by killing their cattle of every kind; and at all times to endeavour to waylay, attack, and desroy their convoys of provision, by land and water, in any part of the country, where they could be found."

With these instructions, I received letters to the Commanding officers at Forts Wm. Henry, and Edward, directing them to forward the service with which I was now charged. . . .

From this time we were constantly employed in patrolling the woods. . . .

3

ALEXANDER HENRY:

Massacre at Mackinac

Alexander Henry (1739–1824), sixteen years a trader in the Old Northwest, seems to have had a penchant for disaster; fortunately, he also possessed two qualities most important to a frontiersman: incredible resilience and extraordinary good luck. Born in New Jersey, he apparently obtained some education before setting out for the wilderness in his twenty-first year, 1760. On this, his first venture in the Northwest fur trade, he saw his boats smashed to pieces and all his trade goods lost in the rapids of the St. Lawrence. But a few months later he was making his way deeper into the wilderness, becoming one of the first English traders to set up shop at Michilimackinac. The longtime French outpost, lying at the junction of the three western Great Lakes and thus at the heart of the richest fur-producing country on the continent, was potentially the most profitable of locations for the young trader; but it was also the most hazardous. Newly won by the English in the French and Indian War, Mackinac was still occupied by Frenchmen jealous of their trade. The neighboring tribes of the Ottawa and Chip-

*pewa viewed the conquerors of their French "Father" with
sullen suspicion, and they were becoming ever more hostile
under the influence of Pontiac, the great Ottawa chief. Henry
scarcely had time to set up his business before the storm broke.
Years later, in a famous book, he told the story of what happened at Mackinac on that June day in 1761, and of his desperate months of captivity among the Indians, during which, by
mere chance, he escaped death again and again. Finally manag-
ing to make his way back to civilization, he returned to the
North Woods only a month later. There he remained until 1776,
trading, exploring for copper, and traveling deep into the Western prairie lands beyond Lake Superior, on the farthest fringes
of the wilderness. Thereafter, until his death almost a half
century later, he lived in Montreal, conducting a thriving business as a fur trader and local merchant, and making visits now
and then to Europe and to the Indian country. His two sons,
William and Charles, were both prominent in the Canadian fur
trade, as was his nephew, also named Alexander Henry (see
Selection 8).*

*Henry's narrative, from which the following excerpt is
taken, was first published in New York in 1809 and is the only
detailed account we have of the massacre at Fort Mackinac.
Written at different times during Henry's later years, and therefore not always as accurate in dates and details as a journal kept
while the events were taking place, the tale nevertheless is
considered generally reliable—as well as eminently readable.
Francis Parkman incorporated it almost word for word in his*
History of the Conspiracy of Pontiac.

When I reached Michilimackinac, I found several other
traders, who had arrived before me, from different parts of
the country, and who, in general, declared the dispositions
of the Indians to be hostile to the English, and even apprehended some attack. M. Laurent Ducharme [a Mackinac
resident] distinctly informed Major Etherington, that a plan

From *Travels and Adventures in Canada and the Indian Territories between the Years 1760
and 1776*, by Alexander Henry (New York, 1809), pp. 71–103, 114–115, 125–126, 131–132.

was absolutely conceived, for destroying him, his garrison and all the English in the upper country; but, the commandant, believing this and other reports to be without foundation, proceeding only from idle or ill-disposed persons, and of a tendency to do mischief, expressed much displeasure against M. Ducharme, and threatened to send the next person, who should bring a story of the same kind, a prisoner, to Détroit.

The garrison, at this time, consisted of ninety privates, two subalterns and the commandant; and the English merchants, at the fort, were four in number. Thus strong, few entertained anxiety concerning the Indians, who had no weapons but small arms.

Meanwhile, the Indians, from every quarter, were daily assembling, in unusual numbers, but with every appearance of friendship, frequenting the fort, and disposing of their peltries, in such a manner as to dissipate almost every one's fears. For myself, on one occasion, I took the liberty of observing to Major Etherington, that in my judgment, no confidence ought to be placed in them, and that I was informed no less than four hundred lay around the fort.

In return, the major only rallied me, on my timidity; and it is to be confessed, that if this officer neglected admonition, on his part, so did I, on mine. Shortly after my first arrival at Michilimackinac, in the preceding year, a Chipeway, named Wa'wa'tam', began to come often to my house, betraying, in his demeanour, strong marks of personal regard. After this had continued for some time, he came, on a certain day, bringing with him his whole family, and, at the same time, a large present, consisting of skins, sugar and dried meat. Having laid these in a heap, he commenced a speech, in which he informed me, that some years before, he had observed a fast, devoting himself, according to the custom of his nation, to solitude, and to the mortification of his body, in the hope to obtain, from the Great Spirit, protection through all his days; that on this occasion, he had dreamed of adopting an Englishman, as his son, brother and friend; that from the moment in which he first beheld me, he had recognised me as the person whom the Great Spirit had been pleased to point out to him for a brother; that he hoped that I would not refuse his present; and that he should forever regard me as one of his family.

I could do no otherwise than accept the present, and declare my willingness to have so good a man, as this appeared to be, for my friend and brother, I offered a present in return for that which I had received, which Wawatam accepted, and then, thanking me for the favour which he said that I had rendered him, he left me, and soon after set out on his winter's hunt.

Twelve months had now elapsed, since the occurrence of this incident, and I had almost forgotten the person of my *brother*, when, on the second day of June, Wawatam came again to my house, in a temper of mind visibly melancholy and thoughtful. He told me, that he had just returned from his *wintering-ground*, and I asked after his health; but, without answering my question, he went on to say, that he was very sorry to find me returned from the Sault; that he had intended to go to that place himself, immediately after his arrival at Michilimackinac; and that he wished me to go there, along with him and his family, the next morning. To all this, he joined an inquiry, whether or not the commandant had heard bad news, adding, that, during the winter, he had himself been frequently disturbed with *the noise of evil birds*; and further suggesting, that there were numerous Indians near the fort, many of whom had never shown themselves within it.—Wawatam was about forty-five years of age, of an excellent character among his nation, and a chief.

Referring much of what I heard to the peculiarities of the Indian character, I did not pay all the attention, which they will be found to have deserved, to the entreaties and remarks of my visitor. I answered that I could not think of going to the Sault, so soon as the next morning, but would follow him there, after the arrival of my clerks. Finding himself unable to prevail with me, he withdrew, for that day; but, early the next morning, he came again, bringing with him his wife, and a present of dried meat. At this interview, after stating that he had several packs of beaver, for which he intended to deal with me, he expressed, a second time, his apprehensions, from the numerous Indians who were round the fort, and earnestly pressed me to consent to an immediate departure for the Sault.—As a reason for this particular request, he assured me that all the Indians proposed to come in a body, that day, to the fort, to demand liquor of the commandant, and that he wished me to be gone, before they should grow intoxicated.

I had made, at the period to which I am now referring, so much progress in the language in which Wawatam addressed me, as to be able to hold an ordinary conversation in it; but, the Indian manner of speech is so extravagantly figurative, that it is only for a very perfect master to follow and comprehend it entirely. Had I been further advanced in this respect, I think that I should have gathered so much information, from this my friendly monitor, as would have put me into possession of the design of the enemy, and enabled me to save as well others as myself; as it was, it unfortunately happened, that I turned a deaf ear to every thing, leaving Wawatam and his wife, after long and patient, but ineffectual efforts, to depart alone, with dejected countenances, and not before they had each let fall some tears.

In the course of the day, I observed that the Indians came in great numbers into the fort, purchasing tomahawks, (small axes, of one pound weight,) and frequently desiring to see silver armbands, and other valuable ornaments, of which I had a large quantity for sale. These ornaments, however, they in no instance purchased; but, after turning them over, left them, saying, that they would call again the next day. Their motive, as it afterward appeared, was no other than the very artful one of discovering, by requesting to see them, the particular places of their deposit, so that they might lay their hands on them in the moment of pillage with the greater certainty and dispatch.

At night, I turned in my mind the visits of Wawatam; but though they were calculated to excite uneasiness, nothing induced me to believe that serious mischief was at hand. The next day, being the fourth of June, was the king's birth-day.*

The morning was sultry. A Chipeway came to tell me that his nation was going to play at *bag'gat'iway*, with the Sacs or Saäkies, another Indian nation, for a high wager. He invited me to witness the sport, adding that the commandant was to be there, and would bet on the side of the Chipeways. In consequence of this information, I went to the commandant, and expostulated with him a little, representing that the Indians might possibly have some sinister end in view; but, the commandant only smiled at my suspicions.

Baggatiway, called, by the Canadians, *le jeu de la crosse*, is played with a bat and ball. The bat is about four feet in length, curved, and terminating in a sort of racket. Two posts are planted in the ground, at a considerable distance from each other, as a mile, or more. Each party has its post, and the game consists in throwing the ball up to the post of the adversary. The ball, at the beginning, is placed in the middle of the course, and each party endeavours as well to throw the ball out of the direction of its own post, as into that of the adversary's.

I did not go myself to see the match which was now to be played without the fort, because, there being a canoe prepared to depart, on the following day, for Montréal, I employed myself in writing letters to my friends; and even when a fellow-trader, Mr. Tracy, happened to call upon me, saying that another canoe had just arrived from Détroit, and proposing that I should go with him to the beach, to inquire the news, it so happened that I still remained, to finish my letters; promising to follow Mr. Tracy, in the course of a few minutes. Mr. Tracy had not gone more than twenty paces from my door, when I heard an Indian warcry, and a noise of general confusion.

Going instantly to my window, I saw a crowd of In-

---

*The events that follow actually took place one June 2.

dians, within the fort, furiously cutting down and scalping every Englishman they found. In particular, I witnessed the fate of Lieutenant Jemette.

I had, in the room in which I was, a fowling-piece, loaded with swan-shot. This I immediately seized, and held it for a few minutes, waiting to hear the drum beat to arms. In this dreadful interval, I saw several of my countrymen fall, and more than one struggling between the knees of an Indian, who, holding him in this manner, scalped him, while yet living.

At length, disappointed in the hope of seeing resistance made to the enemy, and sensible, of course, that no effort, of my own unassisted arm, could avail against four hundred Indians, I thought only of seeking shelter. Amid the slaughter which was raging, I observed many of the Canadian inhabitants of the fort, calmly looking on, neither opposing the Indians, nor suffering injury; and, from this circumstance, I conceived a hope of finding security in their houses.

Between the yard-door of my own house, and that of M. Langlade, my next neighbour, there was only a low fence, over which I easily climbed. At my entrance, I found the whole family at the windows, gazing at the scene of blood before them. I addressed myself immediately to M. Langlade, begging that he would put me into some place of safety, until the heat of the affair should be over; and act of charity by which he might perhaps preserve me from the general massacre; but, while I uttered my petition, M. Langlade, who had looked for a moment at me, turned again to the window, shrugging his shoulders, and intimating, that he could do nothing for me:—"*Que voudriez-vous que j'en ferais?*" ["What do you want me to do?"]

This was a moment of despair; but, the next, a Pani woman, a slave of M. Langlade's, beckoned to me to follow her. She brought me to a door, which she opened, desiring me to enter, and telling me that it led to the garret, where I must go and conceal myself. I joyfully obeyed her directions; and she, having followed me up to the garret-door, locked it after me, and with great presence of mind took away the key.

This shelter obtained, if shelter I could hope to find it, I was naturally anxious to know what might still be passing without. Through an aperture, which afforded me a view of the area of the fort, I beheld, in shapes the foulest and most terrible, the ferocious triumphs of barbarian conquerors. The dead were scalped and mangled; the dying were writhing and shrieking, under the unsatiated knife and tomahawk; and, from the bodies of some, ripped open, their butchers were drinking the blood, scooped up in the hollow of joined hands, and quaffed amid shouts of rage and victory. I was shaken, not only with horror, but with fear. The sufferings which I witnessed, I seemed on the point of experiencing. No long time elapsed, before every one being destroyed, who could be found, there was a general cry, of "All is finished!" At the same instant, I heard some of the Indians enter the house in which I was.

The garret was separated from the room below, only by a layer of single boards, at once the flooring of the one and the ceiling of the other. I could therefore hear every thing that passed; and, the Indians no sooner came in, than they inquired, whether or not any Englishman were in the house? M. Langlade replied, that "He could not say—he did not know of any;"—answers in which he did not exceed the truth; for the Pani woman had not only hidden me by stealth, but kept my secret, and her own. M. Langlade was therefore, as I presume, as far from a wish to destroy me, as he was careless about saving me, when he added to these answers, that "They might examine for themselves, and would soon be satisfied, as to the object of their question." Saying this, he brought them to the garret door.

The state of my mind will be imagined. Arrived at the door, some delay was occasioned by the absence of the key, and a few moments were thus allowed me, in which to look around for a hiding-place. In one corner of the garret was a heap of those vessels of birch-bark, used in maple-sugar making . . .

The door was unlocked, and opening, and the Indians ascending the stairs, before I had completely crept into a small opening, which presented itself, at one end of the heap. An instant after, four Indians entered the room, all armed with tomahawks, and all besmeared with blood, upon every part of their bodies.

The die appeared to be cast. I could scarcely breathe; but I thought that the throbbing of my heart occasioned a noise loud enough to betray me. The Indians walked in every direction about the garret, and one of them approached me so closely that at a particular moment, had he put forth his hand, he must have touched me. Still, I remained undiscovered; a circumstance to which the dark colour of my clothes, and the want of light, in a room which had no window, and in the corner in which I was, must have contributed. In a word, after taking several turns in the room, during which they told M. Langlade how many they had killed, and how many scalps they had taken, they returned down stairs, and I, with sensations not to be expressed, heard the door, which was the barrier between me and my fate, locked for the second time.

There was a feather-bed on the floor; and, on this, exhausted as I was, by the agitation of my mind, I threw myself down and fell asleep. In this state I remained till the dusk of the evening, when I was awakened by a second opening of the door. The person, that now entered, was M. Langlade's wife, who was much surprised at finding me, but advised me not to be uneasy, observing, that the Indians had killed most of the English, but that she hoped I might myself escape.—A shower of rain having begun to fall, she had come to stop a hole in the roof. On her going away, I begged her to send me a little water, to drink; which she did.

As night was now advancing, I continued to lie on the bed, ruminating on my condition, but unable to discover a resource, from which I could hope for life. A flight, to

Détroit, had no probable chance of success. The distance, from Michilimackinac, was four hundred miles; I was without provisions; and the whole length of the road lay through Indian countries, countries of an enemy in arms, where the first man whom I should meet would kill me. To stay where I was, threatened nearly the same issue. As before, fatigue of mind, and not tranquillity, suspended my cares, and procured me further sleep.

The game of baggatiway, as from the description above will have been perceived, is necessarily attended with much violence and noise. In the ardour of contest, the ball, as has been suggested, if it cannot be thrown to the goal desired, is struck in any direction by which it can be diverted from that designed by the adversary. At such a moment, therefore, nothing could be less liable to excite premature alarm, than that the ball should be tossed over the pickets of the fort, nor that having fallen there, it should be followed, on the instant, by all engaged in the game, as well the one party as the other, all eager, all struggling, all shouting, all in the unrestrained pursuit of a rude athletic exercise. Nothing could be less fitted to excite premature alarm—nothing, therefore, could be more happily devised, under the circumstances, than a stratagem like this; and this was, in fact, the stratagem which the Indians had employed, by which they had obtained possession of the fort, and by which they had been enabled to slaughter and subdue its garrison, and such of its other inhabitants as they pleased. To be still more certain of success, they had prevailed upon as many as they could, by a pretext the least liable to suspicion, to come voluntarily without the pickets; and particularly the commandant and garrison themselves.

The respite which sleep afforded me, during the night, was put an end to by the return of morning. I was again on the rack of apprehension. At sunrise, I heard the family stirring; and, presently after, Indian voices, informing M. Langlade that they had not found my hapless self among the dead, and that they supposed me to be somewhere concealed. M. Langlade appeared, from what followed, to be, by this time, acquainted with the place of my retreat, of which, no doubt, he had been informed by his wife. The poor woman, as soon as the Indiɑ·s mentioned me declared to her husband, in the French tongue, that he should no longer keep me in his house, but deliver me up to my pursuers; giving as a reason for this measure, that should the Indians discover his instrumentality in my concealment, they might revenge it on her children, and that it was better that I should die, than they. M. Langlade resisted, at first, this sentence of his wife's; but soon suffered her to prevail, informing the Indians that he had been told I was in his house, that I had come there without his knowledge, and that he would put me into their hands. This was no sooner expressed than he began to ascend the stairs, the Indians following upon his heels.

I now resigned myself to the fate with which I was menaced; and regarding every attempt at concealment as vain, I arose from the bed, and presented myself full in view, to the Indians who were entering the room. They were all in a state of intoxication, and entirely naked, except about the middle. One of them, named Wenniway, whom I had previously known, and who was upward of six feet in height, had his entire face and body covered with charcoal and grease, only that a white spot, of two inches in diameter, encircled either eye. This man, walking up to me, seized me, with one hand, by the collar of the coat, while in the other he held a large carving-knife, as if to plunge it into my breast; his eyes, meanwhile, were fixed stedfastly on mine. At length, after some seconds, of the most anxious suspense, he dropped his arm, saying, "I won't kill you!"—To this he added, that he had been frequently engaged in wars against the English, and had brought away many scalps; that, on a certain occasion, he had lost a brother, whose name was Musinigon, and that I should be called after him.

A reprieve, upon any terms, placed me among the living, and gave me back the sustaining voice of hope; but Wenniway ordered me down stairs, and there informing me that I was to be taken to his cabin, where, and indeed every where else, the Indians were all mad with liquor, death again was threatened, and not as possible only, but as certain. I mentioned my fears on this subject to M. Langlade, begging him to represent the danger to my master. M. Langlade, in this instance, did not withhold his compassion, and Wenniway immediately consented that I should remain where I was, until he found another opportunity to take me away.

Thus far secure, I re-ascended my garret-stairs, in order to place myself, the furthest possible, out of the reach of insult from drunken Indians; but, I had not remained there more than an hour, when I was called to the room below, in which was an Indian, who said that I must go with him out of the the fort, Wenniway having sent him to fetch me. This man, as well as Wenniway himself, I had seen before. In the preceding year, I had allowed him to take goods on credit, for which he was still in my debt; and some short time previous to the surprise of the fort he had said, upon my upbraiding him with want of honesty, that "He would pay me before long!"—This speech now came fresh into my memory, and led me to suspect that the fellow had formed a design against my life. I communicated the suspicion to M. Langlade; but he gave for answer, that "I was not now my own master, and must do as I was ordered."

The Indian, on his part, directed, that before I left the house, I should undress myself, declaring that my coat and shirt would become him better than they did me. His pleasure, in this respect, being complied with, no other alternative was left me than either to go out naked, or to put on the clothes of the Indian, which he freely gave me in exchange. His motive, for thus stripping me of my own apparel, was no other, as I afterward learned, than this, that it might not be stained with blood when he should kill me.

I was now told to proceed; and my driver followed me close, until I had passed the gate of the fort, when I turned toward the spot where I knew the Indians to be encamped. This, however, did not suit the purpose of my enemy, who seized me by the arm, and drew me violently, in the opposite direction, to the distance of fifty yards, above the fort.

Here, finding that I was approaching the bushes and sand-hills, I determined to proceed no further, but told the Indian that I believed he meant to murder me, and that if so, he might as well strike where I was, as at any greater distance. He replied, with coolness, that my suspicions were just, and that he meant to pay me, in this manner, for my goods. At the same time, he produced a knife, and held me in a position to receive the intended blow. Both this, and that which followed, were necessarily the affair of a moment. By some effort, too sudden and too little dependent on thought, to be explained or remembered, I was enabled to arrest his arm, and give him a sudden push, by which I turned him from me, and released myself from his grasp. This was no sooner done, than I ran toward the fort, with all the swiftness in my power, the Indian following me, and I expecting every moment to feel his knife.—I succeeded in my flight; and, on entering the fort, I saw Wenniway, standing in the midst of the area, and to him I hastened for protection. Wenniway desired the Indian to desist; but the latter pursued me round him, making several strokes at me with his knife, and foaming at the mouth, with rage at the repeated failure of his purpose. At length, Wenniway drew near to M. Langlade's house; and, the door being open, I ran into it. The Indian followed me; but, on my entering the house, he voluntarily abandoned the pursuit.

Preserved so often, and so unexpectedly, as it had now been my lot to be, I returned to my garret with a strong inclincation to believe, that through the will of an overruling power, no Indian enemy could do me hurt; but, new trials, as I believed, were at hand, when, at ten o'clock in the evening, I was roused from sleep, and once more desired to descend the stairs. Not less, however, to my satisfaction than surprise, I was summoned only to meet Major Etherington, Mr. Bostwick and Lieutenant Lesslie, who were in the room below.

These gentlemen had been taken prisoners, while looking at the game, without the fort, and immediately stripped of all their clothes. They were now sent into the fort, under

the charge of Canadians, because, the Indians having resolved on getting drunk, the chiefs were apprehensive that
they would be murdered, if they continued in the
camp.—Lieutenant Jemette and seventy soldiers had been
killed; and but twenty Englishmen, including soldiers,
were still alive.* These were all within the fort, together
with nearly three hundred Canadians.

These being our numbers, myself and others proposed
to Major Etherington, to make an effort for regaining possession of the fort, and maintaining it against the Indians.
The Jesuit missionary was consulted on the project; but he
discouraged us, by his representations, not only of the merciless treatment which we must expect from the Indians,
should they regain their superiority, but of the little dependence which was to be placed upon our Canadian aux-
iliaries. Thus, the fort and prisoners remained in the hands
of the Indians, though, through the whole night, the prisoners and whites were in actual possession, and they were
without the gates.

That whole night, or the greater part of it, was passed in
mutual condolence; and my fellow-prisoners shared my
garret. In the morning, being again called down, I found
my master, Wenniway, and was desired to follow him. He
led me to a small house, within the fort, where, in a narrow
room, and almost dark, I found Mr. Ezekiel Solomons, an
Englishman from Détroit, and a soldier, all prisoners. With
these, I remained in painful suspense, as to the scene that
was next to present itself, till ten o'clock, in the forenoon,
when an Indian arrived, and presently marched us to the
lakeside, where a canoe appeared ready for departure, and
in which we found that we were to embark.

Our voyage, full of doubt as it was, would have commenced immediately, but that one of the Indians, who was
to be of the party, was absent. His arrival was to be waited
for; and this occasioned a very long delay, during which we

*According to Major Etherinton's report to his superiors, sixteen soldiers and the
trader Tracy were killed in the massacre, and five of those taken prisoner had since been
killed.—ED.

were exposed to a keen north-east wind. An old shirt was all that covered me; I suffered much from the cold; and, in the extremity, M. Langlade coming down to the beach, I asked him for a blanket, promising, if I lived, to pay him for it, at any price he pleased: but, the answer I received was this, that he could let me have no blanket, unless there were some one to be security for the payment. For myself, he observed, I had no longer any property in that country.—I had no more to say to M. Langlade; but, presently seeing another Canadian, named John Cuchoise, I addressed to him a similar request, and was not refused. Naked as I was, and rigorous as was the weather, but for the blanket, I must have perished.—At noon, our party was collected, the prisoners all embarked, and we steered for the Isles du Castor [the Beaver Islands], in Lake Michigan.

The soldier, who was our companion in misfortune, was made fast to a bar of the canoe, by a rope tied round his neck, as is the manner of the Indians, in transporting their prisoners. The rest were left unconfined; but a paddle was put into each of our hands, and we were made to use it. The Indians in the canoe were seven in number; the prisoners four. I had left, as it will be recollected, Major Etherington, Lieutenant Lesslie and Mr. Bostwick, at M. Langlade's, and was now joined in misery with Mr. Ezekiel Solomons, the soldier, and the Englishman who had newly arrived from Détroit. This was on the sixth day of June. The fort was taken on the fourth; I surrendered myself to Wenniway on the fifth; and this was the third day of our distress.

We were bound, as I have said, for the Isles du Castor, which lie in the mouth of Lake Michigan; and we should have crossed the lake, but that a thick fog came on, on account of which the Indians deemed it safer to keep the shore close under their lee. We therefore approached the lands of the Otawas, and their village of L'Arbe Croche, already mentioned as lying about twenty miles to the westward of Michilimackinac, on the opposite side of the tongue of land on which the fort is built.

Every half hour, the Indians gave their war-whoops, one for every prisoner in their canoe. This is a general custom, by the aid of which all other Indians, within hearing, are apprized of the number of prisoners they are carrying.

In this manner, we reached Wagoshense, a long point, stretching westward into the lake, and which the Otawas make a carrying-place, to avoid gojng round it. It is distant eighteen miles from Michilimackinac. After the Indians had made their war-whoop, as before, an Otawa appeared upon the beach, who made signs that we should land. In consequence, we approached. The Otawa asked the news, and kept the Chipeways in further conversation, till we were within a few yards of the land, and in shallow water. At this moment, a hundred men rushed upon us, from among the bushes, and dragged all the prisoners out of the canoes, amid a terrifying shout.

We now believed that our last sufferings were approaching; but, no sooner were we fairly on shore, and on our legs, than the chiefs of the party advanced, and gave each of us their hands, telling us that they were our friends, and Otawas, whom the Chipeways had insulted, by destroying the English without consulting with them on the affair. They added, that what they had done was for the purpose of saving our lives, the Chipeways having been carrying us to the Isles du Castor only to kill and devour us.

The reader's imagination is here distracted by the variety of our fortunes, and he may well paint to himself the state of mind of those who sustained them; who were the sport, or the victims, of a series of events, more like dreams than realities, more like fiction than truth! It was not long before we were embarked again, in the canoes of the Otawas, who, the same evening, relanded us at Michilimackinac, where they marched us into the fort, in view of the Chipeways, confounded at beholding the Otawas espouse a side opposite to their own.

The Otawas, who had accompanied us in sufficient numbers, took possession of the fort. We, who had changed masters, but were still prisoners, were lodged in the house of the commandant, and strictly guarded.

Early the next morning, a general council was held, in which the Chipeways complained much of the conduct of the Otawas, in robbing them of their prisoners; alleging that all the Indians, the Otawas alone excepted, were at war with the English; that Pontiac had taken Détroit; that the king of France had awoke, and repossessed himself of Quebec and Montréal; and that the English were meeting destruction, not only at Michilimackinac, but in every other part of the world. From all this they inferred, that it became the Otawas to restore the prisoners, and to join in the war; and the speech was followed by large presents, being part of the plunder of the fort, and which was previously heaped in the centre of the room.—The Indians rarely make their answers till the day after they have heard the arguments offered. They did not depart from their custom on this occasion; and the council therefore adjourned.

We, the prisoners, whose fate was thus in controversy, were unacquainted, at the time, with this transaction; and therefore enjoyed a night of tolerable tranquillity, not in the least suspecting the reverse which was preparing for us. Which of the arguments of the Chipeways, or whether or not all were deemed valid by the Otawas, I cannot say; but, the council was resumed at an early hour in the morning, and, after several speeches had been made in it, the prisoners were sent for, and returned to the Chipeways.

The Otawas, who now gave us into the hands of the Chipeways, had themselves declared, that the latter designed no other than to kill us, and *make broth of us*. The Chipeways, as soon as we were restored to them, marched us to a village of their own, situate on the point which is below the fort, and put us into a lodge, already the prison of fourteen soldiers, tied two and two, with each a rope about his neck, and made fast to a pole which might be called the supporter of the building.

I was left untied; but I passed a night sleepless and full of wretchedness. My bed was the bare ground, and I was again reduced to an old shirt, as my entire apparel, the blanket which I had received, through the generosity of M. Cuchoise, having been taken from me among the Otawas, when they seized upon myself and the others, at Wagoshense. I was, besides, in want of food, having for two days ate nothing.

I confess that in the canoe, with the Chipeways, I was offered bread—but, bread, with what accompaniment!—They had a loaf, which they cut with the same knives that they had employed in the massacre— knives still covered with blood. The blood, they moistened with spittle, and rubbing it on the bread, offered this for food to their prisoners, telling them to eat the blood of their countrymen.

Such was my situation, on the morning of the seventh of June, in the year one thousand seven hundred and sixty-three; but, a few hours produced an event which gave still a new colour to my lot.

Toward noon, when the great war-chief, in company with Wenniway, was seated at the opposite end of the lodge, my friend and brother, Wawatam, suddenly came in. During the four days preceding, I had often wondered what had become of him. In passing by, he gave me his hand, but went immediately toward the great chief, by the side of whom and Wenniway, he sat himself down. The most uninterrupted silence prevailed; each smoked his pipe; and this done, Wawatam arose, and left the lodge, saying, to me, as he passed, "Take courgage!"

An hour elapsed, during which several chiefs entered, and preparations appeared to be making for a council. At length, Wawatam re-entered the lodge, followed by his wife, and both loaded with merchandise, which they carried up the chiefs, and laid in a heap before them. Some moments of silence followed, at the end of which Wawatam pronounced a speech, every word of which, to me, was of extraordinary interest:

"Friends and relations," he began, "what is it that I shall say? You know what I feel. You all have friends and brothers and children, whom as yourselves you love; and you—what would you experience, did you, like me, behold your dearest friend—your brother—in the condition of a slave; a slave, exposed every moment to insult, and to menaces of death? This case, as you all know, is mine. See there (*pointing to myself*) my friend and brother among slaves—himself a slave!

"You all well know, that long before the war began, I adopted him as my brother. From that moment, he became one of my family, so that no change of circumstances could break the cord which fastened us together.

"He is my brother; and, because I am your relation, he is therefore your relation too:—and how, being your relation, can he be your slave?

"On the day, on which the war began, you were fearful, lest, on this very account, I should reveal your secret. You requested, therefore, that I would leave the fort, and even cross the lake. I did so; but I did it with reluctance. I did it with reluctance, notwithstanding that you, Menehwehna, who had the command in this enterprise, gave me your promise that you would protect my friend, delivering him from all danger, and giving him safely to me.

"The performance of this promise, I now claim. I come not with empty hands to ask it. You, Menehwehna, best know, whether or not, as it respects yourself, you have kept your word, but I bring these goods, to buy off every claim which any man among you all may have on my brother, as his prisoner."

Wawatam having ceased, the pipes were again filled; and, after they were finished, a further period of silence followed. At the end of this, Menehwehna arose, and gave his reply:

"My relation and brother," said he, "what you have spoken is the truth. We were acquainted with the friendship which subsisted between yourself and the Englishman, in whose behalf you have now addressed us. We knew the danger of having our secret discovered, and the consequences which must follow; and you say truly, that we requested you to leave the fort. This we did, out of regard for you and your family; for, if a discovery of our design had been made, you would have been blamed, whether guilty or not; and you would thus have been involved in difficulties from which you could not have extricated yourself.

"It is also true, that I promised you to take care of your friend; and this promise I performed, by desiring my son, at the moment of assault, to seek him out, and bring him to my lodge. He went accordingly, but could not find him. The day after, I sent him to Langlade's, when he was informed that your friend was safe; and had it not been that the Indians were then drinking the rum which had been found in the fort, he would have brought him home with him, according to my orders.

"I am very glad to find that your friend has escaped. We accept your present; and you may take him home with you."

Wawatam thanked the assembled chiefs, and taking me by the hand, led me to his lodge, which was at the distance of a few yards only from the prison-lodge. My entrance appeared to give joy to the whole family; food was immediately prepared for me; and I now ate the first hearty meal which I had made since my capture. I found myself one of the family; and but that I had still my fears, as to the other Indians, I felt as happy as the situation could allow. . . .

A few days after the occurrence of the incidents recorded in the preceding chapter, Menehwehna, whom I now found to be the great chief of the village of Michilimackinac, came to the lodge of my friend; and when the usual ceremony of smoking was finished, he observed that Indians were now daily arriving from Détroit, some of whom had lost relations or friends in the war, and who would certainly retaliate on any Englishman they found; upon which account, his errand was to advise that I should be dressed like an Indian, an expedient whence I might hope to escape all future insult.

I could not but consent to the proposal, and the chief was so kind as to assist my friend and his family in effecting that very day the desired metamorphosis. My hair was cut off, and my head shaved, with the exception of a spot on the crown, of about twice the diameter of a crown-piece. My face was painted with three or four different colours; some parts of it red, and others black. A shirt was provided for me, painted with vermilion, mixed with grease. A large collar of wampum was put round my neck, and another suspended on my breast. Both my arms were decorated with large bands of silver above the elbow, besides several smaller ones on the wrists; and my legs were covered with *mitusses*, a kind of hose, made, as is the favourite fashion, of scarlet cloth. Over all, I was to wear a scarlet blanket or mantle, and on my head a large bunch of feathers. I parted, not without some regret, with the long hair which was natural to it, and which I fancied to be ornamental; but the ladies of the family, and of the village in general, appeared to think my person improved, and now condescended to call me handsome, even among Indians. . . .

Our next encampment was on the island of Saint-Martin, off Cape Saint-Ignace, so called from the Jesuit mission of Saint Ignatius to the Hurons, formerly established there. Our object was to fish for sturgeon, which we did with great success; and here, in the enjoyment of a plentiful and excellent supply of food, we remained until the twentieth day of August. At this time, the autumn being at hand, and a sure prospect of increased security from hostile Indians afforded, Wawatam proposed going to his intended wintering-ground. The removal was a subject of the greatest joy to myself, on account of the frequent insults, to which I had still to submit, from the Indians of our band or village; and to escape from which I would freely have gone almost any where. At our wintering-ground, we were to be alone; for the Indian families, in the countries of which I write, separate in the winter season, for the convenience, as well of subsistence as of the chase, and re-associate in the spring and summer.

In preparation, our first business was to sail for Michilimackinac, where, being arrived, we procured from a Canadian trader, on credit, some trifling articles, together with ammunition, and two bushels of maize. This done, we steered directly for Lake Michigan. At L'Arbre Croche we stopped one day, on a visit to the Otawas, where all the people, and particularly O'ki'no'chu'ma'ki', the chief, the same who took me from the Chipeways, behaved with great civility and kindness. The chief presented me with a bag of maize. It is the Otawas, it will be remembered, who raise this grain, for the market of Michilimackinac.

Leaving L'Arbre Croche, we proceeded direct to the mouth of the river Aux Sables [near Ludington, Michigan], on the south side of the lake, and distant about a hundred and fifty miles from Fort Michilimackinac. On our voyage, we passed several deep bays and rivers, and I found the banks of the lake to consist in mere sands, without any appearance of verdure; the sand drifting form one hill to another, like snow in winter. Hence, all the rivers, which here entered the lake, are as much entitled to the epithet of *sandy*, as that to which we were bound. . . . In these rivers we killed many wild-fowl and beaver.

To kill beaver, we used to go several miles up the rivers, before the approach of night, and after the dusk came on, suffer the canoe to drift gently down the current, without noise. The beaver, in this part of the evening, came abroad to procure food, or materials for repairing their habitations; and as they are not alarmed by the canoe, they often pass it within gun-shot.

While we thus hunted along our way, I enjoyed a personal freedom of which I had been long deprived, and became as expert in the Indian pursuits, as the Indians.

Racoon-hunting was my more particular and daily employ. I usually went out at the first dawn of day, and seldom returned till sun-set, or till I had laden myself with as many animals as I could carry. By degrees, I became familiarized with this kind of life; and had it not been for the idea of which I could not divest my mind, that I was living among savages, and for the whispers of a lingering hope, that I should one day be released from it—or if I could have forgotten that I had ever been otherwise than as I then was—I could have enjoyed as much happiness in this, as in any other situation.

4

GEORGE CROGHAN:

A Journey down the Ohio

George Croghan (d. 1782) was one of the remarkable men of his time and was as well known in America before the Revolution as Washington and Franklin. Trader, merchant, Indian agent, land speculator, and peace negotiator, Croghan knew the country beyond the Appalachians better than any of his English-speaking contemporaries. In the words of the historian Dale Van Every in Forth to the Wilderness:

Croghan was able to encounter an Indian chief at his council fire on the Wabash, a trader with his pack train on the Tuscarawas, a settler rebuilding his burned cabin on the Susquehanna, a banker in his counting house on the Delaware, a governor in his mansion on the James, a general in his headquarters on the Hudson, or a cabinet minister in a palace on the Thames, and meet each on his own ground.

Young Croghan set out for the Pennsylvania frontier almost as soon as he stepped off the boat from Dublin in 1741. Bold and ambitious, determined to make a fortune in the Indian trade, he settled first on the westernmost edge of the wilderness, near what is now Harrisburg, but was soon venturing beyond the moun-

51

*tains into the Ohio country. There he began building an im-
mensely profitable trading empire. His outposts stood deep
inside French territory, his pack trains spread English influence
throughout the Upper Ohio valley, and his voice was heard at
Indian conferences and at treaty negotiations. The French and
Indian War put an end to his enterprises in the West and brought
Croghan to the verge of bankruptcy. But his frontier genius was
not wasted. During the war he served with General Braddock
and Robert Rogers as a soldier, negotiator, and commander of
friendly Indians, and he was instrumental in swaying the
Northwest tribes to the English cause. When the country
beyond the Appalachians was once more secure, Croghan was
in the forefront of that party of men, including Washington,
Franklin, and Sir William Johnson, who dreamed of opening the
West to colonization—at a large profit to themselves. At one
point he claimed title to upward of 300,000 acres in Pennsylvania and central New York. But with the outbreak of the
Revolution all his land schemes collapsed and he died in pov-
erty, at Passyunk, near Philadelphia, in 1782.*

*Croghan contributed greatly to the opening of the trans-
Appalachian frontier, both by his extensive explorations
beyond the mountains and by his abilities as an agent and peace
negotiator among the Indians. He made his most famous journey
to the West in 1765, immediately after returning from London
where he had been seeking support among English officials for
an imperial Indian department. As Sir William Johnson's Deputy for Indian Affairs, Croghan was to travel down the Ohio to
open the Illinois country to settlers. If possible he was to make
contact with Pontiac and negotiate an end to the Ottawa chief's
war against the English. In his Journals Croghan left a vivid
description of the undisturbed beauty of the Ohio wilderness, of
his capture by the Kickapoo ("I got a stroke of a Hatchet on the
Head," he later wrote a friend, "but my skull being pretty thick,
the hatchet would not enter, so you may see a thick skull is of
service on some occasions"), and of his meeting with Pontiac.*

From "A Selection of George Croghan's Letters and Journals relating to Tours into
the Western Country, November 16, 1750–November, 1765," Reuben Gold Thwaites,
ed., *Early Western Travels*, vol. 1 (Cleveland: Arthur H. Clark Company, 1904), pp.
126–149.

May 15th, 1765.—I set off from fort Pitt with two batteaux, and encamped at Chartier's Island, in the Ohio, three miles below Fort Pitt.

16th.—Being joined by the deputies of the Senecas, Shawnesse, and Delawares, that were to accompany me, we set off at seven o'clock in the morning, and at ten o'clock arrived at the Logs Town, an old settlement of the Shawnesse, about seventeen miles from Fort Pitt, where we put ashore, and viewed the remains of that village, which was situated on a high bank, on the south side of the Ohio river, a fine fertile country round it. At 11 o'clock we re-embarked and proceeded down the Ohio to the mouth of Big Beaver Cree [near the western border of Pennsylvania], about ten miles below the Logs Town: this creek empties itself between two fine rich bottoms, a mile wide on each side from the banks of the river to the highlands. About a mile below the mouth of Beaver Creek we passed an old settlement of the Delawares, where the French, in 1756, built a town for that nation. On the north side of the river some of the stone chimneys are yet remaining; here the highlands come close to the banks and continue so for about five miles. After which we passed several spacious bottoms on each side of the river, and came to Little Beaver Creek, about fifteen miles below Big Beaver Creek. A number of small rivulets fall into the river on each side. From thence we sailed to Yellow Creek, being about fifteen miles from the last mentioned creek; here and there the hills come close to the banks of the river on each side, but where there are bottoms, they are very large, and well watered; numbers of small rivulets running through them, falling into the Ohio on both sides. We encamped on the river bank, and found a great part of the trees in the bottom are covered with grape vines. This day we passed by eleven islands, one of which being about seven miles long. For the most part of the way we made this day, the banks of the river are high and steep. The course of the Ohio from Fort Pitt to the mouth of Beaver Creek inclines to the north-west; from thence to the two creeks partly due west.

17th.—At 6 o'clock in the morning we embarked: and

were delighted with the prospect of a fine open country on each side of the river as we passed down. We came to a place called the Two Creeks, about fifteen miles from Yellow Creek, where we put to shore; here the Senecas have a village on a high bank, on the north side of the river; the chief of this village offered me his service to go with me to the Illinois, which I could not refuse for fear of giving him offence, although I had a sufficient number of deputies with me already. From thence we proceeded down the river, passed many large, rich, and fine bottoms, the highlands being at a considerable distance from the river banks, till we came to the Buffalo Creek, being about ten miles below the Seneca village; and from Buffalo Creek, we proceeded down the river to Fat Meat Creek, about thirty miles. The face of the country appears much like what we met with before; large, rich and well watered bottoms, then succeeded by the hills pinching close on the river; these bottoms, on the north side, appear rather low, and consequently subject to inundations, in the spring of the year, when there never fail to be high freshes in the Ohio, owing to the melting of the snows. This day we passed by ten fine islands, though the greatest part of them are small. They lay much higher out of the water than the main land, and of course less subject to be flooded by the freshes. At night we encamped near an Indian village. The general course of the river from the Two Creeks to Fat Meat Creek inclines to the southwest.

18th.—At 6 o'clock, A.M. we set off in our batteaux; the country on both sides of the river appears delightful; the hills are several miles from the river banks, and consequently the bottoms large; the soil, timber, and banks of the river, much like those we have before described; about fifty miles below Fat Meat Creek, we enter the long reach, where the river runs a straight course for twenty miles, and makes a delightful prospect; the banks continue high; the country on both sides, level, rich, and well watered. At the lower end of the reach we encamped. This day we passed nine islands, some of which are large, and lie high out of the water.

19th.—We decamped at six in the morning, and saile

to a place called the Three Islands, being about fifteen miles from our last encampment; here the highlands come close to the river banks, and the bottoms for the most part—till we come to the Muskingum (or Elk) river—are but narrow: this river empties itself into the Ohio about fifteen miles below the Three Islands; the banks of the river continue steep, and the country is level, for several miles back from the river. The course of the river from Fat Meat Creek to Elk River, is about south-west and by south. We proceeded down the river about fifteen miles, to the mouth of Little Conhawa River, with little or no alteration in the face of the country; here we encamped in a fine rich bottom, after having passed fourteen islands, some of them large, and mostly lying high out of the water. Here buffaloes, bears, turkeys, with all other kinds of wild game are extremely plenty. A good hunter, without much fatigue to himself, could here supply daily one hundred men with meat. The course of the Ohio, from Elk River to Little Conhawa, is about south.

20th.—At six in the morning we embarked in our boats, and proceeded down to the mouth of Hochocken or Bottle River, where we were obliged to encamp, having a strong head wind against us. We made but twenty miles this day, and passed by five very fine islands, the country the whole way being rich and level, with high and steep banks to the rivers. From here I despatched an Indian to the Plains of Scioto, with a letter to the French traders from the Illinois residing there, amongst the Shawnesse, requiring them to come and join me at the mouth of Scioto, in order to proceed with me to their own country, and take the oaths of allegiance to his Britannic Majesty, as they were now become his subjects, and had no right to trade there without license. At the same time I sent messages to the Shawnesse Indians to oblige the French to come to me in case of refusal.

21st.—We embarked at half past 8 o'clock in the morning, and sailed to a place called the Big Bend, about thirty-five miles below Bottle River. The course of the Ohio, from Little Conhawa River to Big Bend, is about south-west by south. The country hereabouts abounds with buffalo, bears, deer, and all sorts of wild game, in such plenty, that we killed out of our boats as much as we wanted. We proceeded down the river to the Buffalo Bottom, about ten miles from the beginning of the Big Bend, where we encamped. The country on both sides of the river, much the same as we passed the day before. This day we passed nine islands, all lying high out of the water.

22d.—At half an hour past 5 o'clock, set off and sailed to a place, called Alum Hill, so called from the great quantity of that mineral found there by the Indians; this place lies about ten miles from Buffalo Bottom; thence we sailed to the mouth of Great Conhawa River, being ten miles from the Alum Hill. The course of the river, from the Great Bend to this place, is mostly west; from hence we proceeded down to Little Guyondott River, where we encamped, about thirty miles from Great Conhawa; the country still fine and level; the bank of the river high, with abundance of creeks and rivulets falling into it. This day we passed six fine islands. In the evening one of our Indians discovered three Cherokees near our encampment, which obliged our Indians to keep out a good guard the first part of the night. Our party being pretty strong, I imagine the Cherokees were afraid to attack us, and so ran off.

23d.—Decamped about five in the morning, and arrived at Big Guyondott, twenty miles from our last encampment: the country as of yesterday; from hence we proceeded down to Sandy River being twenty miles further: thence to the mouth of Scioto, about forty miles from the last mentioned river. The general course of the river from Great Conhawa to this place inclines to the south-west. The soil rich, the country level, and the banks of the river high. The soil on the banks of Scioto, for a vast distance up the country, is prodigious rich, the bottoms very wide, and in the spring of the year, many of them are flooded, so that the river appears to be two or three miles wide. Bears, deer, turkeys, and most sorts of wild game, are very plenty on the banks of this river. On the Ohio, just below the mouth of Scioto, on a high bank, near forty feet, formerly stood the Shawnesse town, called the Lower

Town, which was all carried away, except three or four houses, by a great flood in the Scioto. I was in the town at the time, though the banks of the Ohio were so high, the water was nine feet on the top, which obliged the whole town to take to their canoes, and move with their effects to the hills. The Shawnesse afterwards built their town on the opposite side of the river, which, during the French war, they abandoned, for fear of the Virginians, and removed to the plains on Scioto. The Ohio is about one hundred yards wider here than at Fort Pitt, which is but a small augumentation, considering the great number of rivers and creeks, that fall into it during the course of four hundred and twenty miles; and as it deepens but very little, I imagine the water sinks, though there is no visible appearance of it. In general all the lands on the Scioto River, as well as the bottoms on Ohio, are too rich for any thing but hemp, flax, or Indian corn.

24th, 25th, and 26th.—Stayed at the mouth of Scioto, waiting for the Shawnesse and French traders, who arrived here on the evening of the 26th, in consequence of the message I sent them from Hochocken, or Bottle Creek.

27th.—The Indians requested me to stay this day, which I could not refuse.

28th.—We set off: passing down the Ohio, the country on both sides of the river level; the banks continue high. This day we came sixty miles; passed no islands. The river being wider and deeper, we drove all night.

29th.—We came to the little Miame River, having proceeded sixty miles last night.

30th.—We passed the Great Miame River, about thirty miles from the little river of that name *and in the evening arrived at the place where the Elephants' bones are found,* where we encamped, intending to take a view of the place next morning. This day we came about seventy miles. The country on both sides level, and rich bottoms well watered.

31st.—*Early in the morning we went to the great Lick,**

*Big Bone Lick, In Boone County, Kentucky, was visited by the French in the early eighteenth century. It was a landmark for early Kentucky hunters, who describe it in terms similar to those used by Croghan. At the beginning of the nineteenth century, *where those bones are only found, about four miles from the river, on the south-east side. In our way we passed through a fine timbered clear wood; we came into a large road which the Buffaloes have beaten, spacious enough for two waggons to go abreast, and leading straight into the Lick.* It appears that there are vast quantities of these bones lying five or six feet under ground, which we discovered in the bank, at the edge of the Lick. We found here two tusks above six feet long; we carried one, with some other bones, to our boats, and set off. This day we proceeded down the river about eighty miles, through a country much the same as already described, since we passed the Scioto. In this day's journey we passed the mouth of the River Kentucky. . . .

June 1st.—We arrived within a mile of the Falls of Ohio, where we encamped, after coming about fifty miles this day.

2d.—Early in the morning we embarked, and passed the Falls. The river being very low we were obliged to lighten our boats, and pass on the north side of a little island, which lays in the middle of the river. In general, what is called the Fall here, is no more than rapids; and in the least fresh, a batteau of any size may come and go on each side without any risk. This day we proceeded sixty miles, in the course of which we passed Pidgeon River. The country pretty high on each side of the Ohio River.

3d.—In the forepart of this day's course, we passed high lands; about mid-day we came to a fine, flat, and level country, called by the Indians the Low Lands; no hills to be seen. We came about eighty miles this day, and encamped.

4th.—We came to a place called the Five Islands; these islands are very long, and succeed one another in a chain; the country still flat and level, the soil exceedingly rich, and well watered. The highlands are at least fifty miles from the banks of the Ohio. In this day's course we passed about ninety miles, the current being very strong.

---

scientists took much interest in the remains of the mammoth (or mastodon)—the "elephant's bones" described by Croghan. Thomas Jefferson and several members of the American Philosophical Society, at Philadelphia, attempted to secure a complete skeleton of this extinct giant; and a number of fossils from the lick were also sent to Europe.—THWAITES.

5th.—Having passed the Five Islands, we came to a place called the Owl River. Came about forty miles this day. The country the same as yesterday.

6th.—We arrived at the mouth of the Ouabache [Wabash], where we found a breast-work erected, supposed to be done by the Indians. The mouth of this river is about two hundred yards wide, and in its course runs through one of the finest countries in the world, the lands being exceedingly rich, and well watered; here hemp might be raised in immense quantities. All the bottoms, and almost the whole country abounds with great plenty of the white and red mulberry tree. These trees are to be found in great plenty, in all places between the mouth of Scioto and the Ouabache: the soil of the latter affords this tree in plenty as far as Ouicatonon, and some few on the Miame River. Several large fine islands lie in the Ohio, opposite the mouth of the Ouabache, the banks of which are high, and consequently free from inundations; hence we proceeded down the river about six miles to encamp, as I judged some Indians were sent to way-lay us, and came to a place called the Old Shawnesse Village, some of that nation having formerly lived there. In this day's proceedings we came about seventy-six miles. The general course of the river, from Scioto to this place, is south-west.

7th.—We stayed here and despatched two Indians to the Illinois by land, with letters to Lord Frazer, an English officer, who had been sent there from Fort Pitt, and Monsieur St. Ange, the French commanding officer at Fort Chartres, and some speeches to the Indians there, letting them know of my arrival here; that peace was made between us and the Six Nations, Delawares, and Shawnesse, and of my having a number of deputies of those nations along with me, to conclude matters with them also on my arrival there. This day one of my men went into the woods and lost himself.

8th.—At day-break we were attacked by a party of Indians, consisting of eighty warriors of the Kiccapoos and Musquattimes, who killed two of my men and three Indians, wounded myself and all the rest of my party, except two white men and one Indian; then made myself and all the white men prisoners, plundering us of every thing we had. A deputy of the Shawnesse who was shot through the thigh, having concealed himself in the woods for a few minutes after he was wounded—not knowing but they were Southern Indians, who are always at war with the northward Indians—after discovering what nation they were, came up to them and made a very bold speech, telling them that the whole northward Indians would join in taking revenge for the insult and murder of their people; this alarmed those savages very much, who began excusing themselves, saying their fathers, the French, had spirited them up, telling them that the Indians were coming with a body of southern Indians to take their country from them, and enslave them; that it was this that induced them to commit this outrage. After dividing the plunder, (they left great part of the heaviest effects behind, not being able to carry them,) they set off with us to their village at Ouatto-non, in a great hurry, being in dread of pursuit from a large party of Indians they suspected were coming after me. Our course was through a thick woody country, crossing a great many swamps, morasses, and beaver ponds. We traveled this day about forty-two miles.

9th.—An hour before day we set out on our march; passed through thick woods, some highlands, and small savannahs, badly watered. Traveled this day about thirty miles.

10th.—We set out very early in the morning, and marched through a high country, extremely well timbered, for three hours; then came to a branch of the Ouabache, which we crossed.* The remainder of this day we traveled through fine rich bottoms, overgrown with reeds, which make the best pasture in the world, the young reeds being preferable to shead oats. Here is great plenty of wild game of all kinds. Came this day about twenty-eight, or thirty miles.

---

*This branch of the Wabash is now called the Little Wabash River. The party must have taken a very circuitous route, else Croghan greatly overestimates the distances. Vincennes is about seventy-five miles from the point where they were made prisoners.—THWAITES.

11th.—At day-break we set off, making our way through a thin woodland, interspersed with savannahs. I suffered extremely by reason of the excessive heat of the weather, and scarcity of water; the little sprints and runs being dried up. Traveled this day about thirty miles.

12th.—We passed through some large savannahs, and clear woods; in the afternoon we came to the Ouabache; then marched along it through a prodigious rich bottom, overgrown with reeds and wild hemp; all this bottom is well watered, and an exceeding fine hunting ground. Came this day about thirty miles.

13th.—About an hour before day we set out; traveled through such bottoms as of yesterday, and through some large meadows, where no trees, for several miles together, are to be seen. Buffaloes, deer, and bears are here in great plenty. We traveled about twenty-six miles this day.

14th.—The country we traveled through this day, appears the same as described yesterday, excepting this afternoon's journey through woodland, to cut off a bend of the river. Came about twenty-seven miles this day.

15th.—We set out very early, and about one o'clock came to the Ouabache, within six or seven miles of Port Vincent [Vincennes]. On my arrival there, I found a village of about eighty or ninety French families settled on the east side of this river, being one of the finest situations that can be found. The country is level and clear, and the soil very rich, producing wheat and tobacco. I think the latter preferable to that of Maryland or Virginia. The French inhabitants hereabouts, are an idle, lazy people, a parcel of renegadoes from Canada, and are much worse than the Indians. They took a secret pleasure at our misfortunes, and the moment we arrived, they came to the Indians, exchanging trifles for their valuable plunder. As the savages took from me a considerable quantity of gold and silver in specie, the French traders extorted ten half johannes* from them for

*A johannies was a Portuguese coin current in America about this time, worth nearly nine dollars. The Indians, therefore, paid over forty dollars for their pound of vermilion.—THWAITES.

one pound of vermilion. Here is likewise an Indian village of the Pyankeshaws, who were much displeased with the party that took me, telling them that "our and your chiefs are gone to make peace, and you have begun a war, for which our women and children will have reason to cry." From this post the Indians permitted me to write to the commander, at Fort Chartes, but would not suffer me to write to any body else, (this I apprehend was a precaution of the French, lest their villany should be perceived too soon,) although the Indians had given me permission to write to Sir William Johnson and Fort Pitt on our march, before we arrived at this place. But immediately after our arrival they had a private council with the French, in which the Indians urged, (as they afterwards informed me,) that as the French had engaged them in so bad an affair, which was likely to bring a war on their nation, they now expected a proof of their promise and assistance. Then delivered the French a scalp and part of the plunder, and wanted to deliver some presents to the Pyankeshaws, but they refused to accept of any, and declared they would not be concerned in the affair. This last information I got from the Pyankeshaws, as I had been well acquainted with them several years before this time.

Port Vincent is a place of great consequence for trade, being a fine hunting country all along the Ouabache, and too far for the Indians, which reside hereabouts, to go either to the Illinois, or elsewhere, to fetch their necessaries.

16th.—We were obliged to stay here to get some little apparel made up for us, and to buy some horses for our journey to Ouicatonon, promising payment at Detroit, for we could not procure horses from the French for hire; though we were greatly fatigued, and our spirits much exhausted in our late march, they would lend us no assistance.

17th.—At mid-day we set out; traveling the first five miles through a fine thick wood. We traveled eighteen miles this day, and encamped in a large, beautiful, well watered meadow.

18th and 19th.—We traveled through a prodigious large meadow, called the Pyankeshaw's Hunting Ground: here is no wood to be seen, and the country appears like an ocean: the ground is exceedingly rich, and partly overgrown with wild hemp; the land well watered, and full of buffalo, deer, bears, and all kinds of wild game.

20th and 21st.—We passed through some very large meadows, part of which belong to the Pyankeshaws on Vermilion River; the country and soil much the same as that we traveled over for these three days past, wild hemp grows here in abundance; the game very plenty: at any time, in half an hour we could kill as much as we wanted.

22nd.—We passed through part of the same meadow as mentioned yesterday; then came to a high woodland, and arrived at Vermilion River, so called from a fine red earth found here by the Indians, with which they paint themselves. About half a mile from the place where we crossed this river, there is a village of Pyankeshaws, distinguished by the addition of the name of the river. We then traveled about three hours, through a clear high woody country, but a deep and rich soil; then came to a meadow, where we encamped.

23d.—Early in the morning we set out through a fine meadow, then some clear woods; in the afternoon came into a very large bottom on the Ouabache, within six miles of Ouicatanon; here I met several chiefs of the Kickapoos and Musquattimes, who spoke to their young men who had taken us, and reprimanded them severely for what they had done to me, after which they returned with us to their village, and delivered us all to their chiefs.

The distance from port Vincent to Ouicatanon is two hundred and ten miles. This place is situated on the Ouabache. About fourteen French families are living in the fort, which stands on the north side of the river. The Kickapoos and the Musquattimes, whose warriors had taken us, live nigh the fort, on the same side of the river, where they have two villages; and the Ouicatanons have a village on the south side of the river. At our arrival at this post, several of the Wawcottonans, (or Ouicatonans) with whom

I had been formerly acquainted, came to visit me, and seemed greatly concerned at what had happened. They went immediately to the Kickapoos and Musquattimes, and charged them to take the greatest care of us, till their chiefs should arrive from the Illinois, where they were gone to meet me some time ago, and who were entirely ignorant of this affair, and said the French had spirited up this party to go and strike us.

The French have a great influence over these Indians, and never fail in telling them many lies to the prejudice of his majesty's interest, by making the English nation odious and hateful to them. I had the greatest difficulty in removing these prejudices. As these Indians are a weak, foolish, and credulous people, they are easily imposed on by a designing people, who have led them hitherto as they pleased. The French told them that as the southern Indians had for two years past made war on them, it must have been at the instigation of the English, who are a bad people. However I have been fortunate enough to remove their prejudice, and, in a great measure, their suspicions against the English. The country hereabouts is exceedingly pleasant, being open and clear for many miles; the soil very rich and well watered; all plants have a quick vegetation, and the climate very temperate through the winter. This post has always been a very considerable trading place. The great plenty of furs taken in this country, induced the French to establish this post, which was the first on the Ouabache, and by a very advantageous trade they have been richly recompensed for their labor.

On the south side of the Ouabache runs a big bank, in which are several fine coal mines, and behind this bank, is a very large meadow, clear for several miles. It is surprising what false information we have had respecting this country: some mention these spacious and beautiful meadows as large and barren savannahs. I apprehend it has been the artifice of the French to keep up ignorant of the country. These meadows bear fine wild grass, and wild hemp ten or twelve feet high, which, if properly manufactured, would prove as good, and answer all the purposes of the hemp we cultivate.

July 1st.—A Frenchman arrived from the Illinois with a Pipe and Speech from thence to the Kickapoos & Musquattamies, to have me Burnt, this Speech was said to be sent from a Shawanese Indian who resides at the Ilinois, & has been during the War, & is much attached to the French interest. As soon as this Speech was delivered to the Indians by the French, the Indians informed me of it in Council, & expressed their great concern for what had already happened, & told me they then sett me & my people at liberty, & assured me they despised the message sent them, and would return the Pipe & Belt to their Fathers the French, and enquire into the reason of such a message being sent them by one of his messengers, & desired me to stay with them 'till the Deputies of the Six Nations, Shawanese & Delawares arrived with Pondiac at Ouiatonon in order to settle matters, to which I consented.

From 4th to the 8th—I had several Conferences with the Wawiotonans, Pyankeeshas, Kickapoos & Musquatamies in which Conferences I was lucky enough to reconcile those Nations to his Majesties Interest & obtain their Consent and Approbation to take Possession of any Posts in their country which the French formerly possessed & an offer of their service should any Nation oppose our taking possession of it, all which they confirmed by four large Pipes.

11th—Mr. Maisonville arrived with an Interpreter & a message to the Indians to bring me & my party to the Ilinois, till then I had no answer from Mr. St. Ange to the letter I wrote him of the 16th June, as I wanted to go to the Ilinois, I desired the Chiefs to prepare themselves & set off with me as soon as possible.

12th—I wrote to General Gage & Sir William Johnson, to Colonel Campbell at Detroit, & Major Murray at Fort Pitt & Major Firmer at Mobiel or on his way to the Mississipi, & acquainted [them with] every thing that had happened since my departure from Ft. Pitt.

July 13th—The Chiefs of the Twightwees came to me

from the Miamis and renewed their Antient Friendship with His Majesty & all his Subjects in America & confirmed it with a Pipe.

18th—I set off for the Ilinois with the Chiefs of all those Nations when by the way we met with Pondiac together with the Deputies of the Six Nations, Delawares & Shawanese, which accompanied Mr. Frazier & myself down the Ohio & also Deputies with speeches from the four Nations living in the Ilinois Country to me & the Six Nations, Delawares & Shawanese, on which we return'd to Ouiatonon and there held another conference, in which I settled all matters with the Ilinois Indians—Pondiac & they agreeing to every thing the other Nations had done, all which they confirmed by Pipes & Belts, but told me the French had informed them that the English intended to take their Country from them, & give it to the Cherokees to settle on, & that if ever they suffered the English to take possession of their Country they would make slaves of them, that this was the reason of their Opposing the English hitherto from taking possession of *Fort Chartres* & induced them to tell Mr. La Gutrie & Mr. Sinnott that they would not let the English come into their Country. But being informed since Mr. Sinnott had retired by the Deputies of the Six Nations, Delawares & Shawanese, that every difference subsisting between them & the English was now settled, they were willing to comply as the other Nations their Brethren had done and desired that their Father the King of England might not look upon his taking possession of the Forts which the French had formerly possest as a title for his subjects to possess their Country, as they never had sold any part of it to the French, & that I might rest satisfied that whenever the English came to take possession they would receive them with open arms.

July 25th.—We set out from this place (after settling all matters happily with the natives). . . .

5

DANIEL BOONE:
The Kentucky Hunter

*The American frontiersman was as much a product of myth as of
his own experience, and one of the most potent sources of that
myth was the autobiography of Daniel Boone (1734–1820),
which he dictated in about 1780 and which was edited and
expanded by John Filson, who published it in 1784 as an Appen-
dix to his* Discovery, Settlement, and Present State of Kentucky. *Widely circulated in the United States and Britain, the
book stirred the American imagination and made Boone the
archetypal image of the frontiersman, whose spirit was unconquerable and whose exploits were legendary. He possessed
courage and fortitude and a simple native wisdom, and though
he had little book learning he knew what he needed to know. He
was upright, religious, and independent. And he was a dead
shot with a musket.*

   *In his prime Daniel Boone stood five feet eight or nine inches
tall. He had a large head and blue eyes and his hair was light. He
was strong and lean and a fast runner. Legend has made him the
discoverer of Kentucky, its first explorer, and its first white*

settler. Though he was none of those things, his career is hardly diminished. Born to English parents near Reading, Pennsylvania, he was toting a musket by the time he was twelve. In 1750 his family moved to North Carolina, and there he first began hearing stories of the Kentucky frontier. For several years, however, he continued to lead a settled life, marrying a neighbor's daughter and raising a family of his own. Eventually he set out for the wilderness, exploring, hunting, and setting up outposts in the new land, and returning periodically to North Carolina to lead parties of settlers over the mountains. He was several times captured by the Indians, and during the Revolutionary War he and his companions battled Redcoats as well as redskins. After the war the territory began rapidly filling up with settlers, and Boone, who had opened the road to the West, found himself being pushed from the new-found land by the very people whose path he had cleared. His title to vast tracts of Kentucky forest became the subject of legal disputes, and finally, in about 1798, pursued by debts and having lost all his Kentucky property, Boone moved on to the Missouri territory. In about 1810 he journeyed back to Kentucky, but he only stayed long enough to pay off his debts. Travelers who saw Boone in Missouri in the last years of his life reported that the old man was still fast on his feet and as good a shot as ever. He died one day in 1820 while he was out checking his trap line.

It was on the first of May, in the year 1769, that I resigned my domestic happiness for a time, and left my family and peaceable habitation on the Yadkin River, in North Carolina, to wander through the wilderness of America in quest of the country of Kentucky, in company with John Finley, John Stewart, Joseph Holden, James Monay, and William Cool. We proceeded successfully, and after a long and fatiguing journey through a mountainous wilderness, in a westward direction, on the seventh day of June following, we found ourselves on Red River, where

From "The Adventures of Col. Daniel Boon [*sic*], containing a Narrative of the Wars of Kentucky," *The Discovery, Settlement, and Present State of Kentucky,* by John Filson (London: 1793), pp. 34–49.

John Finley had formerly been trading with the Indians, and, from the top of an eminence, saw with pleasure the beautiful level of Kentucky. Here let me observe, that for some time we had experienced the most uncomfortable weather as a prelibation of our future sufferings. At this place we encamped, and made a shelter to defend us from the inclement season, and began to hunt and reconnoitre the country. We found every where abundance of wild beasts of all sorts through this vast forest; the buffaloes were more frequent than I have seen cattle in the settlements, browzing on the leaves of the cane, or cropping the herbage on those extensive plains, fearless, because ignorant of the violence of man. Sometimes we saw hundreds in a drove, and the numbers about the salt springs were amazing. In this forest (the habitation of beasts of every kind natural to America) we practiced hunting with great success until the twenty-second day of December following.

This day John Stewart and I had a pleasing ramble, but fortune changed the scene in the close of it. We had passed through a great forest on which stood myriads of trees, some gay with blossoms, others with fruits. Nature was here a series of wonders, and a fund of delight; here she displayed her ingenuity and industry in a variety of flowers and fruits, beautifully coloured, elegantly shaped, and charmingly flavoured; and we were diverted with innumerable animals presenting themselves perpetually to our view. In the decline of the day, near Kentucky river, as we ascended the brow of a small hill, a number of Indians rushed out of a thick cane-brake upon us, and made us prisoners. The time of our sorrow was now arrived, and the scene fully opened; the Indians plundered us of what we had, and kept us in confinement seven days, treating us with common savage usage. During this time we discovered no uneasiness or desire to escape, which made them less suspicious of us; but in the dead of night, as we lay in a thick cane brake by a large fire, when sleep had locked up their senses, my situation not disposing me for rest, I touched my companion and gently awoke him. We improved this favourable opportunity and departed, leaving them to take their rest, and speedily directed our course towards our old camp, but found it plundered, and the company dispersed and gone home. About this time my brother, 'Squire Boon, with another adventurer, who came to explore the country shortly after us, was wandering through the forest, determined to find me, if possible, and accidentally found our camp. Notwithstanding the unfortunate circumstances of our company, and our dangerous situation, as surrounded with hostile savages, our meeting so fortunately in the wilderness made us reciprocally sensible of the utmost satisfaction. So much does friendship triumph over misfortune, that sorrows and sufferings vanish at the meeting not only of real friends, but of the most distant acquaintances, and substitute happiness in their room.

Soon after this, my companion in captivity, John Stewart, was killed by the savages, and the man that came with my brother returned home by himself. We were then in a dangerous, helpless situation, exposed daily to perils and death amongst savages and wild beasts, not a white man in the country but ourselves. . . .

We continued not in a state of indolence, but hunted every day, and prepared a little cottage to shelter us from the Winter storms. We remained there undisturbed during the Winter; and on the first day of May, 1770, my brother returned home to the settlement by himself, for a new recruit of horses and ammunition, leaving me by myself, without bread, salt, or sugar, without company of my fellow creatures, or even a horse or dog. I confess I never before was under greater necessity of exercising philosphy and fortitude. A few days I passed uncomfortably. The idea of a beloved wife and family, and their anxiety upon the account of my absence and exposed situation, made sensible impressions on my heart. A thousand dreadful apprehensions presented themselves to my view, and had undoubtedly disposed me to melancholy, if further indulged.

One day I undertook a tour through the country, and the diversity and beauties of nature I met with in this charming season, expelled every gloomy and vexatious thought. Just at the close of day the gentle gales retired, and left the place to the disposal of a profound calm. Not a breeze shook the most tremulous leaf. I had gained the summit of a commanding ridge, and, looking round with astonishing delight, beheld the ample plains, the beauteous tracts below. On the other hand, I surveyed the famous river Ohio that rolled in silent dignity, marking the western boundary of Kentucky with inconceivable grandeur. At a vast distance I beheld the mountains lift their venerable brows, and penetrate the clouds. All things were still. I kindled a fire near a fountain of sweet water, and feasted on the loin of buck, which a few hours before I had killed. The sullen shades of night soon overspread the whole hemisphere, and the earth seemed to gasp after the hovering moisture. My roving excursions this day had fatigued my body, and diverted my imagination. I laid me down to sleep, and I awoke not until the sun had chased away the night. I continued this tour, and in a few days explored a considerable part of the country, each day equally pleased as the first. I returned again to my old camp, which was not disturbed in my absence. I did not confine my lodging to it, but often reposed in thick cane-brakes, to avoid the savages, who, I believe, often visited my camp, but, fortunately for me, in my absence. In this situation I was constantly exposed to danger and death. How unhappy such a situation for a man tormented with fear, which is vain if no danger comes, and if it does, only augments the pain. It was my happiness to be destitute of this afflicting passion, with which I had the greatest reason to be affected. The prowling wolves diverted my nocturnal hours with perpetual howlings; and the various species of animals in this vast forest, in the daytime, were continually in my view.

Thus I was surrounded with plenty in the midst of want. I was happy in the midst of dangers and inconveniences. In such a diversity it was impossible I should be disposed to melancholy. No populous city, with all the varieties of commerce and stately structures, could afford so much pleasure to my mind, as the beauties of nature I found here.

Thus, through an uninterrupted scene of sylvan pleasures, I spent the time until the 27th day of June following, when my brother, to my great felicity, met me, according to appointment, at our old camp; shortly after, we left this place, not thinking it safe to stay there longer, and proceeded to Cumberland river, reconnoitring that part of the country until March, 1771, and giving names to the different waters.

Soon after, I returned home to my family with a determination to bring them as soon as possible to live in Kentucky, which I esteemed a second paradise, at the risk of my life and fortune.

I returned safe to my old habitation, and found my family in happy circumstances. I sold my farm on the Yadkin, and what goods we could carry with us: and on the twenty-fifth day of September, 1773, bade a farewell to our friends, and proceeded on our journey to Kentucky, in company with five families more, and forty men that joined us in Powel's Valley, which is one hundred and fifty miles from the now settled parts of Kentucky. This promising beginning was soon overcast with a cloud of adversity; for upon the tenth day of October, the rear of our company was attacked by a number of Indians, who killed six and wounded one man; of these my eldest son was one that fell in the action. Though we defended ourselves, and repulsed the enemy, yet this unhappy affair scattered our cattle, brought us into extreme difficulty, and so discouraged the whole company, that we retreated forty miles, to the settlement on Clench river. We had passed over two mountains, viz. Powels and Walden's, and were approaching Cumberland mountain when this adverse fortune overtook us. These mountains are in the wilderness, as we pass from the old settlements in Virginia to Kentucky, are ranged in a southwest and northwest direction, are of a great length and breadth, and not far distant from each other. Over these, nature hath formed passes, that are less difficult than might be expected from a view of such huge piles. The aspect of these cliffs is so wild and horrid, that it is impossible to behold them without terror. The spectator is apt to imagine that nature had formerly suffered some violent convulsion; and that these are the dismembered remains of the dreadful shock; the ruins, not of Persepolis or Palmyra, but of the world!

I remained with my family on Clench until the sixth of June, 1774, when I and one Michael Stoner were solicited by Governor Dunmore, of Virginia, to go to the Falls of the Ohio, to conduct into the settlement a number of surveyors that had been sent thither by him some months before; this country having about this time drawn the attention of many adventurers. We immediately complied with the Governor's request, and conducted in the surveyors, completing a tour of eight hundred miles, through many difficulties, in sixty-two days.

Soon after I returned home, I was ordered to take the command of three garrisons during the campaign, which Governor Dunmore carried on against the Shawanese Indians: after the conclusion of which, the militia was discharged from each garrison, and I being relieved from my post, was solicited by a number of North Carolina gentlemen, that were about purchasing the lands lying on the south side of Kentucky River from the Cherokee Indians, to attend their treaty at Wataga, in March, 1775, to negotiate with them, and mention the boundaries of the purchase. This I accepted, and, at the request of the same gentlemen, undertook to mark out a road in the best passage from the settlement through the wilderness to Kentucky, with such assistance as I thought necessary to employ for such an important undertaking.

I soon began this work, having collected a number of enterprising men well armed. We proceeded with all possible expedition until we came within fifteen miles of where Boonsborough now stands, and where we were fired upon by a party of Indians that killed two, and wounded two of our number; yet, although surprised and taken at a disadvantage, we stood our ground.

This was on the twentieth of March, 1775. Three days after, we were fired upon again, and had two men killed, and three wounded. Afterwards we proceeded on to Kentucky river without opposition; and on the first day of April began to erect the fort of Boonsborough at a salt lick, about sixty yards from the river, on the south side.

On the fourth day the Indians killed one of our men. We were busily employed in building this fort, until the fourteenth day of June following, without any farther opposition from the Indians: and having finished the works, I returned to my family, on Clench.

In a short time, I proceeded to remove my family from Clench to this garrison; where we arrived safe without any other difficulties than such as are common to this passage, my wife and daughter being the first white women that ever stood on the banks of Kentucky river.

On the twenty-fourth day of December following we had one man killed, and one wounded, by the Indians, who seemed determined to persecute us for erecting this fortification.

On the fourteenth day of July, 1776, two of Colonel Calaway's daughter's, and one of mine, were taken prisoners near the fort. I immediately pursued the Indians, with only eight men, and on the sixteenth overtook them, killed two of the party, and recovered the girls. The same day on which this attempt was made, the Indians divided themselves into different parties, and attacked several forts, which were shortly before this time erected, doing a great deal of mischief. This was extremely distressing to the new settlers. The innocent husbandman was shot down, while busy cultivating the soil for his family's supply. Most of the cattle around the stations were destroyed. They continued their hostilities in this manner until the fifteenth of April, 1777, when they attacked Boonsborough with a party of above one hundred in number, killed one man, and wounded four. Their loss in this attack was not certainly known to us.

On the fourth day of July following, a party of about two hundred Indians attacked Boonsborough, killed one man, and wounded two. They besieged us forty-eight hours; during which time seven of them were killed, and at last, finding themselves not likely to prevail, they raised the siege and departed. . . .

The savages now learned the superiority of the long knife, as they call the Virginians, by experience; being out-generalled almost in every battle. Our affairs began to wear a new aspect, and the enemy, not daring to venture on open war, practiced secret mischief at times.

On the first day of January, 1778, I went with a party of thirty men to the Blue Licks, on Licking River, to make salt for the different garrisons in the country.

On the seventh day of February, as I was hunting, to procure meat for the company, I met with a party of one hundred and two Indians, and two Frenchmen, on their march against Boonsborough, that place being particularly the object of the enemy.

They pursued, and took me; and brought me on the eighth day to the Licks, where twenty-seven of my party were, three of them having previously returned home with the salt. I knowing it was impossible for them to escape, capitulated with the enemy, and, at a distance in their view, gave notice to my men of their situation, with orders not to resist, but surrender themselves captives.

The generous usage the Indians had promised before in my capitulation, was afterwards fully complied with, and we proceeded with them as prisoners to old Chelicothe, the principal Indian town, on Little Miami, where we arrived, after an uncomfortable journey, in very severe weather, on the eighteenth day of February, and received as good treatment as prisoners could expect from savages. On the tenth day of March following, I and ten of my men were conducted by forty Indians to Detroit, where we arrived the thirtieth day, and were treated by Governor Hamilton, the British commander at that post, with great humanity.

During our travels, the Indians entertained me well; and their affection for me was so great, that they utterly refused to leave me there with the others, although the Governor offered them one hundred pounds Sterling for me, on purpose to give me a parole to go home. Several English gentlemen there, being sensible of my adverse fortune, and touched with human sympathy, generously offered a friendly supply for my wants, which I refused, with many thanks for their kindness; adding, that I never expected it would be in my power to recompense such unmerited generosity.

The Indians left my men in captivity with the British at Detroit, and on the tenth day of April brought me towards Old Chelicothe, where we arrived on the twenty-fifth day of the same month. This was a long and fatiguing march, through an exceeding fertile country, remarkable for fine springs and streams of water. At Chelicothe I spent my time as comfortably as I could expect; was adopted, according to their custom, into a family where I became a son, and had a great share in the affection of my new parents, brothers, sisters, and friends. I was exceedingly familiar and friendly with them, always appearing as chearful and satisfied as possible, and they put great confidence in me. I often went a hunting with them, and frequently gained their applause for my activity at our shooting-matches. I was careful not to exceed many of them in shooting; for no people are more envious than they in this sport. I could observe, in their countenances and gestures, the greatest expressions of joy when they exceeded me; and, when the reverse happened, of envy. The Shawanese king took great notice of me, and treated me with profound respect, and entire friendship, often entrusting me to hunt at my liberty. I frequently returned with the spoils of the woods, and as often presented some of what I had taken to him, expressive of duty to my sovereign. My food and lodging was, in common, with them, not so good indeed as I could desire, but necessity made every thing acceptable.

I now began to meditate an escape, and carefully avoided their suspicions, continuing with them at Old Chelicothe until the first day of June following, and then was taken by them to the salt springs on Sciotha, and kept there, making salt, ten days. During this time I hunted some for them, and found the land, for a great extent about this river, to exceed the soil of Kentucky, if possible, and remarkably well watered.

When I returned to Chelicothe, alarmed to see four hundred and fifty Indians, of their choicest warriors, painted and armed in a fearful manner, ready to march against Boonsborough, I determined to escape the first opportunity.

On the sixteenth, before sun-rise, I departed in the most secret manner, and arrived at Boonsborough on the twentieth, after a journey of one hundred and sixty miles; during which, I had but one meal.

I found our fortress in a bad state of defence, but we proceeded immediately to repair our flanks, strengthen our gates and posterns, and form double bastions, which we completed in ten days. In this time we daily expected the arrival of the Indian army; and at length, one of my fellow prisoners, escaping from them, arrived, informing us that the enemy had an account of my departure, and postponed their expedition three weeks. The Indians had spies out viewing our movements, and were greatly alarmed with our increase in number and fortifications. The grand councils of the nations were held frequently, and with more deliberation than usual. They evidently saw the approaching hour when the long knife would dispossess them of their desirable habitations; and anxiously concerned for futurity, determined utterly to extirpate the whites out of Kentucky. We were not intimidated by their movements, but frequently gave them proofs of our courage.

About the first of August, I made an incursion into the Indian country, with a party of nineteen men, in order to surprise a small town up Sciotha, called Paint-creek-town. We advanced within four miles thereof, where we met a party of thirty Indians, on their march against Boonsborough, intending to join the others from Chelicothe. A smart fight ensued betwixt us for some time: at length the savages gave way, and fled. We had no loss on our side; the enemy had one killed and two wounded. We took from them three horses, and all their baggage; and being informed, by two of our number that went to their town, that the Indians had entirely evacuated it, we proceeded no further, and returned with all possible expedition, to assist our garrison against the other party. We passed by them on the sixth day, and on the seventh we arrived safe at Boonsborough.

On the eighth, the Indian army arrived, being four hundred and forty-four in number, commanded by Captain Duquesne, eleven other Frenchmen, and some of their own chiefs; and marched up within view of our fort, with British and French colours flying; and having sent a summons to me, in his Britannic Majesty's name, to surrender the fort, I requested two days consideration, which was granted.

It was now a critical period with us. We were a small number in the garrison: a powerful army before our walls, whose appearance proclaimed inevitable death, fearfully painted, and marking their footsteps with desolation. Death was preferable to captivity; and if taken by storm, we must inevitably be devoted to destruction. In this situation we concluded to maintain our garrison, if possible. We immediately proceeded to collect what we could of our horses, and other cattle, and bring them through the posterns of the fort: and in the evening of the ninth, I returned answer, that we were determined to defend our fort [while] a man was living. "Now," said I, to their commander, who stood attentively hearing my sentiments, "we laugh at all your formidable preparations: but thank you for giving us notice and time to provide for our defence. Your efforts will not prevail; for our gates shall for ever deny you admittance." Whether this answer affected their courage, or not, I cannot tell; but, contrary to our expectations, they formed a scheme to deceive us, declaring it was their orders, from Governor Hamilton, to take us captives, and not to destroy us; but if nine of us would come out, and treat with them, they would immediately withdraw their forces from our walls, and return home peaceably. This sounded grateful in our ears; and we agreed to the proposal.

We held the treaty within sixty yards of the garrison, on purpose to divert them from a breach of honour, as we could not avoid suspicions of the savages. In this situation the articles were formally agreed to, and signed; and the Indians told us it was customary with them, on such occasions, for two Indians to shake hands with every whiteman in the treaty, as an evidence of entire friendship. We agreed to this also, but were soon convinced their policy was to take us prisoners. They immediately grappled us; but, although surrounded by hundreds of savages, we extricated ourselves from them, and escaped all safe into the garrison, except one that was wounded, through a heavy fire from their army. They immediately attacked us on every side, and a constant heavy fire ensued between us day and night for the space of nine days.

In this time the enemy began to undermine our fort, which was situated sixty yards from Kentucky river. They began at the water-mark, and proceeded in the bank some distance, which we understood by their making the water muddy with the clay; and we immediately proceeded to disappoint their design, by cutting a trench a-cross their subterranean passage. The enemy discovering our counter-mine, by the clay we threw out of the fort, desisted from that stratagem: and experience now fully convincing them that neither their power nor policy could effect their purpose, on the twentieth day of August they raised the siege and departed.

During this dreadful siege, which threatened death in every form, we had two men killed, and four wounded, besides a number of cattle. We killed of the enemy thirty-seven, and wounded a great number. After they were gone, we picked up one hundred and twenty-five pounds weight of bullets, besides what stuck in the logs of our fort; which certainly is a great proof of their industry. Soon after this, I went into the settlement, and nothing worthy of a place in this account passed in my affairs for some time. . . .

About [the end of June, 1780] I returned to Kentucky with my family; and here, to avoid an enquiry into my conduct, the reader being before informed of my bringing my family to Kentucky, I am under the necessity of informing him that, during my captivity with the Indians, my wife, who despaired of ever seeing me again, expecting the Indians had put a period to my life, oppressed with the distresses of the country, and bereaved of me, her only happiness, had, before I returned, transported my family and goods, on horses, through the wilderness, amidst a multitude of dangers, to her father's house, in North-Carolina.

Shortly after the troubles at Boonsborough, I went to them, and lived there peaceably until this time. The history of my going home, and returning with my family, forms a series of difficulties, an account of which would swell a volume, and being foreign to my purpose, I shall purposely omit them.

I settled my family in Boonsborough once more, and shortly after, on the sixth day of October, 1780, I went in company with my brother to the Blue Licks, and, on our return home, we were fired upon by a party of Indians; they shot him, and pursued me, by the scent of their dog, three miles, but I killed the dog, and escaped. The winter soon came on, and was very severe, which confined the Indians to their wigwams.

The severity of this winter caused great difficulties in Kentucky. The enemy had destroyed most of the corn the summer before; this necessary article was scarce and dear, and the inhabitants lived chiefly on the flesh of buffaloes. The circumstances of many were lamentable; however, being a hardy race of people, and accustomed to difficulties and necessities, they were wonderfully supported through all their sufferings, until the ensuing fall, when we received abundance from the fertile soil.

Towards spring we were frequently harassed by Indians, and, in May, 1782, a party assaulted Ashton's station, killed one man, and took a negro prisoner. Captain Ashton, with twenty-five men, pursued, and overtook the savages, and a smart fight ensued, which lasted two hours; but they being superior in number, obliged Captain Ashton's party to retreat, with the loss of eight killed, and four mortally wounded; their brave commander himself being numbered among the dead.

The Indians continued their hostilities, and about the tenth of August following, two boys were taken from Major Hoy's station. This party was pursued by Captain Holder and seventeen men, who were also defeated, with the loss of four men killed and one wounded. Our affairs became more and more alarming; several stations which had lately been erected in the country were continually infested with savages, stealing their horses and killing the men at every opportunity. In a field near Lexington, an Indian shot a man, and running to scalp him, was himself shot from the fort, and fell dead upon his enemy.

Every day we experienced recent mischiefs. The barbarous savage nations of Shawanese, Cherokees, Wyandots, Tawas, Delawares, and several others near Detroit, united in a war against us, and assembled their choicest warriors at old Chelicothe, to go on the expedition, in order to destroy us, and entirely depopulate the country. Their savage minds were inflamed to mischief by two abandoned men, Captains M'Kee and Girty. These led them to execute every diabolical scheme; and on the fifteenth day of August, commanded a party of Indians and Canadians, of about five hundred in number, against Briant's station, five miles from Lexington. Without demanding a surrender, they furiously assaulted the garrison, which was happily prepared to oppose them; and after they had expended much ammunition in vain, and killed the cattle round the fort, not being likely to make themselves masters of this place, they raised the siege, and departed in the morning of the third day after they came, with the loss of about thirty killed, and the number of wounded uncertain. Of the garrison four were killed, and three wounded.

On the eighteenth day, Colonel Todd, Colonel Trigg, Major Harland, and myself, speedily collected one hundred and seventy-six men, well armed, and pursued the savages. They had marched beyond the Blue Licks to a remarkable bend of the main fork of Licking river, about forty-three miles from Lexington . . . where we overtook them on the nineteenth day. The savages observing us, gave way, and we, being ignorant of their numbers, passed the river. When the enemy saw our proceedings, having greatly the advantage of us in situation, they formed the line of battle . . . from one bend of Licking to the other, about a mile from the Blue Licks. An exceeding fierce battle immediately began, for about fifteen minutes, when we, being over powered by numbers, were obliged to retreat, with the loss of sixty-seven men, seven of whom were taken prisoners. The brave and much-lamented Colonels Todd and Trigg, Major Harland, and my second son, were among the dead. We were informed that the Indians, numbering their dead, found they had four killed more than we; and therefore four of the prisoners they had taken, were, by general consent, ordered to be killed, in a most barbarous manner by the young warriors, in order to train them up to cruelty, and then they proceeded to their towns. . . .

I cannot reflect upon this dreadful scene, but sorrow fills my heart; a zeal for the defence of their country led these heroes to the scene of action, though with a few men, to attack a powerful army of experienced warriors. When we gave way, they pursued us with the utmost eagerness, and in every quarter spread destruction. The river was difficult to cross, and many were killed in the flight, some just entering the river, some in the water, others after crossing, in ascending the cliffs. Some escaped on horse-back, a few on foot; and being dispersed every where, in a few hours brought the melancholy news of this unfortunate battle to Lexington. Many widows were now made. The reader may guess what sorrow filled the hearts of the inhabitants, exceeding any thing that I am able to describe. Being reinforced, we returned to bury the dead, and found their bodies strewed every where, cut and mangled in a dreadful manner. This mournful scene exhibited a horror almost unparalleled: some torn and eaten by wild beats; those in the river eaten by fishes; all in such a putrified condition, that no one could be distinguished from another.

As soon as General Clark, then at the Falls of the Ohio, who was ever our ready friend, and merits the love and gratitude of all his country men, understood the circumstances of this unfortunate action, he ordered an expedition, with all possible haste, to pursue the savages, which was so expeditiously effected, that we overtook them within two miles of their towns, and probably might have obtained a great victory, had not two of their number met us about two hundred poles before we come up. These returned quick as lightning to their camp with the alarming news of a mighty army in view. The savages fled in the utmost disorder, evacuated their towns, and reluctantly left their territory to our mercy. We immediately took possession of Old Chelicothe without opposition, being deserted by its inhabitants; we continued our pursuit through five towns on the Miami rivers, Old Chelicothe, Pecaway, New Chelicothe, Will's towns, and Chelicothe; burnt them all to ashes, entirely destroyed their corn, and other fruits, and every where spread a scene of desolation in the country. In this expedition we took seven prisoners and five scalps, with the loss of only four men, two of whom were accidentally killed by our own army.

This campaign in some measure damped the spirits of the Indians, and made them sensible of our superiority. Their connections were dissolved, their armies scattered, and a future invasion put entirely out of their power; yet they continued to practice mischief secretly upon the inhabitants, in the exposed parts of the country.

In October following, a party made an excursion into that district called the Crab Orchard, and one of them being advanced some distance before the others, boldly entered the house of a poor defenceless family, in which was only a negro man, a woman, and her children, terrified with the apprehensions of immediate death. The savages, perceiving their defenceless situation, without offering violence to the family, attempted to captivate the negro, who happily proved an overmatch for him, threw him on the ground, and in the struggle, the mother of the children drew an ax from a corner of the cottage, and cut his head off, while her little daughter shut the door. The savages instantly appeared, and applied their tomahawks to the door. An old rusty gun barrel, without a lock, lay in a corner, which the mother put through a small crevice, and the savages, perceiving it, fled. In the mean time, the alarm spread through the neighbourhood, the armed men collected immediately, and pursued the ravagers into the wilderness. Thus Providence, by the means of this negro, saved the whole of the poor family from destruction. From that time, until the happy return of peace between the United States and Great Britain, the Indians did us no mischief. Finding the great king beyond the water disappointed in his expectations, and conscious of the importance of the long knife, and their own wretchedness, some of the nations immediately desired peace, to which, at present, they seem universally disposed. . . .

To conclude, I can now say that I have verified the saying of an old Indian who signed Colonel Henderson's deed. Taking me by the hand at the delivery thereof, Brother, says he, we have given you a fine land, but I believe you will have much trouble in settling it. My footsteps have often been marked with blood, and therefore I can truly subscribe to its original name. Two darling sons and a brother have I lost by savage hands, which have also taken from me forty valuable horses, and abundance of cattle. Many dark and sleepless nights have I been a companion for owls, separated from the cheerful society of men, scorched by the summer's sun, and pinched by the winter's cold, an instrument ordained to settle the wilderness: but now the scene is changed; peace crowns the sylvan shade. . . .

This account of my adventures will inform the reader of the most remarkable events of this country. I now live in peace and safety, enjoying the sweets of liberty, and the bounties of Providence, with my once fellow-sufferers in this delightful country, which I have seen purchased with a vast expence of blood and treasure, delighting in the prospect of its being in a short time one of the most opulent and powerful states on the continent of North America; which, with the love and gratitude of my countrymen, I esteem a sufficient reward for all my toil and danger.

DANIEL BOON.

Fayette county, Kentucky.

6

PETER POND:

A Connecticut Yankee
in the Old Northwest

Peter Pond (1740–1807), a Connecticut shoemaker turned fur trader, spent more than twenty years exploring and trading, on foot and by canoe, amid the forests and prairies of the Upper Mississippi area and the Canadian Northwest. Having first set out for the fur country in 1765 as a young man of twenty-five, Pond traveled far into the wilderness in search of new trapping and trading grounds and in search, too, of the elusive Northwest Passage to the Pacific. He traveled deeper into the interior of the continent than any white man had been known to travel before, and the information he brought back, and the maps he later made, contributed greatly to the white man's knowledge of that distant and unknown land (and provided the basis for the Canadian explorations of Alexander Mackenzie).

Among many of his fellow voyageurs of the north—men who were not known for their even dispositions or for moral business practices—Peter Pond was regarded as an irascible character with a violent temper: proud, bold, and utterly ruthless in competition. He was long believed to have murdered two of his arch-rivals in the fur trade, even though he was aquitted in one case and never brought to trial for the other. There was probably some truth in the portrait of Pond drawn by his contemporaries, but much of the enmity directed toward him may also have been a reflection of the bitterness felt by those who were beaten out by a clever and tenacious competitor. In any case, historians find little evidence that Pond was involved in the deaths of his rivals, and Pond's own account of his early life, although crude in form and spelling, reveals a man of sensitivity and good humor. In the excerpt that follows, Pond gives a vivid and picturesque description of a trading expedition in through Wisconsin in 1773–1774, beginning with his arrival at Mackinac from Montreal, and continuing along the old French traders' route up the Fox River and down the Wisconsin.

[At Mackinac] I found my Goods from New York Had Arived Safe. Hear I Met with a Grate meney Hundred People of all Denominations—Sum trading with the tribes that Came a Grate Distans with thare furs, Skins &Mapel Suga &c to Market. To these May be added Dride Venson, Bares Greas, and the Like which is a Considerable Part of trade. Others ware Imployd in Making up thare Equipments for to Send in to the Differant Parts of the Country to Pas the Winter with ye Indan tribes and trade what thay Git from the Hunt of ye Winter Insewing. I was one of this Discription. I Divided my Goods into twelve Parts and fited out twelv Larg Canoes for Differant Parts of the Mississippy River. Each cannew was mad of Birch Bark and white Leader [cedar] thay would Carry seven Thousand wate. . . .

. . . In . . . In Sept [1773] I Had my Small fleat Readey to Cross Lake Mishegan. On my Way to Grean Bay at the Mouth of fox river I Engaged Nine Clarkes for Differant Parts of the Northan & Westarn Countrey and Beaing Mand we Imbarkt & Crost the Lake without Seaing an Indian

From "The Journal of Peter Pond," *The Connecticut Magazine*, vol. 10 (1906), pp. 244–252.

or Eney Person Except our One. In three or four Days we arive at the Mouth of the Bay which is two or three Mile Brod. In the Mouth is Som Islands which we follow in Crossing to the South West Sid & then follow ye Shore to the Bottom is Seventey Miles whare the fox River Empteys in to the Bay. We went a Short Distans up the River whare is a small french village and thare Incampt for two Days. This Land is Exalent. The Inhabitans Rase fine Corn and Sum Artickels for fammaley youse in thare Gardens. Thay Have Sum trad with ye Indans which Pas that way. On the North Part of this Bay is a small Villeag of Indans Cald the Mannomaneas [Menominees] who Live By Hunting Cheafley. Thay have another Resois [resource]—the Bottom of the Bay Produces a Large Quantity of Wilde Rice which thay Geather in Sept for food. I ort to have Menshand that the french at ye Villeg whare we Incampt Rase fine black Cattel & Horses with Sum swine.

At the End of two Days we asended the fox river til We Came to a Villeg which Lies on the East End of a small Lake that Emties into the fox River. These People are Cald Penans [Puans] & the Lake by the same Name. These People are Singelar from the Rest of thare Neighbors. Thay Speake a Hard Un Couth Langwidge scarst to be Learnt By Eney People. Thay will not a Sosheat with or Convars with the other tribes Nor Inter-marey among them. I Enquird into the Natral Histrey of these People when I was at Detroit of the Oldest and Most Entelagent frenchmen Who had Bin aquanted with them for Meney Years. The Information amounted to this that thay formerley Lived West of ye Misrarey [Missouri] River—that thay Had Etarnal Disputes among themselves and Dispute with the Nations about them—at Length thare Neighbors In Grate Numbers fel upon them and what was Saved flead across the Misesarea to ye eastward and Over the Mississippey and on to this Lake whare thay now live thare thay met with a trib of Indans Who Suferd them to Seat Down. It was as is Suposed the foxe Nation who lived Near them. . . .

. . . The Land about them on the Lake is Exalant. Thare women Rase Corn & Beens Punkins &c But the Lake afords

no Variety of fish thare Wood Produce Sum Rabits & Par-
treageis, a small Quantaty of Vensen. Thay Live in a Close
Connection among themselves. We made But a Small Stay
Hear and Past a Small Distans on the Lake and Enterd the
fox River agane Which Leads up to the Cairing [carrying]
Plase of Osconston [Wisconsin].

We asended that River til we Cam to a High Pece of
Ground whare that Nation yous to Entan thare Dead when
thay Lived in that Part [Butte des Morts, at Oshkosh,
Wisconsin]. We stopt hear awhile finding Sum of that Nation on the Spot Who Came thare to Pay thare Respect to
thare Departed frend. Thay Had a small Cag of Rum and sat
around the grave. Thay fild thar Callemeat [calumet] and
Began thar saremony By Pinting the Stem of the Pipe
upward—then giveing it a turn in thare and then toward ye
head of the Grav—then East & West, North & South after
which thay smoaked it out and fild it agane & Lade By
—then thay took Sum Rum out of the Cag in a Small Bark
Vessel and Pourd it on the Head of the Grave By way of
giving it to thar Departed Brother—then thay all Drank
themselves—Lit the Pipe and seamed to Enjoi themselves
Verey well. Thay Repeated this till the Sperit Began to
Operate and thare harts Began to Soffen. Then thay Began
to Sing a Song or two But at the End of Every Song thay
Soffened the Clay. After Sumtime Had Relapst the Cag had
Bin Blead often. Thay Began to Repete the Satisfaction thay
had with that friend while he was with them and How fond
he was of his frends While he Could Git a Cag of Rum and
how thay youst to Injoy it togather. They Amused themselves in this manner til thay all fell a Crying and a woful
Nois thay Mad for a While til thay thought Wisely that thay
Could Not Bring him Back and it would Not Due to Greeve
two much—that an application to the Cag was the Best Way
to Dround Sorrow & Wash away Greefe for the Moshun was
soon Put in Execution and all Began to be Marcy as a Party
Could Bea. Thay Continued til Near Nite. Rite Wen thay
Ware More than Half Drunk the men began to approach the
females and Chat frelay and apearantley friendley. At
Lengh thay Began to Lean on Each other, Kis & apeared

Verey amaras. . . . I Could Observe Clearley this Bisiness
was first Pusht on by the Women who made thare visit to
the Dead a Verey pleasing one in thare Way. One of them
who was Quit Drunk, as I was By Self Seating on the
Ground observing thare Saremones, Cam to me and askt
me to take a Share in her Bountey. . . . But I thought it was
time to Quit and went about Half a mile up the River to my
Canoes whare My men was Incampt But the Indans never
cam Nigh us. The Men then shun that three of the Women
had bin at the Camp In the Night In Quest of Imploy. The
next Morning we Proseaded up the River which was Verey
Sarpentine inded til we Cam to a Shallo Lake whare you
Could Sea water But Just in the Canoe track the Wilde Oates
ware so thick that the Indans Could Scarse Git one of thare
Small Canoes into it to Geather it and the Wild Ducks When
thay Ris Made a Nois like thunder. We Got as meney of
them as we Chose fat and Good. We Incampt hear Would
not undertake to Cross til Morning—the Water was two
Deap to wade and ye Bottom Soft—the Rode so narrow that
it toock the Most of ye next Day to get about three Miles
With our Large Cannoes the track was so narrow. Near Nite
we Got to Warm Ground whare we Incampt and Regaled
Well after the fateages of the Day. The Next Day we Proseaded up the River which was slack water But Verey
Sarpentine—we Have to go two Miles Without Geating
fiftey yards ahead so winding—But Just at nite we reacht
within Site of ye Caring Plase and Incampt. Next morning
Near noon we Arived and unLoded our Canoes & toock
them out of the water to dry that thay mite be liter. On the
Caring Plase On account of the fox River and its Neghber-
ing Cuntrey A Long its Shores from the Mouth to the
Pewans Lake is A good Navagation. One or two Small
Rapeds from that Lake the water up to the Caring plase is
Verey Gental But Verey Sarpentine. In Maney Parts In
Going three Miles you due not advans one. The Bank is
almost Leavel With the Water and the Medoes on Each Sid
are Clear of Wood to a Grate Distans and Clothd with a
Good sort of Grass the Openings of this River are Cald
Lakes But thay are no more than Larg Opeings. In these

Plases the Water is about four or five feet deap. With a Soft Bottom these Places Produce the Gratest Quantaties of Wild Rise of Which the Natives Geather Grat Quantaties and Eat what thay Have Ocation for & Dispose of the Remainder to People that Pass & Repass on thare trade. This Grane Looks in its Groth & Stock & Ears Like Ry and the Grane is of the same Culler But Longer and Slimer. When it is Cleaned fit for youse thay Baile it as we Due Rise and Eat it with Bairs Greas and Suger But the Greas thay ad as it is Bileing which helps to Soffen it and make it Brake in the same Maner as Rise. When thay take it out of thare Cettels for yous thay ad a Little suger and is Eaten with fresh Vensen or fowls we yoused it in the Room of Rise and it Did very well as a Substatute for that Grane as it Busts it turns out perfeckly White as Rise. Back from this River the Lands are as Good as Can be Conseaved and Good timber But not Overthick it is Proverbel that the fires Which Ran threw these . . . and Meadows Stops the Groth of ye Wood and Destroise Small wood. I Have Menshund the Vast Numbers of Wild Ducks which faten on ye Wild Rise Eaverey fall. It would Sound two much Like a travelers Storey to Say What I Realey Beleve from What I Have Sean. You Can Purchis them Verey Cheape at the Rate of two Pens Per pese. If you Parfer shuting them yourself you may Kill what you Plese. On account of the Portage of Wisconstan the South End of this Caring plase is Verey Leavel But in Wet Weather it is Bad On acount of the Mud & Water which is two thirds of a Mile and then the Ground Riseis to a Considerabel Hith and Clothed with fine Open Wood & a Hansom Varder [verdure].

This Spot is about the Senter of ye Portage and takes up about a Quorter Part of it. The South End is Low, flat and Subject to Weat. . . .

After Two Days Hard Labor We Gits our Canoes at the Carring plase with all Our Goods and Incampt on the Bank of the River Wisconstan and Gund our Canoes fit to descend that River. About Midday we Imbarkt. The River is a Gentel Glideing Streame and a Considerabell Distans to the first Villeag which Lise on the North Side. The River Runs near west from the Portage to the Missippey. Its a Gentel Glideing Streame. As we Descended it we saw Maney Rattel Snakes Swimming Across it and Kild them. The Next Day we Arived at the Villeag whare we tarread two Days. This Beaing the Last Part of Sept these People had Eavery artickel of Eating in thare way In abandans. I shall Give Sum acount of these People and the Countrey. These People are Cald Sankeas. Thay are of a Good Sise and Well Disposed—Les Inclind to tricks and Bad manners than thare Nighbers. Thay will take of the traders Goods on Creadit in the fall for thare youse. In Winter and Except for Axedant thay Pay the Deapt Verey Well for Indans I mite have sade Inlitend or Sivelised Indans which are in General made worse by the Operation. Thare Villeag is Bilt Cheafely with Plank thay Hugh Out of Wood—that is ye uprite—the top is Larch Over with Strong Sapplins Sufficient to Support the Roof and Covered with Barks which Makes them a tile roof. Sum of thare Huts are Sixtey feet Long and Contanes Several fammalayes. Thay Rase a Platfoarm on Each Side of thare Huts About two feet high and about five feet Broad on which thay Seat & Sleap. Thay have no flores But Bild thar fire on the Ground in the Midel of the Hut and have a Hole threw the Ruf for the Smoke to Pas. In the fall of ye Year thay Leave thare Huts and Go into the Woods in Quest of Game and Return in the Spring to thare Huts before Planting time. The Women Rase Grate Crops of Corn, Been, Punkens, Potatoes, Millans and artickels—the Land is Exaleant—& Clear of Wood Sum Distans from the Villeag. Thare Sum Hundred of Inhabitants. Thare amusements are Singing, Dancing, Smokeing, Matcheis, Gameing, Feasting, Drinking, Playing the Slite of Hand, Hunting and thay are famas in Mageack. Thay are Not Verey Gellas of thare Women. In General the Women find Meanes to Grattafy them Selves without Consent of the Men. The Men often join War parties with other Nations and Go aganst the Indans on the Miseure & west of that. Sometimes thay Go Near St. Fee in New Mexico and Bring with them Spanish Horseis. I have sean meney of them. The River aford But a few fish. Thare Woods aford Partrageis, a few Rabeat, Bairs

& Deear are Plenty In thare Seasons. Wild foul thay have But few. Thar Religion is Like Most of the tribes. Thay alow thare is two Sperits—One Good Who Dweles a Bove the Clouds, Superintends over all and helps to all the Good things we have and Can Bring Sickness on us if He pleases—and another Bad one who dweles in the fire and air, Eavery whare among men & Sumtimes Dose Mischehef to Mankind.

Cortship & Marriages—At Night when these People are Seating Round thare fires the Elderly one will be teling what thay Have Sean and Heard or Perhaps thay may be on Sum Interesting Subject. The family are lisning. If thare be aney Young Garl in this Lodg or hut that aney Man of a Differant Hut Has a Likeing for he will Seat among them. The Parson of his Arrant Being Prasent hea will Watch an Opertunety & through a Small Stick at Hair. If She Looks up with a Smile it is a Good Omen. He Repets a Second time. Perhaps ye Garle will Return the Stick. The Semtam ar Still Groing Stronger and when thay think Proper to Ly Down to Slepe Each Parson Raps himself up in his One Blanket. He take Notis whar the Garl Seats for thare she slepes. When all the famaley are Quite a Perhaps a Sleap he Slips Soffely into that and Seat himself Down By her Side. PresantLey he will Begin to Lift Her Blanket in a Soft maner. Perhaps she may twich it Out of his hand with a Sort of a Sie & Snore to Gather But this is no Kiling Matter. He Seats awhile and Makes a Second Atempt. She May Perhaps Hold the Blankead Down Slitely. At Lengh she turns Over with a Sith and Quits the Hold of the Blanket. . . . This Meatherd [method] is Practest a Short time and then ye young Indan will Go ahunting and [if] he is Luckey to Git meat he Cum and Informs the famaley of it and where it is he Brings the Lung and hart with him and thay Seat of after the Meat and Bring it Home this Plesis [pleases] and he Begins to Gro Bold in the famerley. The Garl after that will not Refuse him . . . He Will then Perhaps Stay about the famerley a Year and Hunt for the Old father But in this Instans he gives his Conseant that thay may Sleap togather and when thay Begin to have Children thay save what thay can git for thare One youse and Perhaps Live in a Hut apart. After I had Given them a number of Cradeat to Receve Payment the Next Spring I Desended to the fox Villeage on the Same River and Same Sid about fiftey Miles Distans. Hear I meat a differant Sort of People who was Bread at Detroit under the french Government and Clarge [clergy]; till thay By Chrisanising Grew so Bad thay ware Oblige to Go to War aganst them. Tho thay Lived Within thre Miles of the Garrson and among the Inhabatans, thay Was Obliged to fite them and killed Grate Numbers of them. The Remander flead to the fox River whare thay made a Stand and treated the traders Going to the Missaseepey Verey Ill and Pilleaged them. At Lengh thay went a Strong Partey aganst them and Beat them back to whare thay Now are But in Sad Sarkamstanis to what thay ware Before thay took So much on them selves. As I Aprocht the Banks of the Villeag I Perseaved a Number of Long Panted Poles on which Hung a Number of Artickels, Sum Panted Dogs and also a Grate Number of Wampam Belts with a Number of Silver Braslets and Other Artickels in the Indan way. I Inquired the Cause. Thay told me thay Had a Shorte time Before had a Sweapeing Sicknes among them which had Caread of Grate Numbers of Inhabitans & thay had offered up these Sacrafisces to Apease that Beaing who was Angrey with them and sent the Sickness—that it was much Abated tho thar was Sum Sick. Still I told them thay Had Dun Right and to take Cair that thay Did not Ofend him Agane for fear a Grater Eavel myte befall them. Thare Villeag was Bilt in the Sam form & ye the sam Like Materls as the Sankeas Produse of the Ground—the Sam & Brote in the Same By the Women But not in so Grate Plentey as the former one on Account of thare Late Sickness. I taread hear One Day.

After Suplying myself with such Artickels as I wanted and thay Had to Spare I gave them Sum Creadeat and Descended the River to the Mouth which Emteys into the Masseippey and Cros that River and Incampt. The Land along the River as you desend Apears to be Exalant. Just at Night as we ware InCampt we Perseaved Large fish Cuming on the Sarfes of the Water. I had then a Diferant trader with me who had a number·of Men with him. We were Incampt Near Each other. We Put our Hoock and Lines into the Water & Leat them Ly all nite. In the Morning we Perseaved thare was fish at the Hoocks and went to the Wattr Eag and halld on our line. Thay Came Heavey. At Lengh we hald one ashore that wade a Hundered and four Pounds—a Seacond that was One Hundered Wate—a third of Seventy five Pounds. The Men was Glad to Sea this for thay Had not Eat mete for Sum Days nor fish for a long time. We asked our men How meney Men the Largest would Give a Meale. Sum of the Largest Eaters Sade twelve men Would Eat it at a Meal. We Agread to Give ye fish if thay would find twelve men that would undertake it. Thay Began to Dres it. The fish was what was Cald the Cat fish. It Had a large flat Head Sixteen Inches Betwene the Eise. Thay Skind it—Cut it up in three larg Coppers Such as we have for the Youse of our men. After it was Well Boild thay Sawd it up and all Got Round it. Thay Began and Eat the hole without the least thing with it But Salt and Sum of them Drank of the Licker it was Boild in. The Other two was Sarved out to the Remainder of the People who finished them in a Short time. Thay all Declard thay felt the Beater of thare Meale Nor did I Perseave that Eney of them ware Sick or Complaind. Next Morning we Recrost ye River which was about a Mile Brod and Mounted about three Miles til we Come to the Planes of the Dogs [Prairie du Chien] so Cald the Grate Plase of Rondavues for the traders and Indans Before thay Dispars for thare Wintering Grounds. Hear we Meat a Larg Number of french and Indans Makeing out thare arrangements for the InSewing winter and sending of thare cannoes to Differant Parts—Like wise Giveing Creadets to the Indans who war all to Rondaveuse thare in Spring. I Stayed ten days Sending of my men to Differant Parts. I had Nine Clarks which I Imploid in Differant Rivers that fel into the River.

When I had finished my Matters Hear in October I Seat of with two traders in Company for St. Peters River which was a Hundred Leags up the River But the Season was faverabel and we went on Sloley to Leat the Nottawaseas

[Sioux] Git Into the Plain that we Mite not be trubeld with them for Creadit as thay are Bad Pay Marsters. In Going up the River we had Plenty of fat Gease and Duks with Venson—Bares Meat in abandans—so that we Lived as Well as hart Could Wish on Such food—Plenty of flower tea, Coffee, Sugar and Buter, Sperits and Wine, that we faird Well as Voigers. The Banks of ye River aforded us Plentey of Crab Apels which was Verey Good when the frost Had tuchd them at a Sutabel tim. We Enter St. Peters River and Proseaded up it as far as we thought Best Without Seaing an Indan Except what we toock with us. We Incampt on a High Bank of the River that we mite not Be Overflone in the Spring at the Brakeing up of the Ice, and Bilt us Comfortbel Houseis for the Winter and trade During the Winter & Got our Goods under Cover.

To be Intelagabel I Go back to the Planes of the Dogs—this Plain is a Very Handsum one Which is on the East Side of the River on the Pint of Land Betwene the Mouth of Wisconstan whare it Emties in to the Masseppey & the Last River. The Plane is Verey Smooth hear. All the traders that Youseis [uses] that Part of the Countrey & all the Indans of Several tribes Meat fall & Spring whare the Grateist Games are Plaid Both By french & Indans. The french Practis Billiards—ye latter Ball. Hear the Botes from New Orleans Cum. Thay are navagated By thirty Six men who row as maney oarse. Thay Bring in a Boate Sixtey Hogseats of Wine on one . . . Besides Ham, Chese &c—all to trad with the french & Indans. Thay Cum up the River Eight Hundred Leages. These Amusements Last three or four weakes in the Spring of the Year. As we Proseaded up the River we found the Land & timber to be Exalant—fit for Eney Improvement. As we Past up St Peters River about fourteen miles We Stopt to Sea Carnes Hut whare he Past his Winter when in that Countrey. It was a Log House about Sixteen feet long Covered With Bark—With a fireplase—But one Room and no flore. This was the Extent of his travels. His Hole toure I with One Canoe Well maned Could make in Six weeks. We Go Forward to the Goods—we made Ourselves Comfortbel for the Winter. In Desember the Indans Sent Sum young men from the Planes a Long the River to Look for traders & thay found us. After Staying a few days to Rest them thay Departed with the Information to thare frends. In Jany thay Began to Aproach us & Brot with them Drid & Grean Meet, Bever, Otter, Dear, fox, Woolaef, Raccone & other Skins to trade. Thay ware Welcom and we Did our bisnes to advantage. Threw the Winter I had a french man for my Nighber Who had Winterd among the Nottawase Several Winters in this River Well Knone By the Differant Bands. I perseaved that he Seamd to have a Prefrans & Got more trade than myself. We ware good frends. I told him he Got more than his Share of trade But Obsarved at ye Same time it was not to be Wonderead at as he had Bin Long a Quanted. He Sade I had not Hit on ye Rite Eidea. He Sade that the Indans of that Quorter was Given to Stealing and aspachely the women. In Order to Draw Custom he Left a few Brass things for the finger on the Counter—Sum needels & awls which Cost But a trifel, Leattel Small Knives, . . . Bell and such trifles. For the sake of Stealing these trifels thay Com to Sea him and what thay Had for trade he Got. I Beleaved what he sade and tried the Expereament—found it to Prove well after which I kept up Sides. Well thare was not Eney thing Extrodnerey Hapend Dureing the Winter. We Proseaded eastward with ease & Profet till Spring. At the Brakeing up of the Ice In the River in Spring the Water Rose twentey Six feat from its Common sarfes & Made Sad Work with its Banks.

At the yousal time We prepard to Desend to the Planes of the Dogs. . . . The Waters Sun went of or fell and we Imbarkt & Drifted Down with the Currant till we Came to the Plane whare we Saw a Large Colection from Eavery Part of the Misseppey who had arived Before us—Even from Orleans Eight Hundred Leages Belowe us. The Indans Camp Excaded a Mile & a half in Length. Hear was Sport of All Sorts. We went to Colecting furs and Skins . . . By the Differant tribes with Sucksess. The french ware Veray Numeres. Thare was Not Les than One Hundred and thirtey Canoes which Came from Mackenaw Caring from Sixtey to

Eightey Hundred wate Apease all Made of Birch Bark &
white Seder for the Ribs. Those Boates from Orleans &
Ilenoa and other Parts ware Numeres. But the natives I have
no true Idea of thair Numbers. The Number of Packs of
Pottrey of Differant Sorts was Cald fifteen Hundred of a
Hundred wt Each which went to Mackana. All my outfits
had Dun well. I had Grate Share for my Part as I furnish
Much the Largest Cargo on the River. After all the Bisness
Was Dun and People Began to Groe tirde of Sport, thay
Began to Draw of for thare Differant Departments and Pre-
pare for the Insewing winter.

7

GEORGE ROGERS CLARK:
Hannibal of the West

For sheer daring and courage, few exploits in the early history of the frontier matched the conquest of the Northwest Territory in 1778 and 1779 by George Rogers Clark (1752–1818) and his small army of frontiersmen. Clark, the tall, graceful, red-haired son of a Virginia planter, was not yet twenty when he first set out for the Kentucky wilderness in 1772. Traveling far down the Ohio, he hunted and explored the green new land, fought Indians, and surveyed the country for the ever-increasing numbers of settlers. His reputation as a leader of men grew, and when the Revolution reached the frontier, Clark, at twenty-four, was commissioned a major and given charge of Kentucky's defenses.

Time and again in the "year of the bloody sevens," 1777, Indian war parties descended on the Kentuckians' isolated stockades, in a succession of raids that were organized and supplied at Detroit by the British lieutenant governor, Henry Hamilton, and that were launched from Britain's Illinois outposts at Kaskaskia, Cahokia, and Vincennes. But Clark's few short years in the wilderness had taught him what James Smith and Robert Rogers had learned not long before: that the only effective way to defend the frontier settlements was to take the offensive. Rather than huddling in a stockade and waiting to be attacked, Clark would take the war to the enemy's doorstep. He would capture the British outposts and convince the Indians of American superiority.

Winning meager support from Virginia's governor, Patrick Henry, who was worried about defenses in the East, Clark gathered what men and supplies he could and set off for Illinois in the spring of 1778, with a tiny army of 175 men. Traveling by flatboat down the Ohio to the mouth of the Tennessee, then overland across prairies and forests, the Americans took the British outposts completely by surprise. Kaskaskia, Cahokia, and Vincennes were captured in quick succession, and Clark's wise diplomacy soon won the allegiance of the French inhabitants and the neighboring tribes. Governor Hamilton quickly retaliated, marching from Detroit at the outset of winter and recapturing Vincennes from the handful of militiamen that Rogers had left behind. Clearly, Hamilton would have no difficulty in retaking the other forts in the spring, once the winter floods had subsided. He could then conquer Kentucky at will.

Clark decided to move immediately, when Hamilton would least expect an attack. The forced winter march of 180 miles from Kaskaskia to Vincennes was an epic of endurance that prompted the Virginia statesman John Randolph to call Clark "the Hannibal of the West." During that incredible trek across rain-soaked prairies and overflowing rivers, Clark's men were hardly ever dry, and they went for days without food. Clark joked and cajoled and cheered them on—and gave orders for the rear guard to shoot all deserters. The result was all that Clark had hoped for. Tricked by cunning ruses and threats, Hamilton's Indians deserted and Hamilton himself finally surrendered. With the capture of Vincennes, the Northwest Territory passed into American hands—although "for want of a few men" Clark was never able to march against Detroit—and after the war American possession of the area north of the Ohio was formalized by the treaty of 1783.

Clark's original account of the winter march, the capture of Vincennes, and his subsequent pacification of the Indians is contained in a letter he wrote a few months later to his Virginia friend and supporter, George Mason. The letter, dated November 19, 1779, is thought to have been written with the help of a companion.

We were now Sensible that St. Vincents was in possession of the English; and consequently we might shortly expect an Attact. . . . Governour Hamiltons Party consisted of about eight hundred when he took possession of that Post on the 17th day of december past: finding the Season too far spent for his intention against Kaskaskias [he] had sent nearly the whole of his Indians out in different Parties to War: But to embody as soon as the weather would Permit and compleat his design: He had also sent messengers to the southern Indians, five hundred of whom he expected to join him. [Since I had] only eighty Troops in Garrisson (our Situation still appeard desperate, it was at this moment I would have bound myself seven years a Slave to have had five hundred Troops) I saw the only probability of our maintaining the Country was to take the advantage of his present weakness, perhaps we might be fortunate: I considered the Inclemency of the season, the badness of the Roads &c—as an advantage to us, as they would be more off their Guard on all Quarters. I collected the Officers, told them the probability I thought there was of turning the scale in our favour: I found it the sentiment of every one of them and eager for it. . . .

I had a Large Boat prepared and Rigged mounting two four pounders six [*illegible*] large swevels Manned with a fine Company Commanded by Lieutenant [John] Rogers: She set out in the evening of the 4th of January with orders to force her way if possible within ten Leagues of St. Vin-

From "George Rogers Clark Papers, 1771–1781," edited with introduction and notes by James Alton James, *Collections of the Illinois State Historical Library*, vol. VIII (Springfield, 1914), pp. 138–149. Reprinted by permission.

cents and lay until further Orders. . . . By the 4th day of January [actually February 5] I got every thing Compleat and on the 5th I marched being joined by two Volunteer Companies of the Principal Young Men of the Illinois Commanded by Captain McCarty & Francis Charlaville. Those of the Troops was Captains Bowman & William Worthingtons of the light Horse. we were Conducted out of the Town by the Inhabitants: and Mr. Jeboth the Priest, who after a very suitable Discourse to the purpose, gave us all Absolution And we set out on a Forlorn hope indeed; for our whole Party with the Boats Crew consisted of only a little upwards of two hundred. I cannot account for it but I still had inward assurance of success; and never could when weighing every Circumstance doubt it: But I had some secret check. We had now a Rout before us of two hundred and Forty miles in length, through, I suppose one of the most beautiful Country in the world; but at this time in many parts flowing with water and exceading bad marching. my greatest care was to divert the Men as much as possible in order to keep up their spirits; the first ob-struction of any consequence that I met with was on the 13th Arriveing at the two little Wabachces [Wabashes] al-though three miles asunder they now make but one, the flowed water between them being at Least three feet deep, and in many places four: Being near five miles to the oppo-site Hills, the shallowest place, except about one hundred Yards was three feet. This would have been enough to have stop'ed any set of men that was not in the same temper that we was But in three days we contrived to cross, by building a large Canoe, ferried across the two Channels, the rest of the way we waded; Building scaffolds at each [shore] to lodge our Baggage on until the Horses Crossed to take them; it Rained nearly a third of our March; but we never halted for it; In the evening of the 17th we got to the low Lands of the River Umbaera which we found deep in water, it being nine miles to St. Vincents which stood on the East side of the Wabache and every foot of the way covered with deep water, we Marched down the little River in order to gain the Banks of the main [river] which we did in about three Leagues, made a small Canoe and sent an Express to meet the Boat and hurry it up from the spot we now lay on was about ten miles to Town, and every foot of the way put together that was not three feet and upwards under water would not have made the length of two miles and a half and not a mouthful of Provision; To have waited for our Boat, if possible to avoid it, would have been Impolitic If I was sensible that You wou'd let no Person see this relation I would give You a detail of our suffering for four days in crossing those waters, and the manner it was done; as I am sure that You wou'd Credit it. but it is too incredible for any Person to believe except those that are as well acquainted with me as You are, or had experienced something similar to it I hope You will excuse me until I have the pleasure of seeing You personally. But to our inexpressible Joy in the evening of the 23rd we got safe on Terra firma within half a League of the Fort, covered by a small Grove of Trees had a full view of the wished for spot (I should have crossed at a greater distance from the Town but the White River comeing in jest below us we were affraid of getting too near it) we had Already taken some Prisoners that was coming from the Town: Laying in this Grove some time to dry our Clothes by the Sun we took another Prisoner known to be a friend by which we got all the Intiligence we wished for: but would not suffer him to see our Troops except a few.

A thousand Ideas flashed in my Head at this moment I found that Governor Hamilton was able to defend himself for a considerable time, but knew that he was not able to turn out of the Fort; that if the Seige Continued long a Superior number might come against us, as I knew there was a Party of English not far above in the River: that if they found out our Numbers might raise the disaffected Savages and harass us. I resolved to appear as Darring as possible, that the Enemy might conceive by our behaviour that we were very numerous and probably discourage them. I immediately wrote to the Inhabitants in general. Informing them where I was and what I determined to do desireing the Friends to the States to keep close in their Houses those in the British Interest to repair to the fort and fight for their

King: otherways there should be no mercy shewn them &c—&c—Sending the Compliments of several Officers that was known to be Expected to reinforce me, to several Gentlemen of the Town: I dispatched the Prisoner off with this letter waiting until near sunset, giving him time to get near the Town before we marched. As it was an open Plain from the Wood that covered us; I march'd time enough to be seen from the Town before dark but taking advantage of the Land, disposed the lines in such a manner that nothing but the Pavilions [war banners] could be seen, having as many of them as would be sufficient for a thousand Men, which was observed by the Inhabitants, who had Just Receiv'd my letter counted the different Colours and Judged our number accordingly But I was careful to give them no oppertunity of seeing our Troops before dark, which it would be before we could Arrive: The Houses obstructed the Forts observing us and were not Allarmed as I expected by many of the Inhabitants: I detached Lieutenant Bayley and party to Attact the Fort at a certain Signal, and took possession of the strongest Posts of the Town with the main Body. The Garrisson had so little suspicion of what was to happen that they did not believe the Fireing was from an Enemy, until a Man was wounded through the Ports (which hapned the third or fourth shot) Expecting it to be some drunken Indians—The Fireing commenced on both sides very warm; a second Division Joined the first A considerable number of British Indians made their escape out of Town: The Kickepous and Peankeshaws to the amount of about one hundred that was in Town immediately Armed themselves in our favour and Marched to attact the Fort. I thanked the Chief for his intended service, told him the Ill consequence of our People being mingled in the dark; that they might lay in their Quarters until light. he Approved of it and sent off his Troops appeared to be much elivated himself and staid with me giving all the Information he could. (I knew him to be a friend) The Artillery from the Fort played briskly but did no execution. The Garrisson was intirely surrounded within eighty and a hundred Yards behind Houses Palings and Ditches &c—&c.—Never was a heavier fireing kept up on both sides for eighteen Hours with so little damage done. In a few hours I found my Prize sure, Certain of taking every Man that I could have wished for, being the whole of those that incited the Indians to War: all my past sufferings vanished: never was a Man more happy. It wanted no encouragement from any Officer to inflame our Troops with a Martial Spirit. The Knowledge of the Person they attacted and the thoughts of their massecred friends was Sufficient. I Knew that I could not afford to loose Men, and took the greatest care of them that I possibly could: at the same time encouraged them to be daring, but prudent. every place near the fort that could cover them was crowded, and a very heavy firing during the Night. having flung up a considerable Intrenchment before the gate where I intended to plant my Artillery when Arrived. I had learnt that one Masonville had arived that evening with two prisoners taken on the Ohio discovering some sign of us, supposed to be spies from Kentucky, immediately on his arival Captain Lemote was sent out to intercept them; being out on our Arival could not get in the Fort; in attempting several of his men was made Prisoners, himself and party hovering round the Town; I was convinced that they wou'd make off to the Indians at daybrake if they cou'd not join their friends; finding all endeavours fruitless to take him I withdrew the Troops a little before from the Garrisson in order to give him an oppertunity to get in which he did (much to his Credit and my satisfaction: as I would rather it should Receive that Reinforcement, than they should be at Large among the Savages. The firing again commenced, A number of the Inhabitants Joining the Troops & Behaved exceeding well in General; . . . about Eight o'clock in the morning I ordered the fireing to cease and sent a flag into the Garrisson with a hard Bill Recommended Mr. Hamilton to surrender his Garrisson & severe threats if he should destroy any Letters &c. He return'd an Answer to this purpose; that the Garrisson was not disposed to be awed into any thing unbecomeing British Soldiers: the Attact was Renewed with greater Vigour than ever and continued for about two hours; I was determined to listen to no Terms whatever until I was in Possession of the Fort; and only ment to keep them in Acttion with part of my Troops, while I was making necessary preparations with the other (neglected calling on any of the Inhabitants for Assistants although they wished for it) A flag appeard from the Fort with a Proposition from Mr. Hamilton for three days Cessation—A desire of a Conference with me immediately, that if I should make any difficulty of comeing into the Fort, he would meet me at the Gate: I at first had no notion of listening to any thing he had to say as I could only consider himself & Officers as Murderers, And intended to treat them as such: but after Some deliberation I sent Mr. Hamilton my Compliments, and beged leave to inform him that I should agree to no other terms than his surrendering himself and Garrisson Prisoners at discretion; but if he was desirous of a Conference with me I would meet him at the Church. We accordingly met, he Offered to surrender but we could not agree upon terms. He received such treatment on this Conference as a Man of his known Barbarity deserv'd. I would not come upon terms with him, recommended to him to defend himself with spirit and Bravery, that it was the only thing that would induce me to treat him and his Garrisson with Lenity in case I stormed it which he might expect. He asked me what more I could Require than the offers he had already made I told him (which was really the truth) that I wanted a sufficient excuse to put all the Indians & partisans to death, as the greatest part of those Villians was then with him: all his propositions was refus'd: he asked me if nothing would do but fighting. I knew of nothing else: he then begged me to stay until he should return to the Garrisson and consult his Officers: being indiferent about him and wanted a few moments for my Troops to refresh themselves I told him that the firing should not commence until such an hour, that during that time he was at Liberty to pass with safety. Some time before a Party of Warriers sent by Mr. Hamilton against Kentucky, had taken two Prisoners, was discovered by the Kickebues [Kickapoos] who gave information of them. A Party was immediately Detached to meet them which hapned in the Commons: they conceived our Troops to be a Party sent by Mr. Hamilton to conduct them in; an honour commonly paid them. I was highly pleased to see each Party hooping, hollowing and Striking each others Breasts as they approached in the open fields each seemed to try to out do the other in the greatest signs of Joy: the Poor Devils never discovered their mistake until it was too late for many of them to escape; Six of them was made Prisoners, two of them Scalped and the rest so wounded as we afterwards learnt, but one Lived. I had now a fair oppertunity of making an impression on the Indians that I could have wished for; that of convincing them that Governour Hamilton could not give them that protection that he had made them to believe he could in some measure to insence the Indians against him for not Exerting himself to save their Friends: Ordered the Prisoners to be Tomahawked in the face of the Garrisson: It had the effect that I expected: insted of making their friends inviterate against us, they upbraided the English Parties in not trying to save their frineds and gave them to understand that they believed them to be liers and no Warriers—A remarkable Circumstance hapned that I think worthy our notice: An old French Gentleman of the name of St. Croix Lieutenant of Captain McCarthy's Volunteers from Cohos had but one Son who headed these Indians and was made Prisoner. The Question was put whether the White Man Should be saved. I ordered them to put him to Death, through Indignation which did not extend to the Savages. for fear he would make his escape, his father drew his Sword and stood by him in order to Run him through in case he should stir; being painted [the father] could not know him. The Wretch on seeing the Executioners Tomahawk raised to give the fatal Stroke, raised his eyes as if making his last Addresses to heaven; Cried out O Save me. The father knew his Son's voice you may easily guess of the adgetation and behaviour of these two Persons comeing to the knowledg of each other at so critical a moment. I had so little mercy for such Murderers, and so valuable an oppertunity for an Example; knowing there would be the greatest selicitations made to save him, that I immediately absconded myself: but by the warmest Selicitations from his father who have behaved so exceedingly well in our Service; and some of the Officers, I granted his Life on certain conditions

Mr. Hamilton and myself again met: he produced certain Articles which was refused; but towards the close of the Evening I sent him the following Articles—

First: That Lieutenant Governour Hamilton engages to deliver up to Colonel Clark, Fort Sackville [as the British had renamed Vincennes] as it is at present with all the Stores &c—

Second: The Garrisson are to deliver themselves up Prisoners of War and March out with their Arms and Acoutriments &c &c—

Third: The Garrison to [be] Delivered up tomorrow at ten Oclock—

Fourth: Three days time be allowed the Garrison to settle their Accompts with the Traders and Inhabitants of this Place—

Fifthly The Officers of the Garrisson to be allowed their necessary Baggage &c—&c—

Which was agreed to and fulfilled the next day knowing that Governour Hamilton had sent a Party of Men up the Ouabach to Ome for Stores that he had left there which must be on the return; I waited about twelve hours for the Arival of the Galley to Intercept them; but fearing their getting Intiligence, dispatchd Captain Helms with a Party in Armed Boats who Supprised and made Prisoners of forty, among which was Dejeane, Grand Judge of Detroit with a large Packet from Detroit, and seven Boats load of Provisions, Indian Goods &c—Never was a Person more mortified than I was at this time to see so fair an opportunity to push a Victory; Detroit lost for want of a few Men; knowing that they would immediately make greater Preparations expecting me—The Galley had taken upon her passage the Express from Williamsburg with letters from his Excellency—Having at once all the intiligence I could wish for from both sides. I was better able to fix my future Plans of operation against Du Troit. By his Excellencies

Letter I might expect to have a Compleat Batallian in a few months, the Militia of the Illinois I knew would turn out, did not doubt of getting two or three hundred Men from Kentucky Consequently put the matter out of doubt.

I contented myself on that Presumption having almost as many Prisoners as I had Men—Seeing the necessity of geting rid of many of the Prisoners, not being able to guard them; not doubting but my good treatment of the Volunteers Inhabitants of Detroit would Promote my Interest there I discharged the greatest Part of them that had been with Indian Parties, on their taking the Oath of Neutrality. They went off huzzaing for the Congress and declared though they could not fight against the Americans they would for them. (As I after this had Spies constant to and from Detroit I learnt they answered every purpose that I could have wished for, by prejudiceing their friends in favour of America. So certain was the Inhabitants of that Post, of my Marching immediately against it, that they made Provision for me in defiance of the Garrison Many of them has paid dear for it since.

I dispatched off Captain Williams and Company with Governour Hamilton, his principal Officers and a few Soldiers to the Falls of Ohio, to be sent to Williamsburg, and in a few days sent my letters to the Governour. Having matters a little setled, the Indian Department became the next Object. I knew that Mr. Hamilton had endeavoured to make them believe that we intinded at last to take all their Lands from them and that in case of Success we should shew no greater Mercy for those that did not join him than those that did. I indeavoured to make myself acquainted [with] the Arguments he used: And calling together the Neighbouring Nations, Peankeshaws, Kickepoes, & others that would not listen to him Indeavoured to undeceive them; I made a very long Speach to them in the Indian manner, Extol'd them to the Skies for their Manly behaviour and fedility; told them that we were so far from having any design on their Lands, that I looked upon it that we were on their Land where the Fort stood, that we claimed no Land in their Country; that the first Man that offered to take their Lands by Violence must strike the tomahawk in my head; that it was only necessary that I should be in their Country during the War and keep a Fort in it to drive off the English, who had a design against all People; after that I might go to some place where I could get Land to support Me: The Treaty was concluded to the satisfaction of both parties; they were much pleased at what they hear'd and begged me to favour them the next day with my Company at a Council of theirs I accordingly Attended: greatest part of the time spent in Ceremony; They at last told me they had been meditating on what I had said the day before: that all the Nations would be rejoiced to have me always in their Country as their great Father and Protector: And as I had said I would claim no Land in their Country, they were determin'd that they would not loose me on that Accounp: and Resolved to give me a piece, but larger than they had given to all the French at that Village, and laying down what they would wish me to do &c—I was well pleased at their offer as I had then an oppertunity to deny the exceptance, & farther convince them that we did not want their Land; they appear'd dejected at my Refusial; I waved the discourse upon other Subjects: Recommended a frolick to them that night as the Sky was clearer than ever; gave them a quantity of [rum] and Provisions to make merry on and left them. In a few days some Chipoways and others who had been with Mr. Hamilton, came in and begged me to excuse their blindness and take them into favour; after the warmest Silicitations for Mercy, I told them that the Big Knives was mercifull which Proved them to be Warriers; that I should send Belts and a Speech to all the Nations: that they after hearing of it might do as they pleased but must blame themselves for future misfortunes and dispatched them. Nothing destroys Your Interest among the Savages so soon as wavering sentiments or speeches that shew the least fear. I consequently had observed one steady line of conduct among them: Mr. Hamilton, who was almost Deified among them being captured by me, it was a sufficient confirmation to the Indians of every thing I had formerly said to them and gave the greatest weight to the Speeches I intended to send them: expecting that I should shortly be able to fulfill my threats with a Body of Troops sufficient to penetrate into any part of their Country: and by Reducing Detroit bring them to my feet—I sent the following Speech to the different Tribes near the Lakes that was at war with us. to wit—

To the Warriers of the different Nations—
Men and Warriers; it is a long time since the Big Knives [the Americans] sent Belts of peace among You Siliciting of you not to listen to the bad talks and deceit of the English as it would at some future day tend to the Destruction of your Nations. You would not listen, but Joined the English against the Big Knives and spilt much Blood of Women & Children. The Big Knives then resolved to shew no mercy to any People that hereafter would refuse the Belt of Peace. . . .

I now send two Belts to all the Nations, one for Peace and the other for War. The one that is for War has your great English fathers Scalp tied to it, and made red with his Blood; all you that call yourselves his Children, make your Hatchets sharp & come out and Revenge his Blood on the Big knives fight like Men that the Big Knives may not be ashamed when they fight you; that the old Women may not tell us that we only fought Squaws. If any of you is for taking the Belt of Peace send the Bloody Belt back to me that I may know who to take by the hand as Brothers, for you may be Assured that no peace for the future will be granted to those that do not lay down their Arms immediately. Its as you will I dont care whether you are for Peace or War; as I Glory in War and want Enemies to fight us, as the English cant fight us any longer, and are become like Young Children begging the Big Knives for Mercy and a little Bread to eat; this is the last Speech you may ever expect from the Big knives, the next thing will be the Tomahawk. And You may expect in four Moons to see Your Women & Children given to the Dogs to eat, while those Nations that have kept their words with me will Flourish and grow like the Willow Trees on the River Banks under the care and nourishment of their father the Big Knives.

In a few weeks great Numbers came into St. Vincents and treated for Peace being laughed at by those that had strictly adhear'd to their former Treaty with me. After fixeing every Department so as to promise future advantage . . . [and] leaving a sufficient Garrison on the 20th of march I set out for Kaskaskias by Water with a Guard of eighty Men. . . .

8

ALEXANDER HENRY THE YOUNGER:
The Red River Brigade

Among the famous Northmen who traveled the lakes and rivers of the Old Northwest, one of the few to leave a detailed account of the trader's life was Alexander Henry the Younger (d. 1814), nephew of the other Alexander Henry, the long-time trader on the Upper Great Lakes (see Selection 3). The younger Henry, a partner and fur trader in the Northwest Fur Company, spent fifteen years, from 1799 to 1814, trading among the Indians, learning their ways, and taking their women for his wives. Traveling by canoe, on horseback, and by dog sled, he journeyed from Montreal to the Pacific, living in or passing through the Canadian provinces of Ontario, Manitoba, Saskatchewan, Alberta, and the Northwest Territories, and through the states of Wisconsin, Minnesota, North Dakota, Idaho, Oregon, and Washington. Most of the time he diligently kept a journal of his travels and adventures, making his last entry the day before his death by drowning at the mouth of the Columbia River. In minute and graphic detail he described the grandeur of the countryside and the agony of saddle sores, the migrations of the birds and the patching of a damaged canoe. He recorded his battles with the Sioux. He noted the customs of the various tribes, the changes in the weather, and the day-to-day business of the fur trade, from setting traps to building a fort to cheating the Indians with watered-down liquor. His journals, copied in 1824, then long forgotten, were reissued in 1897–though much of his flowery prose had to be edited and condensed to make it readable. The opening of the following excerpt, from the edited journals of the years 1800–1801, finds Henry at the Grand Portage on Lake Superior's north shore. His route westward followed the usual passage to the interior: along the Rainy River (now the boundary of Minnesota and Ontario), through the Lake of the Woods, then along the Winnipeg River and through Lake Winnipeg to the Red River of the north.

Saturday, July 19th, 1800, 3 p. m. Our baggage and other necessaries having been carried over the portage, which is about nine miles, our men fully equipped for the year, and their accounts settled, I set off for Fort Charlotte, where I arrived at 5 p. m. The portage was very bad in some places, being knee-deep in mud and clay, and so slippery as to make walking tedious.

Sunday, July 20th. The canoes having been given out to the men, to gum and prepare, I found everything ready for our departure; and early this morning gave out to all their respective loading, which consisted of 28 packages per cánoe, assorted for the Saulteur trade on Red river, namely:

Merchandise, 90 pounds each,...........	5 bales
Canal tobacco, ...	1 bale
Kettles,...	1 bale
Guns,..	1 case
Iron works, ...	1 case
New twist tobacco,.........................	2 rolls

From *New Light on the Early History of the Greater Northwest*, Elliot Coues, ed. (New York: 1897), pp. 6–8, 22–24, 28–30, 42–45, 91, 93–103, 122–123, 152, 155–157, 159, 167, 168–169, 171–174, 177–178, 183–184.

Leaden balls, ...	2 bags
Leaden shot, ...	1 bag
Flour, ...	1 bag
Sugar, ...	1 keg
Gunpowder, ...	2 kegs
High wine, 9 gallons each, ...	10 kegs
Total, ...	28 pieces

Equipage for the voyage: Provisions for four men to Red river, 4 bags corn, 1½ bushels in each; ½ keg grease; 4 packages, of about 90 pounds each, private property belonging to the men, consisting of clothing, tobacco, etc., for themselves and families for the year; so that when all hands were embarked, the canoes sunk to the gunnel.

At ten o'clock the brigade were all off, and at three o'clock I followed. The water was very low. In a short time we came to Partridge portage, of about 600 paces over. The road was very slippery and muddy. Having got our baggage over, we embarked and proceeded to the Prairie, where our people were camped. All were merry over their favorite regale, which is always given on their departure, and generally enjoyed at this spot, where we have a delightful meadow to pitch our tents, and plenty of elbow-room for the men's antics. . . .

Aug. 4th. . . . came to the entrance of Lake of the Woods; when, having a fine calm, we made the traverse and camped at the [Big] island. A terrible storm during the night.

Aug. 5th. This morning early embarked; wind aft; came to the Rocher Rouge, where we found a number of Indians who had made canoes and were all intoxicated with liquor received for them. . . . we purchased a few fish and dried hurtleberries, and proceeded on our journey without molestation. We had left them but a short time when a sturgeon almost jumped into my canoe; his head struck the gunnel near one of the men who, instead of taking hold of him, gave a scream, and the fish fell into the water again. The wind came on so strong as to oblige us to put ashore, where we passed the rest of the day in drying our goods at L'Anse de Sable. . . .

Aug. 9th. At daybreak we embarked. . . . We were troubled by a thick fog, which caused us to lose much time in going round the bays. We at last got astray and were obliged to wait until the weather cleared up about ten o'clock, when we proceeded to Portage de l'Isle, about 50 paces over. One of my canoes, to avoid the trouble of making this portage, passed down near the N. shore with a full load. As my own canoe was soon over the portage, we loaded and embarked, and on pushing from shore I perceived the canoe on the N. side coming off to sault [shoot] the rapids. She had not gone many yards when, by some mismanagement of the foreman, the current bore down her bow full upon the shore, against a rock, upon which the fellow, taking the advantage of his situation, jumped, whilst the current whirled the canoe around. The steersman, finding himself within reach of the shore, jumped upon the rock with one of the midmen; the other midman, not being sufficiently active, remained in the canoe, which was instantly carried out and lost to view amongst the high waves. At length she appeared and stood perpendicular for a moment, when she sank down again, and I then perceived the man riding upon a bale of dry goods in the midst of the waves. We made every exertion to get near him, and did not cease calling out to him to take courage and not let go his hold; but alas! he sank under a heavy swell, and when the bale arose the man appeared no more. At this time we were only a few yards from him; but while we were eagerly looking out for him, poor fellow! the whirlpool caught my canoe, and before we could get away she was half full of water. We then made all haste to get ashore, unload, and go in search of the property. The canoe we found flat upon the water, broken in many places. However, we hauled her ashore, and afterward collected as many pieces as we could find. The men had landed a few packages above the rapid, otherwise our loss would have been still greater. The loss amounted to five bales merchandise, two bales new tobacco, one bale canal tobacco, one bale kettles, one bale balls, one bale shot, one case guns. I was surprised that a keg of sugar drifted down about half a mile below the rapid, as its weight was 87 lbs.; it proved to be but little damaged. The kegs of gunpowder also floated a great distance, and did not leak. . . .

Aug. 18th. . . . we arrived at the Forks [now the site of Winnipeg], where the Assiniboine joins Red river, the former coming in from the W., while the latter keeps its direct course from the S.

I found about 40 Saulteurs awaiting my arrival; they were provided with a plentiful stock of dried buffalo meat, and anxious for a dram. I accordingly gave liquor in return for their provisions; they fell to and kept drinking all night, during which we were plagued by mosquitoes, and prevented from sleeping by the howling the Indians and their dogs kept up.

Aug. 19th. We began early this morning to unpack, assort, and divide the goods, one-half intended for Portage la Prairie on the Assiniboine, and the remainder for Red river. This employed us most of the day, during which we also settled the men, delivered the baggages, and attended to the Indians, who were still drinking. . . .

[Having split his party in two at the Forks, Henry proceeded south up the Red River, into the country of the hostile Sioux. His company consisted of twenty-one *voyageurs*, four of whom had brought along their wives and children. Close behind came a party of forty-one Ojibway Indians and their families, intending to trap and trade for the white man's merchandise. Early in September the parties reached Park River, near the present town of Grafton, in northeastern North Dakota, where Henry decided to build his winter quarters.]

Sept. 9th. Early this morning I . . . went in search of a proper place to build. I found none so well situated for defense, with timber at hand, as a point of wood on the W. side, about a quarter of a mile from the entrance of Park river, with a beautiful level plain intervening. I should have preferred to build at the entrance, but there was no wood on the one side, and the land was too low on the other. We also examined the E. side of Red river, but there the land was low, subject to overflow in the spring, with no wood but very large elms and oaks, too heavy for the men to stir.

This being settled, the canoes drifted down to the place I had chosen. Our first work was to unload and carry our baggages and canoes up the hill, which is about 30 feet high. We then arranged camp in the best order possible for defense, and made a suitable stage near by, to hold fresh meat, etc. I opened a case of ironworks [hardware]; gave each man a large ax to put in order, and then a dram of high wine. I then trenched out the spot for our fort, which I wished to make as compact as possible. . . .

Sept. 10th. All hands were up early . . . I gave them all a dram and set them at work to build a storehouse, to get the goods under cover as soon as possible. Some were employed chopping logs, others cutting hay to cover, and others making wooden shovels. We have no other wood for building but oak.

This afternoon Crow arrived on horseback, having left the [Ojibways] at the Bois Percé; they were coming up slowly. He was happy to find us building, and tells me that I shall take out some good packs of beaver. . . .

Park river, near which we are settled, derives its name from the fact that the Assiniboines once made a park or pound on this river for buffalo. It receives its waters from a large lake and marshes in the Hair hills, which come down in three branches [present South fork, Middle fork, and Cart creek] to within about 15 miles of Red river, in a direct line, where they join nearby at the same spot to form one stream. . . . The water is thick and muddy until it empties into Red river; its banks are almost level with the plain, and but partially wooded. Between this and Panbian river is one continual level plain, where not the least hillock nor wood of any kind is to be seen. The country southward appears to be the same as that we have already passed through.

Sept. 11th. I climbed up a tall oak, which I had trimmed for that purpose, at the entrance of the plain, from the top of which I had an extensive view of the country. Buffalo and red deer were everywhere in sight, passing to and fro. The weather being perfectly serene, I could distinguish the Hair hills on the W., though they were scarcely perceptible—nothing more than a blue stripe, running N. and S. The interval is a level meadow, with nothing to attract the eye but the winding course of Park river, whose wood is lost to the sight long before it reaches the hills. The distance may be between 12 and 15 leagues.

. . . This afternoon Charlo and family arrived on foot. He wanted liquor for four bearskins, but I would give him none until all the Indians arrived, when I proposed to sell them liquor for what few skins and provisions they might have; as giving them rum for nothing was out of the question. I had already given them as much as they deserved, and for the future, if they wanted liquor, they must expect to pay for it.

This afternoon my storehouse was finished; I immediately put everything into it, and a padlock on the door. I now desired each man to cut 50 oak stockades 12 feet long, and carry them to the spot where I proposed erecting the fort. Maymiutch, Liard, and Aceguemanche arrived and camped; they had killed 12 bears. Crow, who had gone hunting, returned, having killed two bears. I shot a wolf that was passing on the opposite side of the river, and killed him dead. My double-barreled gun is an excellent piece. Buffaloes come down to drink, both day and night, near our camp; we seldom molest them, but allow them to return in quiet. The Indians this evening loaded our stage with bears' fat and choice meat. This would have been a glorious time for my men, had not dread of the Sioux deprived them of their appetite and made them only anxious to finish the fort.

Sept. 12th. The Indians left early to hunt and make discoveries above. My men were hard at work cutting and carrying the stockades. It required the full strength of two men to carry one log at a time on their shoulders, and though the distance was only about 200 paces, this was laborious, and soon took the skin off. Fear was an excellent overseer, and the work went on with expedition. At twelve o'clock the rest of the Indian families arrived, and soon after the hunters returned, having been up about four leagues to Salt river, where they saw no sign of an enemy; they had killed four bears. I supposed they might now drink in safety, and therefore began to trade rum; they were all soon drunk, men, women, and even some of the children. I settled with Little Crane to hunt for me. I promised that if he would behave well, and kill as many animals as I might require for the season, I would pay him 60 skins, furnish a gun, and ammunition, and give a clothing to himself and his wife.

Sept. 13th. . . . This evening I settled a plan with Maymiutch for future operations, as he apprehended no danger from the enemy at present, the season being advanced when the Sioux resort to St. Peter's river [the Minnesota] to see their traders. He told me that the Indians would go up Red river a few miles where there were bears and beaver cabins, and plenty of other animals; there they would remain some time and do for the best. . . .

Sunday, Sept. 14th. The men began early to plant the stockades, the women went for meat, and some of the Indians killed four bears. . . .

Sept. 15th. I equipped my hunter with clothing for himself and his wife, and then gave out to the Indians their necessaries for debts to the amount of 20 skins each, and an assortment of small articles gratis, such as one scalper, two folders, and four flints apiece to the men, and to the women two awls, three needles, one seine of net thread, one fine steel, a little vermilion, and half a fathom of tobacco. My hunter killed a large bear near camp; when I instantly sent for it; the hunter, returning with the men, killed another, and Maymiutch killed four more. Desmarais this evening went to seine with the men in two small canoes. They caught one sturgeon, two catfish, six brim, and a number of other small fish. Bulls continued near camp, but the cows kept at a distance. The Indians, proposing to embark to-morrow, were gumming their canoes. . . .

Sept. 17th. . . . My men were employed in cutting up and melting bears' fat, which we pour into red deer skins

and wooden troughs; but we have collected such a quantity
that we can find no place to store it, and the weather being
sultry great quantities spoil. The raw fat will not keep many
days, particularly when the weather is sultry, soon turning
rancid; but when melted down and properly taken care of,
it will keep good and sweet at any season.

Sept. 18th. I took my usual morning view from the top of
my oak and saw more buffaloes than ever. They formed one
body, commencing about half a mile from camp, whence
the plain was covered on the W. side of the river as far as the
eye could reach. They were moving southward slowly, and
the meadow seemed as if in motion. . . . At ten o'clock part
of the women returned to camp, informing me that their
husbands had altered their minds and intended to go up
Red river. They had taken their bear-traps on their backs
and proceeded S. W. toward the Hair hills, to a place where
they had seen beaver last summer. . . . They had sent me
word to take care of their families, as they would being me
beaver or lose their heads.

This afternoon I rode a few miles up Park river. The few
spots of wood along it have been ravaged by buffaloes;
none but the large trees are standing, the bark of which is
rubbed perfectly smooth, and heaps of wool and hair lie at
the foot of the trees. The small wood and brush are entirely
destroyed, and even the grass is not permitted to grow in
the points of wood. The bare ground is more trampled by
these cattle than the gate of a farm-yard. This is a delightful
country, and, were it not for perpetual wars, the natives
might be the happiest people upon earth. . . .

Sept. 20th. At daybreak I awoke my men to begin work;
but they assembled around the fire and each began to relate
his discoveries. This discourse brought up other matters of
their own, and what with cutting tobacco and smoking the
sun was high before they thought about their work. I was
therefore obliged to reprimand them for their indolence,
and remind them of our defenseless situation in case the
Sioux should fall upon us. This had the desired effect; they
labored with redoubled ardor, and our work went on with
great dispatch. At noon two Indians came from above to ask
me to send a large canoe for what they had collected at their

tents.* They informed me they had killed forty bears, some red deer, moose, and a few beavers and raccoons. This afternoon the men finished planting the stockades and hung the gates, so we are in a position to defend ourselves, and might defy several hundred Sioux. The Indian lad killed two bears.

Sunday, Sept. 21st. The men began to fell trees for our dwelling-houses. It was at their own option to work this day or not; their excuse is the necessity of forwarding their work as fast as possible to get under cover before cold weather. They are but few, badly provided with axes, and have much work still to do, cutting firewood, etc. I sent Desmarais and another man in a large canoe to the Indians' tent above, with nine gallons of mixed liquor for them. He returned with a canoe-load of bear's oil, fat, meat, skins, etc. He says the beach is covered with bear's fat where the Indians are tented, the women being too lazy to melt and preserve it in red deer skins. . . .

Sept. 23rd. Last night great numbers of swans and geese passed, flying S., and this morning they continued. The weather was cold, with a strong N. wind. . . .

Sept. 24th. The stench about camp being so great from the quantities of flesh and fat thrown away since our arrival, and the bastions of my tent being complete, with a flooring about nine feet from the ground, I caused it to be pitched up in the S. W. bastion, on this flooring. Here, from the door of my tent, I could see everything that went on, both within and without the stockade, and also had a fine view of the country around us. I cut down a number of the small oaks, which intercepted the full view of the plains. My men also pitched their tents inside the stockade, and we determined to be regular in shutting the gates at night. Our situation appeared very comfortable and my people began to enjoy their kettle more than heretofore. . . .

Sept. 25th. . . . Wind, N. E., wild fowl passing in abundance; the leaves are falling, having turned yellow a few days ago. . . .

---

*The Indians had no tents, properly so called; Henry means the huts, or whatever shelter they made for themselves where they were camped. . . .—Coues.

Sept. 27th. An Indian came in early from the Salt River camp, and informed me they had been alarmed and were all gone on discoveries. One of them positively said he saw a man, who hid in the grass and willows. Another said he found the spot on the beach where a person had laid grass and sticks on the mud on purpose to drink, the prints of the hands being very plain. It appeared to them this must have been done by a stranger. We awaited with anxiety the result of this affair. . . .

This alert will injure my returns, as the Indians had found some beavers' cabins and were preparing to hunt when they got alarmed. We had a hard frost last night; the water in our kettles this morning had a covering of ice about a quarter of an inch thick. . . .

Oct. 22d. I desired my men to begin to cut our winter stock of fuel—120 cords of oak will suffice for the four fireplaces, as we shall leave early in the spring. . . .

Nov. 14th. . . . I had my three canoes put in safety for the winter, between my house and the stockades, bottom upward, on three cross poles, and well covered with about a foot thick of straw, having loosened the ribs. . . .

Nov. 22d. My chimney smoked intolerably; therefore, the weather being moderate, I had it torn down and built anew. My men came in with a load of meat from the hunter's tent. Bulls are numerous. Ten Red Lake Indians arrived from Riviere aux Voleurs. . . . They brought a tolerably good trade. I treated them well, and they made great promises—probably more than they will perform.

Sunday, Nov. 23d. The Indians set off early on their return, well pleased with their reception. The mice destroy everything; they eat my skins and peltries—indeed, anything that is not iron or steel goes down with them.

Nov. 24th. My men making dog sleighs to haul meat home. They have excellent oak for that purpose. Desmarais making snowshoes. . . .

Nov. 25th. I sent two men early, with letters to Portage la Prairie, to inform our gentlemen to the N. of my transactions in this quarter. They take on sleigh and two dogs, to draw their provisions and blankets. . . .

Nov. 28th. Two men from Portage la Prairie arrived with

the two I had sent from here on the 25th. They met at Reed river, where both parties arrived the same day. They bring me letters from all my friends on the Assiniboine, and dispatches from Grand Portage of Aug. 9th.

I find myself obliged to send Desmarais to join Mr. [Charles Jean Baptiste] Chaboillez at Portage la Prairie. Larocque, senior, came in from his traps, with a skunk, a badger, and a large white wolf, all three caught in the same trap at once, as he said. This we thought extraordinary—indeed, a falsehood—until he explained the affair. His trap was made in a hollow stump, in the center of which there was a deep hole in the ground. He found the wolf just caught, and still alive; he dispatched him, and on taking him out, noticed something stirring and making a noise in the hole in the ground. Upon looking in he perceived the badger, which he killed with a stick, and on pulling him out, smelled the horrid stench of the skunk, which was in one corner of the hole; he soon dispatched him also. From this the Indians all predicted some great misfortune, either to the person to whom the traps belonged, or to our fort. Some supposed the Sioux would destroy us all.

Nov. 29th. Desmarais prepared for his departure with a heavy heart, as he fond of this place. . . .

Monday, Dec. 1st. . . . I have frequent visits from the Red Lake Indians, who bring a few skins.

Jan. 14th. At daybreak I was awakened by the bellowing of buffaloes. I got up, and was astonished when I climbed into the S. W. bastion. On my right the plains were black, and appeared as if in motion, S. to N. Opposite the fort the ice was covered; and on my left, to the utmost extent of the reach below us, the river was covered with buffalo moving northward. Our dogs were confined within the fort, which allowed the buffalo to pass within a few paces. I dressed and climbed my oak for a better view. I had seen almost incredible numbers of buffalo in the fall, but nothing in comparison to what I now beheld. The ground was covered at every point of the compass, as far as the eye could reach, and every animal was in motion. All hands soon attacked them with a tremendous running fire, which put them to a quicker pace, but had no effect in altering their course. The first roads beaten in the snow were followed by those in the rear. They passed at full speed until about nine o'clock, when their numbers decreased and they kept further off in the plain. There was about 15 inches of snow on a level, in some places drifted in great banks. Notwithstanding the buffalo were so numerous, and 12 guns were employed, we killed only three cows and one old bull, but must have wounded a great number.

Jan. 15th. The plains were still covered with buffalo moving slowly northward. . . .

Jan. 19th. Most of the Indians camped at the fort, having left off hunting. . . .

My winter stock of provision is complete—all good, fat buffalo meat, and my men have little to do. They, therefore, amuse themselves by sliding down the bank on sleighs from the S. gate. Their descent is so great as to cause their trains to run across Red river. The Indian women join them, and they have excellent sport. They have given over trapping since Christmas, as they took nothing worth their while. Indians go hunting on the E. side of the river, where the buffalo are as numerous as on the W., and much easier to approach in the willows and long grass. My men have finished hauling in fire-wood, with the assistance of their dogs. . . .

Mar. 5th. The snow being entirely melted, and the ground thawing about noon, renders it very muddy, at times over the shoes. . . .

. . . My men have raised and put their traps in order for the spring hunt, as the raccoons begin to come out of their winter quarters in the daytime, though they retire to the hollow trees at night. On the 8th it rained for four hours; fresh meat thawed. On the 9th we saw the first spring bird. . . .

Mar. 14th. My two men that I sent to Portage la Prairie Feb. 1st, arrived with Messrs. Chaboillez . . . and John Cameron. They bring the Northwest Company's northern winter express, which will proceed with all dispatch to Grand Portage; there to be put on board the vessel and conveyed to Sault Ste. Marie, where it arrives about June 1st, and sometimes in May, according to the state of the ice in Lake Superior. It generally starts from Athabasca Jan. 1st.

The ice is rising in a body, in consequence of the melting snow. Being apprehensive the water would come into the fort and overflow the property, I set all hands to erect a large stage, on which we laid most of our property. On the 15th we saw six swans and several outardes going N., and on the 17th had a terrible snowstorm; buffaloes near the fort. . . . *19th*. Mr. Chaboillez and his men set off with two of mine, loaded with goods. The river continues to rise, and is now only a few feet from the gate. Got out my canoes, repaired and gummed them, and placed them in the fort ready to load, to save ourselves in the plain, in case the water rises suddenly. *20th*. I saw a sturgeon jump. . . . *30th*. Rain broke up the ice; it drifted in large masses, making a great noise by crushing, tumbling, and tossing in every direction, driven by a strong current. Many trunks of trees and much mud are carried down on the ice. It continued to drift on the 31st, bearing great numbers of dead buffalo from above, which must have been drowned in attempting to cross while the ice was weak. My four men returned from Portage la Prairie. The water is falling fast, leaving us an ugly, dirty bank, covered with nearly a foot of slime and mud; had it risen two feet more, we should have had it in our houses. A heavy fall of snow.

Wednesday, Apr. 1st. The river clear of ice, but drowned buffalo continue to drift by entire herds. . . .

May 1st. The stench from the vast numbers of drowned buffalo along the river was intolerable. Gummed my canoes. *2d*. Two hunters arrived in a skin canoe from Grandes Fourches with 30 beaver and 7 bear skins. They tell me the number of buffalo lying along the beach and on the banks above passes all imagination; they form one continuous line, and emit a horrid stench. I am informed that every spring it is about the same.

May 4th. All hands up early, prepared for embarkation; Indians still drinking, and troublesome for liquor. At ten o'clock I sent off the canoes with 45 pieces of 90 pounds each per canoe, but only two men, there being no room for more on board. Quantities of fresh meat remain in my provision store, perfectly good to eat. The canoes were no sooner off than the women and children began to rummage the buildings, even raising the floors, to search for any trifle that might have been lost during the winter. I remained till noon, wishing them to embark on board their skin canoes, which they then did; and, having seen them all off, I bid adieu to Park river. . . .

[*May 20th.*] At sunset we arrived at the Forks, where I found my people waiting for me. No news from Assiniboine river. . . .

May 22d. Gave my people directions to take care of the baggage, and set off on horseback for Portage la Prairie, where I arrived at dusk. Found all hands actually starving. I remained here until June 1st, when I embarked for Grand Portage in a light canoe with eight men.

RETURNS OF LOWER RED RIVER DEPARTMENT, 1800–01.

	REED RIVER, M. LANGLOIS.	PARK RIVER, A. HENRY.	TOTALS, IN 4 CANOES.
Beaver skins; weight, 1,904 lbs	832	643	1,475
Black bear skins	52	125	177
Brown bear do	20	23	43
Grizzly bear do	4	2	6
Wolf do	111	83	204
Red fox do	82	102	184
Kitt do	9	7	16
Raccoon do	37	160	197
Fisher do	108	70	178
Otter do	60	36	96
Marten do	26	36	62
Mink do	68	29	97
Wolverene do	2	3	5
Loup-cervier do	9	11	20
Dressed moose and biche skins	1	20	21
Shaved and parchment do	63	29	92
Muskrat do	1	26	27
Buffalo robes	26	31	56
Badger skins	1	9	10
Packs of 90 lbs. each	26	34	60
Bag of pemmican of 90 lbs. each	20	57	77
Kegs of grease		4	4
Kegs of beef		7	7
Bales of dried meat		10	10

Gain, Halifax currency, £1,958 11s. 11d.

9

PHILIP TOME:

Elk Hunting on the Susquehanna

Philip Tome (1782–1855), the greatest hunter of the Pennsylvania frontier, was born in Dauphin County, near present-day Harrisburg, in 1782, when the Iroquois and Susquehannock Indians were still making life difficult for the settlers in the area. His father had been a hunter before him, and young Philip learned to read the signs of the woods like other men read books. Like James Fenimore Cooper's Leatherstocking he was a trusted friend of the Indians, serving the Seneca chiefs Cornplanter and Blacksnake as an interpreter for fifteen years. Little else is known of Tome's life, but he wrote down his hunting tales and had them published in a small edition in 1854, the year before he died. Thus he preserved a record of his encounters with bear, wolf, panther, elk, and other big game on the Allegheny frontier, telling his tales with the quiet humor and matter-of-fact pride of a man who, by his own account, "was never conquered by man or beast." The story that follows describes one of Tome's most daring feats, the capture of a live elk, which he exhibited— at great profit–throughout New York State and Pennsylvania.

From *Pioneer Life; or, Thirty Years a Hunter. Being Scenes and Adventures in the Life of Philip Tome* . . . Published for the Author (Buffalo, N.Y., 1854). Reprinted (Harrisburg, Pa., 1928), pp. 53–59.

When I lived on Kenzua Flats, in 1816, I went to see Cornplanter, about catching some elk. He said that I could not do it; that no Indian of the Six Nations had done it, or any white man that he knew of. He said that young elk three or four months old had been caught, but no live, full-grown one could be—they were lords of the forest. I told him that I had caught or assisted in catching and leading in three. He asked how we led them, and I informed him. He said he did not know but it was possible, but he did not believe I could take one that winter on the Allegany, as he thought they were larger and wilder than those on the Susquehannah. I told him that if he would show me the track of an elk—I did not care how large—the larger the better; I would willingly wager a small sum of money that I would being on in alive. He said that he could show plenty of elk-tracks. I told him to find a man that I could hire, and I would employ him. He brought a man who charged a dollar a day, which I agreed to pay him on condition that he would find a track. He said there was no doubt but that we could find one. There was no rope to be procured except one that belonged to Cornplanter, for which he wanted two dollars, but agreed to refund the money if I returned the rope uninjured. I agreed to his terms, and left the money. As we parted he wanted to shake hands, saying that he never expected to see me again if I attempted to catch an elk alive. The next morning the Indian I had engaged joined me, and I entered into a partnership with a Mr. Campbell, each of us to stand half the expense and have half the profits. We hired two other men who were to have all they killed and half that we killed. On the third day of January, Campbell and myself, the two white men, the Indian, and four dogs started up Kenzua Creek. We went about twelve miles up the south branch, and encamped for the night. The next morning we continued about six miles, to the top of a hill, and halted. The Indian said we would find elk within four or five miles of this spot. I proposed to divide, Campbell, myself and the Indian each taking a separate course while the two others should remain to build a camp where we would all meet at night. Accordingly, as soon as we had eaten dinner we all started, and remained out until dark, when we met at the camp. No one had discovered any indications of elk. The next morning I told them we would hunt one day more, each upon a different course. I took a direct easterly course, and the others chose each his own route. At night all but the Indian came in, without having discovered any signs of an elk. I told Campbell I thought it useless to hunt here longer, as there were probably no elk in the vicinity. About eight o'clock one of the party discovered the Indian coming in, followed apparently by one of the dogs. He remarked that one of the dogs was loose, and following the Indian in. I found the dogs all in their places, and told the men I thought it was a wolf they saw. At this moment he stopped and we saw at a glance that it was a panther. We sprang forward with our guns, when he turned, and moved off. We followed him two miles, without obtaining a shot at him, when we returned to our camp. We paid the Indian and let him go. I told Campbell I would not be disappointed in this manner, but would hunt all winter rather than give up. We concluded to go to the headwaters of the Susquehannah, and accordingly started on the eighth of January, going about fifteen miles up the Kenzua, and encamped for the night. The next day, when we had proceeded about twelve miles we arrived at a place where a village now stands, but at that time there was but a solitary house in which lived a family named Smith. The man had gone to procure a barrel of flour, and since his departure a deep snow had fallen. He had now been gone three days beyond the expected time, and the supply of provisions and fuel which he had left was nearly exhausted. In addition to the prospect of starvation which stared them in the face, his family were harrassed with fear that he had perished in the snow. The next day we prepared her a supply of fire-wood, left a loaf of bread and flour enough to supply her for two days, and promised to send her man back, on our arrival at the canoe place. We arrived there a little before night, and engaged a man named Burt to go back to the distressed family. He took with him some corn meal and potatoes, and we continued on to Isaac Lyman's, about twelve miles farther. He asked us to come in; we got to talking about elk-hunting, and I asked him what a full-grown live elk would be worth. He said from three to four hundred dollars. I asked him if he would purchase one if I had the luck to catch one. He replied that he had not the means, but would like to join us, and would furnish three men, a horse, and all the provisions necessary, and have one-half the profits. After some consultation, Campbell and I finally consented to accept the proposal. The whole party, consisting of Campbell, myself, three assistants, a horse and four dogs, started the next morning, taking the road to the Susquehannah River. About twelve miles from Lyman's we came upon the track of eight elk, going west. We followed about four miles and encamped for the night. The next morning Campbell, myself, and one of the men continued on the track of the elk, leaving the others to build a shanty. We went about five miles, started the elk and killed one, with which we returned to camp. We sent one of the men home with the meat, and started with the other two for the Susquehannah. The man who went home was to return to the camp in three days, with a supply or provisions. After traveling seven or eight miles, we came to where a large drove of elk had been some time before. We hunted during the day to ascertain what course they had taken, and about five miles distant we came to where they had lain the preceding night. Campbell and one of the men George Ayres, went forward, while the other man and myself remained behind with the dogs. They were to call to us when they saw the elk, and we were to let the dogs loose, though I told him I did not believe there were any there we would want to catch, as I thought they were all fawns and does. After they had gone a short distance they saw them, and counted forty-two. They called to us, and we let the dogs loose. The elk scattered, and each of the dogs took after a separate animal, but none of them stopped, and we did not kill any. The dogs all came back that night, and the next morning we went so[u]theast, and found signs of elk, but they all appeared to be small ones. By this time Mr. Lyman's hands wished to go home, so we told them we would keep on to the southeast, and they might go. The following morning they said they did not like to go, as the tracks might be filled with snow. We then said we would strike the road and they might go home from there, while we would go to our log hut, and procure some more provisions. When we reached the road, we told them they might as well go to the shanty and stay with us that night, as it was late. We found two men there with an abundance of provisions. The next morning two men left, while Ayres and another remained. We hunted the next three days without seeing any tracks which we thought best to follow. We then came back to the road, and the remaining two men left for home with two dogs. We sent word by them to Lyman to send provisions to the camp on Kettle Creek, where we should be in a few days. We hunted the next two days without accomplishing any thing, when we returned to the camp. On our arrival there I told Campbell he might take his choice to make a fire or kill some game. He preferred to kill the game, and I proceeded to cut wood and make a fire. He had not been gone more than half an hour when I heard the report of his gun. He soon came in, dragging a large fat deer, which enabled us to make an excellent supper. After we had eaten, we began to talk about our success, when Campbell said he would hunt but three days longer unless we were more successful. I told him I should hunt until the snow went off before I would give up. The next morning we went south toward Sinemahoning, seeing no signs of elk, and at night we returned to our camp. The following day Campbell was somewhat unwell, and I told him if he would remain and keep camp and dry some of the venison, I would go out toward Pine Creek, to which he consented. After proceeding about seven miles, I found where an elk had been browsing. The manner in which the limbs had been pulled down showed that it must have been a very large animal. I hunted in the vicinity several hours to ascertain the direction in which he went, but the tracks were so old that I could not decide. As I arrived at the camp a man came along who said that he had seen in the road the largest elk-tracks he ever saw. I told Campbell of the indications I had discovered, and that the tracks were probably those of the same animal. We invited the man to eat supper with us, as we were greatly obliged to him for the information he had given us. Campbell thought we could not catch him, as we had not sufficient force. I told him I could take the elk alone. The next morning we started at daybreak, and found the tracks of the elk, going west. A mile and a half farther he had lain the previous night. In a moment Campbell saw him, and cried out, "There he stands: the largest elk I ever saw!" I let the dogs go, they attacked him vigorously, and he ran south ten miles to Kettle Creek. He then ran around a hill, and turned up the east branch which he ascended four miles on the ice when he broke through, into water about four feet deep. Here the dogs worried him, as we judged, about two hours, when he started again, ran up a hill, and halted on a rock. The dogs pursued him to the rock, and then returned to us. We met them two or three miles from the elk, which had taken a circuitous course, so that the track at one place was but a fourth of a mile from the rock on which he was stationed, while it was two miles to follow the track. The dogs tried to go directly to the elk, but we thought they saw something else, and compelled them to keep the track, reaching the elk about dark. Campbell made ready the rope, while I cut a pole about fifteen feet long. He went to the south side of the rock with the dogs, to call his attention in that direction, while I mounted the rock on the north side, and endeavored to put the rope over his horns with the pole. He wheeled and came toward me, when I jumped from the rock, and he turned again to the dogs. About eight feet from the rock stood a hemlock tree, about two feet in diameter, with branches six or eight feet above the ground. It occurred to me that if I could climb this it would be an easy matter to slip the noose over the horns of the elk. I made the attempt, but did not succeed as my moccasins were frozen. I pulled them off and tried again, but with no better success. I then took off my coat, which was by no means pleasant, as the weather was intensely cold, but it enabled me to climb the tree. Campbell then passed the pole and rope to me, and called off the dogs. I shouted, and the elk turned and advanced toward me, when I slipped the noose over his horns, and with a jerk drew it tight. I then descended and attached the end of the rope to a tree about forty feet from the elk, and we pulled him from the rock, when we left him for the night. It was then half-past eleven, and we were compelled to go three-quarters of a mile to find a suitable place for encamping. Arriving there I was attacked so severely with nervous headache that I could scarcely walk. Campbell, in looking for a suitable camping-place, found a shanty which had been built by a party of hunters the previous night. We found here a bed of coals and plenty of wood cut. Campbell replenished the fire, and prepared a decoction of hemlock boughs, which greatly relieved me. He then cooked supper, and when we had eaten, it was two o'clock. Our next thought was to procure assistance enough to convey home our elk. The nearest settlement was forty miles distant, and I told Campbell that as I was the stronger I had better go. He said he preferred going himself, as he did not understand how to take care of an elk. As he desired it I consented. He started the next morning, taking with him the dogs, went to Cowdersport, the nearest settlement, and in 4 days returned with three men and a horse.

About ten o'clock one night during his absence I heard bells on the east side of Kettle Creek. I walked down to the creek, and as I reached the bank a sleigh drawn by two horses drove into the creek on the opposite side. The weight of the horses broke the ice the entire width of the stream, and when they reached the bank they could not draw the sleigh out of the water. The man then went to the hind end of the sleigh with a bar of iron, which he used as a lever, and spoke to the horses. They made another attempt to extricate the sleigh, and fell. He came to the forward end, and for the first time saw me. He was startled at the unexpected appearance of a human form in the wilderness, and cried out, "In the name of God, what are you? A man, or a ghost?" I assured him that I was flesh and blood, and he said I should have spoken to him. I replied that I was so intent in watching his operations that I had not thought of speaking. He asked me to start the horses, while he went behind and pushed with the lever. I told him it was useless; the horses had already tried, and were unable to draw the sleigh out. He went in, however, and spoke to the horses, when they made another effort and fell again. I told him to come out of the water and go to the camp, and I would be there soon with his horses and sleigh. He was quite willing to accept my offer, and started for the camp. I detached the horses from the sleigh, brought them to the top of the bank and connected them by a chain which I found in the sleigh to the end of the tongue. As they could now obtain firm footing, they brought the sleigh to the top of the bank without difficulty. Just as I was starting for the camp, another man arrived at the opposite bank, with a horse and cutter, and wished to cross. I advised him to leave his cutter and ride his horse through the creek, which he did, and we went to the camp together. On our arrival there we found the other man in excruciating pain. His clothes were so frozen before he reached the camp, that he could scarcely walk, and he had nearly perished. They both believed that they would have frozen, had it not been for the assistance I rendered. The following morning as they did not like to leave me there alone, I accompanied them to their destination, ten miles distant, where we left the sleighs and harness, and rode the horses back to the camp. Quite early the next morning Campbell arrived with the four men, the horses and sleigh. We immediately set to removing the elk, and in two days we arrived with him at Cowdersport. We there settled with Lyman, he to be one-half owner of the elk, and Campbell and myself, each a quarter. Lyman sold one-half his share to a man named Waterman, for two hundred and fifty dollars, the elk being valued at a thousand dollars. We all four went with him to Olean, forty miles distant, where we obtained twelve dollars by exhibiting him. We then exhibited him at a place six miles farther, and made six dollars more. At the latter place a man bet five dollars that he could hold him by grasping his nose with one hand, with his other arm around his horns. He lost the money, however, the animal striking him in the back with one of its hind feet, so severely that it drew blood.

10

JOHN TANNER:

Man in the Middle

The American frontiersman's way of life, neither wholly savage nor wholly civilized, placed him in a curiously ambiguous position. Relative to the Indians among whom he lived he considered himself a civilized man; yet relative to his native society he was a barbarian, crude of language, dress, and manners, and unfit for civilized company. True, few men of the wilderness probably ever gave much thought to such things; but to John Tanner (c. 1780–1847), who had been thrust into the wilds against his will, life between two worlds became as painful as it was difficult. Captured by Shawnees near his father's home on the Ohio when he was about nine years old, and later adopted by an old Ottawa squaw, Tanner eventually became as wild as any Indian. He forgot his native language and acquired an Indian name ("the Falcon"), numerous Indian relatives, and even some of the Indians' mystical and visionary powers. He lived among the Ottawas and Ojibways for thirty years, hunting and trapping in Wisconsin, Michigan, northern Minnesota, and the Lake of the Woods district of Canada. (His tribe was among

*those that traded with the younger Alexander Henry on the Red
River of the North.)*

*Had he remained among the Indians Tanner might have
lived out his life in contentment. However, a persistent longing
to return someday to his own people brought him back to the
Ohio in 1820. Three of his six halfbreed children came with him.
But, though Tanner was eventually reunited with those of his
family who were still alive, his attempts to become white once
again were frustrated time after time. His white heritage was
forever at war with his Indian ways, and the whites were hostile
and abusive toward him. As time went on Tanner grew increas-
ingly bitter. He was described in his later years by Henry
Schoolcraft, the Mackinac trader and chronicler, as being "a
grey-headed, hard-featured old man, at war with everyone.
Suspicious, revengeful, bad-tempered." Finally, in 1846,
wrongly accused of murdering Schoolcraft's brother, Tanner
disappeared into the woods and was never heard from again.
The following excerpt from his* Narrative, *dictated in the 1820s
to Dr. Edwin James, a botanist and Western traveler, describes
his first attempts to readjust to the white man's way of life.*

In the spring of 1822, I started to go again to the north,
not finding that I was content among my friends in
Kentucky. . . . Being now destitute of employment, I engaged to Mr. Stewart, the agent of the American Fur Company, to go with the traders into the Indian country. . . .
For my services with the people of the American Fur Company, I was to receive two hundred and twenty-five dollars
per years, and a suit of clothes.

My children I placed at school at Mackinac, and went to
the Saut De St. Marie with Mr. Morrison, one of the
company's principal clerks. Thence they sent me, in a boat,
with some Frenchmen, to Fond Du Lac. I was unacquainted

From *A Narrative of the Captivity and Adventures of John Tanner (U.S. Interpreter at the
Saut de Ste. Marie,) During Thirty Years Residence Among the Indians in the Interior of North
America,* prepared for the press by Edwin James, M.D. (New York: 1830), pp. 261,
263–281.

with the manners of these people, and should have suffered, and perished for want of provisions, had I not purchased some occasionally from the crew. From Fond Du Lac I went to Rainy Lake with [the trader] Mr. Cote; but my ignorance of the business in which I had embarked, exposed me to much inconvenience. I had still some of my traps with me, with which I took a considerable number of musk rats on this journey, and I was not less surprised than displeased, to be told that the skins did not belong to me. But I was not only compelled to give them up; I was made to paddle by myself a canoe, heavily loaded with wild rice, and to submit to various other laborious employments, which I did very reluctantly.

When we arrived at Rainy Lake, I went to hunt, but killed nothing. Soon afterwards, they sent me to the rapids of Rainy Lake River; and before the ice had formed so as to put an end to the fishing, I had taken one hundred and fifty sturgeons. The winter had now commenced, and Mr. Cote sent me, with one clerk, four Frenchmen, and a small outfit of goods, equal to one hundred and sixty dollars in value, to trade among the Indians. . . .

When I [returned to the trader's house], I accounted for my whole outfit; having the peltries I had purchased in exchange for every article, except some powder and shot, which we had ourselves expended in hunting. The price of this was deducted from my pay, in my final settlement with the agent of the American Fur Company. . . . But Mr. Cote did not consider my return a good one, and complained of me for having refused to take whiskey with my outfit. I told him that if I had taken whiskey, I could certainly have obtained a much greater quantity of peltries, but I was averse to trading with the Indians when intoxicated, and did not wish to be one, on any occasion, to introduce whiskey among them. But as he had determined on sending me out again, and insisted I should take whiskey, I told him I would for once, conform entirely to his instructions, which were "to use every method to procure the greatest possible quantity of skins, at the lowest price." This time I went to the country about the Lake of the Woods, and with an outfit valued at two hundred dollars, I purchased, by means of whiskey, more than double the amount of peltries I had before brought in. Now Mr. Cote expressed the highest satisfaction at my success; but I told him, if he wished to have his goods sold in that way, he must employ some other person, as I could not consent to be the instrument of such fraud and injustice. I had been so long among the Indians, that many of them were personally my friends, and having seen the extent of the mischiefs occasioned by the introduction of intoxicating liquors, I had become desirous of preventing it, as far as in my power, at least; I was not willing to be myself active in spreading such poison among them; nor was I willing to use the advantage, their unconquerable appetite for spirits might give me, in bargaining with them, as I knew, that though they might easily be defrauded, any fraud thus practised must be known to them, and they would feel resentment and dislike, in proportion as they were made to suffer; more particularly against me, whom they looked upon as one of their own number.

I remained fifteen months in the American Fur Company's employ, during all which time, I slept only thirteen nights in the house, so active and laborious were my occupations. It had been an item in my agreement with Mr. Stewart, that I should be allowed to go to Red River to see my children, and make an attempt to bring them out with me. Accordingly, when the traders were about to make their yearly visit to Mackinac, I was allowed to go by myself, but having been disappointed of moccasins and other articles that had been promised me by Mr. Cote, I suffered much inconvenience, travelling as I did by myself in a small canoe. My children were three in number, two daughters and one son, and had been a long time separated from me, even before I first left the Indian country.

Mr. Clark, of the Hudson's Bay Company, who was now stationed at Red River, and to whom I had a letter, refused to give me any assistance in recovering my children. In the morning, when I arrived there, I had left my blanket in his house, expecting, at least, that I should sleep there; but when at the approach of night I was about to go in, he sent the blanket out to me. From the manner in which this was done, I knew if I went in again, it would only be to be driven out, and I went immediately to select a place to sleep in the woods at a little distance. But Mr. Bruce, the interpreter saw me, and calling me into his lodge, invited me to remain, and while I did so, treated me in the most friendly and hospitable manner. Knowing that I had no reason to expect any assistance from Mr. Clark, who was soon to leave the country, I went to Captain Bulger, the military commandant, to state my business, and received from him a most attentive and friendly hearing. Immediately on my calling to see him, he asked me where I had slept, as he knew that I had arrived the day before. When he heard that I had been refused a lodging in the trading house, he invited me to come and eat with him, and sleep in his house as long as I should remain there. He knew of my business to the country, and asked me if I could tell where my children were. I had ascertained that they were with the Indians about the Prairie Portage.

Some Indians about the Fort, told me that those of the band with whom my children were, had heard of my arrival, and were determined to kill me if I should attempt to take my children from them. Nevertheless, I visited the band as soon as I could make the journey, and went into the lodge of the principal chief, who treated me kindly. I remained some time, always staying in the lodge with my children, who appeared pleased to see me; but I easily discovered that it was by no means the intention of the Indians to suffer me to take them away. Giah-ge-wa-go-mo, the man who had long before stolen away my son, and whom I had been compelled to beat, as well as to kill his horse, now treated me with some insolence, and threatened even to take my life. I said to him, "if you had been a man, you would have killed me long ago, instead of now threatening me. I have no fear of you." But being entirely alone, I could accomplish no more at present, than to induce the band to remove, and encamp near the fort at Red River. This was a considerable journey, and on all of it, my children and myself were made to carry heavy burthens, and were treated like slaves. They did not indeed give me a load to carry, but they were careful so far to overload my children, that when I had taken as much as I could move under, there were heavy loads left for them. After they had encamped near the fort, I asked them for my children, but they utterly refused to give them up. Giah-ge-wa-go-mo was the princial man who was active in resisting me, and with him the dispute had grown to so open a quarrel, that I was about to proceed to violent measures, but I bethought me that I should do wrong to attempt to shed blood without first making my intentions known to Captain Bulger, who had expressed so much friendly feeling towards me. I went accordingly, and told him my situation, and that I was now convinced I could not take my children without using violent measures with Giah-ge-wa-go-mo. He approved of my having told him what I was about to do, and immediately sent Mr. Bruce to call my children into the fort. They came accordingly, and stood before his house, but with ten or twelve Indians accompanying them, and who were careful to stand near by on each side of them. Having pointed out my children to him, the captain directed his servant to feed them. Something was accordingly brought from his own table, he having just then eaten, and given to them; but the Indians immediately snatched it away, leaving them not a mouthful. A loaf of bread was then brought, but it went in the same way, not a particle of it being left to them. Captain Bulger now directed a store house to be opened, and told me to go in and get them something to eat. Finding there some bags of pemmican, I took the half of one, about twenty pounds, and making them sit down, all partook of it.

The Indians refused the children to the demand of Captain Bulger, as they had done to me; but next day he called all the principal men, and among others Giah-ge-wa-go-mo, to come and council with him. The chief man of the band was very willing that I should take away the children, and when we all went into the council room, he took a seat with Captain Bulger and myself, thereby placing the four men who were principally active in detaining them, in the situation of persons who were acting in open contravention to his wishes.

Presents to the amount of about one hundred dollars in value, were brought in, and placed on the floor between the two parties. Captain Bulger then said to the Indians:

"My children, I have caused to be placed before you here, a pipe full of tobacco, not because I am willing to have you suppose I would purchase from you a right for this man to come and take what is his own, but to signify to you, that I still hold you by the hand, as long as you are ready to listen attentively to my words. As for this man, he comes to you not in his own name only, and speaking his own words; but he speaks the words of your great father who is beyond the waters, and of the Great Spirit, in whose hand we all are, and who gave these children to be his. You must, therefore, without venturing to give him any farther trouble, deliver to him his children, and take these presents, as a memorial of the good will that subsists between us."

The Indians began to deliberate, and were about to make a reply, when they saw a considerable armed force brought and paraded before the door of the council house, and finding themselves completely surrounded, they accepted the presents, and promised to surrender the children.

The mother of these children was now an old woman, and as she said she wished to accompany them, I readily consented. The boy, who was of age to act for himself, preferred to remain among the Indians, and as the time for giving him an education, and fitting him to live in any other manner than as the Indians do, had passed, I consented he should act as he thought best. Several Indians accompanied us four days' journey on our return, than all went back, except my two daughters and their mother.

I did not return to the Lake of the Woods by the way of the Be-gwi-o-nus-ko Se-be, but chose another route, in which I had to travel a part of the way by water, a part by land. In ascending the Bad River, there is a short road by what is called Sturgeon River, and a portage to come again into the principal river. Not far from the mouth of Sturgeon River was, at this time, an encampment, or village, of six or seven lodges. A young man belonging to that band, and whose name was Ome-zhuh-gwutoons, had not long previous to this been whipped by Mr. Cote, for some real or alleged misconduct about the trading-house, and feeling dissatisfied, he, when he heard I had passed up Sturgeon River, started after me in his little canoe, and soon overtook me. After he had joined me, he showed, I thought, an unusual disposition to talk to me, and claimed to be, in some manner, related to me. He encamped with us that night, and the next morning we started on together. This day, when we stopped, and were resting on shore, I noticed that he took an opportunity to meet one of my daughters in the bushes; but she returned immediately, somewhat agitated. Her mother, also, was several times, in the course of the day, in close conversation with her; but the young woman continued sad, and was several times crying.

At night, after we stopped to encamp, the young man very soon left us; but as he remained at a little distance, apparently much busied about something, I went and found him with his medicines all opened about him, and he was inserting a thong of deer's sinew, about five inches in length, into a bullet. I said ot him, "My brother," [for this was the name he had himself given me,] "if you want powder, or balls, or flints, I have plenty, and will give you as much as you wish." He said that he also had plenty, and I left him and returned to camp. It was some time before he came in; when at last he made his appearance, he was dressed and ornamented as a warrior for battle. He continued, during the first part of the night, to watch me much too closely, and my suspicions, which had been already excited, were now more and more confirmed. But he continued to be as talkative, and to seem as friendly as ever. He asked me for my knife, as he said, to cut some tobacco, and instead of returning it to me, slipped it into his own belt; but I thought, perhaps he would return it to me in the morning.

I laid myself down at about the usual time, as I would not appear to suspect his intentions. I had not put up my tent, having only the little shelter afforded by a piece of painted cloth that had been given me at Red River. When I lay down, I chose such a position as would enable me to watch the young man's motions. I could see, as he sat opposite the fire, that his eyes were open and watchful, and that he felt not the least inclination to sleep. When at length a thunder shower commenced, he appeared more anxious and restless than before. When the rain began to fall, I asked him to come and place himself near me, so as to enjoy the benefit of my shelter, and he did so. The shower was very heavy, and entirely extinguished our fire; but soon after it had ceased, the mosquitoes becoming very troublesome, Ome-zhuh-gwut-oons rekindled it, and breaking off a branch of a bush, he sat and drove them away from me. I was conscious that I ought not to sleep; but drowsiness was gaining some hold on me, when another thunder shower, more violent than the first, arose. In the interval of the showers, I lay as one sleeping, but almost without moving or opening my eyes. I watched the motions of the young man; at one time, when an unusually loud clap of thunder alarmed him, he would throw a little tobacco into the fire, as an offering; at another, when he seemed to suppose me asleep, I saw him watching me like a cat about to spring on its prey; but I did not suffer myself to sleep.

He breakfasted with us as usual, then started by himself, before I was quite ready. My daughter, whom he had met in the bushes, was now apparently more alarmed than before, and absolutely refused to enter the canoe; but her mother was very anxious to quiet her agitation, and apparently very desirous to prevent my paying any particular attention to her. At last, she was induced to get into the canoe, and we went on. The young man kept along before us, and at a little distance, until about ten o'clock, when, at turning a point in a difficult and rapid part of the river, and gaining a view of a considerable reach above, I was surprised that I could see neither him nor his canoe. At this place the river is about eighty yards wide, and there is, about ten yards from the point before mentioned, a small island of naked rock. I had taken off my coat, and I was, with great effort, pushing up my canoe against the powerful current, which compelled me to keep very near the shore, when the discharge of a gun at my side arrested my progress. I heard a bullet whistle past my head, and felt my side touched, at the same instant that the paddle fell from my right hand, and the hand itself dropped powerless to my side. The bushes were obscured by the smoke of the gun, but at a second look I saw Ome-zhuh-gwut-oons escaping. At that time the screams of my children drew my attention to the canoe, and I found every part of it was becoming covered with blood. I endeavoured, with my left hand, to push the canoe in shore, that I might pursue after him; but the current being too powerful for me, took my canoe on the other side, and threw it against the small rocky island before mentioned. I now got out, pulled the canoe a little on to the rock, with my left hand, and then made an attempt to load my gun. Before I could finish loading I fainted, and fell on the rock. When I came to myself again, I was alone on the island, and the canoe, with my daughters, was just going out of sight in the river below. Soon after it disappeared, I fainted a second time; but consciousness at length returned.

As I believed that the man who had shot me was still watching from his concealment, I examined my wounds, and finding my situation deperate, my right arm being much shattered, and the ball having entered my body, in the direction to reach my lungs, and not having passed out, I called to him, requesting him to come, and by putting an immediate end to my life, to release me from the protracted suffering I had in prospect. "You have killed me," said I; "but though the hurt you have given me must be mortal, I fear it may be some time before I shall die. Come, therefore, if you are a man, and shoot me again." Many times I called to him, but here turned me no answer. My body was now almost naked, as I had on, when shot, beside my pantaloons, only a very old and ragged shirt, and much of this

had been torn off in the course of the morning. I lay exposed
to the sun, and the black and green headed flies, on a naked
rock, the greater part of a day in July or August, and saw no
prospect before me, but that of a lingering death; but as the
sun went down, my hope and strength began to revive, and
plunging into the river, I swam across to the other side.
When I reached the shore, I could stand on my feet, and I
raised the sas-sah-kwi, or war whoop, as a cry of exultation
and defiance to my enemy. But the additional loss of blood,
occasioned by the exertion in swimming the river, caused
me another fainting fit, from which, when I recovered, I
concealed myself near the bank, to watch for him. Presently
I saw Ome-zhuh-gwut-oons come from his hiding place,
put his canoe into the water, embark, and begin to descend
the river. He came very near my hiding place, and I felt
tempted to make a spring, and endeavour to seize and
strangle him in the water; but fearing that my strength
might not be sufficient, I let him pass without discovering
myself.

I was now tormented with the most excessive thirst, and
as the bank was steep and rocky, I could not, with my
wounded arm, lie down to drink. I was therefore compelled
to go into the water, and let my body down into it, until I
brought my mouth to a level with the surface, and this I was
able to drink. By this time, the evening growing somewhat
cooler, my strength was, in part, restored; but the blood
seemed to flow more freely. I now applied myself to dressing the wound in my arms. I endeavoured, though the
flesh was already much swollen, to replace the fragments of
the bone; to accomplish which, I tore in strips the remainder of my shirt, and with my teeth and my left hand I
contrived to tie these around my arm, at first loosely, but by
degrees tighter and tighter, until I thought it had assumed,
as nearly as I could give it, the proper form. I then tied on
small sticks, which I broke from the branches of trees, to
serve as splints, and then suspended my hand in a string,
which passed around my neck. After this was completed, I
took some of the bark of a choke cherry bush, which I
observed there, and chewing it fine applied it to the

wounds, hoping thus to check the flowing of the blood. The bushes about me, and for all the distance between me and the river, were covered with blood. As night came on, I chose a place where was plenty of moss, to lie down on, with the trunk of a fallen tree for my pillow. I was careful to select a place near the river, that I might have a chance of seeing any thing that might pass; also, to be near the water in case my thirst should again become urgent. I knew that one trader's canoe was expected, about this time, to pass this place, on the way towards Red River, and it was this canoe from which I expected relief and assistance. There were no Indians nearer than the village from which Ome-zhuh-gwut-oons had followed me, and he, with my wife and daughters, were the only persons that I had any reason to suppose were within many miles of me.

I laid myself down, and prayed to the Great Spirit, that he would see and pity my condition, and send help to me, now in the time of my distress. As I continued praying, the mosquitoes, which had settled on my naked body in vast numbers, and were, by their stings, adding greatly to the torment I suffered, began to rise, and after hovering at a little distance above and around me, disappeared entirely. I did not attribute this, which was so great a relief, to the immediate interposition of a Superior Power, in answer to my prayer, as the evening was, at that time, becoming somewhat cool, and I knew it was entirely the effect of change of temperature. Nevertheless, I was conscious, as I have ever been in times of distress and danger, that the Master of my life, though invisible, was yet near, and was looking upon me. I slept easily and quietly, but not without interruption. Every time I awoke, I remembered to have seen, in my dream, a canoe with white men, in the river before me.

It was late in the night, probably after midnight, when I heard female voices, which I supposed to be those of my daughters, not more than two hundred yards from me, but partly across the river. I believed that Ome-zhuh-gwut-oons had discovered their hiding place, and was, perhaps, offering them some violence, as the cry was that of distress;

but so great was my weakness, that the attempt to afford them any relief seemed wholly beyond my power. I learned afterwards, that my children, as soon as I fainted and fell on the rock, supposing me dead, had been influenced by their mother to turn the canoe down the river, and exert themselves to make their escape. They had not proceeded far, when the woman steered the canoe into a low point of bushes, and threw out my coat, and some other articles. They then ran on a considerable distance, and concealed themselves; but here it occurred to the woman, that she might have done better to have kept the property belonging to me, and accordingly returned to get it. It was when they came to see these things lying on the shore, that the children burst out crying, and it was at this time that I heard them.

Before ten o'clock the next morning, I heard human voices on the river above me, and from the situation I had chosen, I could see a canoe coming, like that I had seen in my dream, loaded with white men. They landed at a little distance above me, and began to make preparations for breakfast. I knew that this was the canoe belonging to Mr. Stewart, of the Hudson's Bay Company, who, together with Mr. Grant, was expected about this time; and being conscious that my appearance would make a painful impression upon them, I determined to wait until they had breakfasted, before I showed myself to them. After they had eaten, and put their canoe again in the water, I waded out a little distance into the river, to attract their attention. As soon as they saw me, the Frenchmen ceased paddling, and they all gazed at me, as if in doubt and amazement. As the current of the river was carrying them rapidly past me, and my repeated calls, in the Indian language, seemed to produce no effect, I called Mr. Stewart by name, and spoke a few words of English, which I could command, requesting them to come and take me. In a moment their paddles were in the water, and they brought the canoe so near where I stood, that I was able to get into it.

No one in the canoe recognized me, though Mr. Stewart and Mr. Grant were both well known to me. I had not been able to wash the blood off my body, and it is probable that the suffering I had undergone, had much changed my appearance. They were very eager and rapid in their inquiries, and soon ascertained who I was, and also became acquainted with the principal facts I have related. They made a bed for me in the canoe, and at my urgent request went to search for my children, in the direction where I had heard them crying, and where I told them I feared we should find they had been murdered; but we sought here, and in other places, to no purpose.

Having ascertained who it was that had wounded me, these two traders agreed to take me immediately to the village of Ome-zhuh-gwut-oons, and they were determined, in case of discovering and taking him, to aid me in taking my revenge, by putting him immediately to death. They therefore concealed me in the canoe, and on landing near the lodges, an old man came down to the shore, and asked them, "what was the news in the country they came from?" "All is well there," answered Mr. Stewart; "we have no other news," "This is the manner," said the old man, "in which white people always treat us. I know very well something has happened in the country you have come from, but you will not tell us of it. Ome-zhuh-gwut-oons, one of our young men, has been up the river two or three days, and he tells us that the Long Knife, called Shaw-shaw-wa-ne-ba-se, (the falcon,) who passed her a few days since, with his wife and children, has murdered them all; but I am fearful that he himself has been doing something wrong, for he is watchful and restless, and has just fled from this place before you arrived." Mr. Stewart and Mr. Grant, notwithstanding this representation, sought for him all the lodges, and when convinced that he had indeed gone, said to the old man, "It is very true that mischief has been done in the country we come from; but the man whom Ome-zhuh-gwut-oons attempted to kill, is in our canoe with us; we do not yet know whether he will live or die." They then showed me to the Indians, who had gathered on the shore.

We now took a little time to refresh ourselves, and to examine my wounds. Finding that the ball had entered my body, immediately under the broken part of my arm, and gone forward and lodged against the breast bone, I tried to persuade Mr. Grant to cut it out; but neither he nor Mr. Stewart being willing to make the attempt, I was compelled to do it myself, as well as I could, with my left hand. A lancet, which Mr. Grant lent me, was broken immediately, as was a pen knife, the flesh of that part of the body being very hard and tough. They next brought me a large white handled razor, and with this I succeeded in extracting the ball. It was very much flattened, and the thong of deer's sinew, as well as the medicines Ome-zhuh-gwut-oons had inserted in it, were left in my body. Notwithstanding this, when I found that it had not passed under my ribs, I began to hope that I should finally recover, though I had reason to suppose, that the wound being poisoned, it would be long in healing.

After this was done, and the wound in my breast taken care of, we went on to Ah-kee-ko-bow-we-tig, (the Kettle Fall,) to the village of the chief Waw-wish-e-gah-bo, the brother of Ome-zhuh-gwut-oons. Here Mr. Stewart used the same precaution of hiding me in the canoe, and then giving tobacco, which he called every man in the village, by name, to receive; but when there appeared no prospect of finding him, they made me again stand up in the canoe, and one of them told the chief that it was his own brother who had attempted to kill me. The chief hung his head, and to their inquiries about Ome-zhuh-gwut-oons he would make no answer. We, however, ascertained from other Indians, that my daughters and their mother had stopped here a moment, in their way towards Rainy Lake.

When we arrived at the North West Company's house, at Rainy Lake, we found that my daughters and their mother had been detained by the traders, on account of suspicions arising from their manifest agitation and terror, and from the knowledge that I had passed up with them but a few days before. Now, when I first came in sight of the fort, the old woman fled to the woods, taking the two girls with her. But the Company's people sent out and brought them in again. Mr. Stewart and Mr. Grant now left it to me to say what punishment should be inflicted on this woman, who, as we all very well knew, had been guilty of aiding in an attempt to kill me. They said they considered her equally criminal with Ome-zhuh-gwut-oons, and thought her deserving of death, or any other punishment I might wish to see inflicted. But I told them I wished she might be sent immediately, and without any provisions, away from the fort, and never allowed to return to it. As she was the mother of my children, I did not wish to see her hung, or beaten to death by the labourers, as they proposed; but as the sight of her had become hateful to me, I wished she might be removed, and they accordingly dismissed her without punishment.

Mr. Stewart left me at the Rainy Lake trading house, in the care of Simon M'Gillevray, a son of him who many years ago was so important a partner in the North West Company. He gave me a small room, where my daughters cooked for me, and dressed my wounds. I was very weak, and my arm badly swollen, fragments of bone coming out from time to time. I had lain here twenty-eight days, when Major Delafield, the United States commissioner for the boundary, came to the trading house, and having heard something of my history, proposed to bring me in his canoe to Mackinac. But I was too weak to undertake such a journey, though I wished to have accompanied him. Finding that this was the case, Major Delafield gave me a large supply of excellent provisions, two pounds of tea, some sugar and other articles, a tent and some clothing, and left me.

Two days after this, I pulled out of my arm the thong of deer's sinew which had been attached, as I have before stated, to the bullet. It was still about five inches long, but nearly as large as my finger, and of a green colour. Ome-zhuh-gwut-oons had two balls in his gun at the time he shot me; one had passed near my head.

Immediately after the departure of Major Delafield, the unfriendly disposition of Mr. M'Gillevray made itself manifest; it had been only fear of Major Delafield that had induced him hitherto to treat me with some attention.

Insults and abuses were heaped upon me, and at last I was forcibly turned out of the house. But some of the Frenchmen had so much compassion as to steal out at night, and without Mr. M'Gillevray's knowledge, furnish tent poles, and set up my tent. Thanks to the bounty of Major Delafield, I had a supply of every thing needful, and my daughters still remained with me, though Mr. M'Gillevray repeatedly threatened that he would remove them. His persecutions did not abate when I left the fort, and he went so far as to take my daughters from me, and send them to sleep in the quarters of the men; but they escaped, and fled to the house of the old Frenchman, near by, who was Mr. M'Gillevray's father-in-law, and with whose daughters mine had become intimate.

Forty-three days I had lain in and near this trading house, and was now in a most miserable condition, having been for some time entirely deprived of the assistance of my daughters, when my former acquaintance and friend, Mr. Bruce, unexpectedly entered my tent late in the evening. He was with Major Long,* and a party of gentlemen then returning from Lake Winnipeg, who, as Mr. Bruce thought, would be willing and able to afford me some assistance in taking my daughters out of the hands of Mr. M'Gillevray, and perhaps in getting out to Mackinac.

Three times I visited Major Long at his camp, at that late hour of the night, though I was scarce able to walk, and each time he told me that his canoes were full, and that he could do nothing for me; but at length becoming a little acquainted with my history, he seemed to take more interest in me, and when he saw the papers I had from Governor Clark and others, he told me I was a fool not to have shown him these before. He had, he said, taken me for one of those worthless white men, who remain in the Indian country from indolence, and for the sake of marrying squaws; but now that he understood who I was, he would try to do something for me. He went himself, with several men, and

*Major Stephen H. Long, then on the return leg of his 1823 exploration of the Red River region.—ED

sought in the trading house for my daughters. He had intended to start early the next morning after his arrival; but having been stirring nearly all night in my affairs, he determined to remain over the next day, and make farther exertions for the recovery of my children. All the search we could make for my daughters, at and about the trading house, resulted in the conviction, that through the agency of Mr. M'Gillevray, and the family of his father-in-law, they had fallen into the hands of Kaw-been-fush-kwaw-naw, a chief of our village at Me-nau-zhe-tau-naung. This being the case, I was compelled to relinquish the hope of bringing them out the present year, and miserably as I was situated, I was anxious to come to my own people, and to my three children at Mackinac, to spend the winter.

I knew the character of Mr. M'Gillevray, and also that the traders of the North West Company generally, had less cause to feel friendly towards me, than they might have had, if I had not concerned myself with [the Hudson Bay Company] in the capture of their post at Red River. I knew, also, that my peculiar situation with respect to the Indians, would make it very difficult for me to gain permission to remain at or near either of the houses of the North West, or of the American Fur Company. I had been severely and dangerously wounded by an Indian, and according to their customs, I was bound, or at least expected, to avenge myself on any of the same band that might fall in my way; and should it be known that I was at either of the trading houses, very few Indians would venture to visit it. Taking these things into consideration, I determined to accept the friendly offer of Major Long, to bring me to the States, and accordingly took a place in one of his canoes. But after proceeding on our way an hour or two, I became convinced, as did Major Long and the gentlemen with him, that I could not safely undertake so long and difficult a journey in my present situation. Accordingly they put me in charge of some people belonging to the traders, and sent me back to the fort.

I knew that the doors of the North West Company's house would be closed against me, and accordingly made application to my late employers, the American Fur Company. Young Mr. Davenport, in whose care the house then was, granted a ready compliance with my request, and gave me a room; but as provisions were scarce on that side, I was supplied daily by Dr. M'Laughlin, of the North West, who had now taken the place of Mr. M'Gillevray. He sent every day as much as sufficed to feed me and Mr. Davenport, together with his wife.

I had not been long here, when Mr. Cote arrived, and took charge of the house in place of Mr. Davenport. Mr. Cote came to my room, and seeing me on the bed, only remarked, "well, you have been making a war by yourself." That night he allowed my supper to be brought me, and early next morning turned me out of doors. But he was not content with driving me from the house; he forbade me to remain on the United States side of the boundary; and all my entreaties, together with the interference of Dr. M'Laughlin, could in influence Mr. Cote to change his determination. In this emergency, Dr. M'Laughlin, though he knew that the success of his post in the winter's trade, must be injured by the measure, consented to receive me on the British side, where he fed and took care of me. . . .

In the spring, I was again able to hunt. I killed considerable numbers of rabbits, and some other animals, for the skins of which the Doctor paid me in money, a very liberal price. As the time approached for the traders to leave the wintering grounds, he told me, the North West had no boats going to Mackinac, but that he would oblige Mr. Cote to carry me out. It was accordingly so arranged, and Mr. Cote promised to take me to Fond Du Lac in his own canoe. But instead of this, he sent me in a boat with some Frenchmen. In the route from Fond Du Lac to the Saut De St. Marie, I was dependent upon Mr. Morrison; but the treatment I received from the boatmen was so rough, that I induced them to put me on shore, to walk thirty-five miles to the Saut. . . . as I heard that the little property I had left at Mackinac had been seized to pay my children's board, and as I knew their situation required my presence, I went thither accordingly, and was engaged by Col. Boyd as Indian interpreter, in which situation I continued till the summer of 1828, when being dissatisfied with the treatment, I left Mackinac, and proceeded to New-York, for the purpose of making arrangements for the publication of my narrative; and upon my return to the north, was employed by Mr. [Henry] Schoolcraft, Indian agent at the Saut De St. Marie, as his interpreter; to which place I took my family, and have since resided there.

Three of my children are still among the Indians in the north. The two daughters would, as I am informed, gladly join me, if it were in their power to escape. The son is older, and is attached to the life he has so long led as a hunter. I have some hope that I may yet be able to go and make another effort to bring away my daughters.

11

DAVY CROCKETT:

Half-Horse, Half-Alligator

Davy Crockett (1786–1836) appeared on the American scene at a time when the buckskin-clad frontiersman was just emerging as a national folk hero. The country's rough frontier heritage, long a source of embarrassment to a nation that identified itself largely with European values and traditions, was now being boasted with patriotic enthusiasm. Daniel Boone was celebrated in an epic poem. The Leatherstocking Tales were being bought out as fast as James Fenimore Cooper could write them. And in 1828 Andrew Jackson, himself a native of the Carolina and Tennessee frontier, was elected President. Crockett came to national attention at about the same time, having been elected a Congressman from Tennessee in 1826—largely, it was said, because he was a dead shot and a good storyteller. Restless and independent, honest and good humored and full of manly self-confidence, this "half-horse, half-alligator" personified the popular image of the frontiersman—so much so that he became a legendary figure even before his death at the Alamo in 1836.

Crockett presented that image as he wanted it to be in his

Narrative of the Life of David Crockett, Written by Himself *(but more probably by a ghost writer). Framed in plain, unadorned language, with humor and a good deal of bragging, the book was widely read and contributed greatly to Crockett's fame. It tells the story of Crockett's life on the Tennessee frontier; of his boyhood, his romances, and his half-hearted efforts to acquire an education; of his service under Andrew Jackson during the Creek wars; of his indifferent attempts at farming and his ill-fated schemes for making money (a grist mill he built was destroyed in a flood; a shipment of pipe staves he was taking to market was lost on the Mississippi). But most of all the book tells the story of the consummate woodsman and hunter; for, whatever Crockett's other schemes and ambitions, he was always relieved when he could return to the woods, to test his skill against his favorite quarry, the bear.*

In the fall of 1825, I concluded I would build two large boats, and load them with pipe staves for market. So I went down to the lake, which was about twenty-five miles from where I lived [on the Obion River, in western Tennessee], and hired some hands to assist me, and went to work; some at boat building, and others to getting staves. I worked on with my hands till the bears got fat, and then I turned out to hunting, to lay in a supply of meat. I soon killed and salted down as many as was necessary for my family; but about this time, one of my old neighbors who had settled down on the lake about twenty-five miles from me, came to my house and told me he wanted me to go down and kill some bears about in his parts. He said they were extremely fat, and very plenty. I knowed that when they were fat they were easily taken, for a fat bear can't run fast or long. But I asked a bear no favors, no way, further than civility, for I now had eight large dogs, and as fierce as painters, so that a bear stood no chance at all to get away from them. So I went

From *A Narrative of the Life of David Crockett of the State of Tennessee, Written by Himself.* (Philadelphia, 1834). Reprinted in *Life of Col. David Crockett* . . . (Philadelphia, 1859), pp. 141–157.

home with him and then went on down towards the Mississippi and commenced hunting.

We were out two weeks, and in that time killed fifteen bears. Having now supplied my friend with plenty of meat, I engaged occasionally again with my hands in our boat building, and getting staves. But I at length couldn't stand it any longer without another hunt. So I concluded to take my little son and cross over the lake, and take a hunt there. We got over, and that evening turned out and killed three bears in little or no time. The next morning we drove up four forks, and made a sort of scaffold, on which we salted up our meat, so as to have it out of the reach of the wolves, for as soon as we would leave our camp, they would take possession. We had just eat our breakfast, when a company of hunters came to our camp who had fourteen dogs, but all so poor, that when they would bark they would almost have to lean up against a tree and take a rest. I told them their dogs couldn't run in smell of a bear, and they had better stay at my camp and feed them on the bones I had cut out of my meat. I left them there and cut out; but I hadn't gone far, when my dogs took a first rate start after a very large fat old he-bear, which run right plumb towards my camp. I pursued on, but my other hunters had heard my dogs coming, and met them and killed the bear before I got up with him. I gave him to them, and cut out again for a creek called Big Clover, which wasn't very far off. Just as I got there, and was entering a cane brake, my dogs all broke and went ahead, and in a little time they raised a fuss in the cane, and seemed to be going every way. I listened a while, and found my dogs was in two companies, and that both was in a snorting fight. I sent my little son to one and I broke for t'other. I got to mine first, and found my dogs had a two-year-old bear down a-wooling away on him, so I just took out my big butcher, and went up and slapp'd it into him, and killed him without shooting. There was five of the dogs in my company. In a short time I heard my little son fire at his bear; when I went to him he had killed it too. He had two dogs in his team. Just at this moment we heard my other dog barking a short distance off, and all the rest immediately broke to him. We pushed on too, and when we got there, we found that he had still a larger bear than either of them we had killed, treed by himself. We killed that one also, which made three we had killed in less than half an hour. We turned in and butchered them, and then started to hunt for water and a good place to camp. But we had no sooner started, than our dogs took a start after another one, and away they went like a thundergust and was out of hearing in a minute. We followed the way they had gone for some time, but at length we gave up the hope of finding them, and turned back. As we were going back, I came to where a poor fellow was grubbing, and he looked like the very picture of hard times. I asked him what he was doing away there in the woods by himself? He said he was grubbing for a man who intended to settle there; and the reason why he did it was, that he had no meat for his family, and he was working for a little.

I was mighty sorry for the poor fellow, for it was not only a hard but a very slow way to get meat for a hungry family; so I told him if he would go with me, I would give him more meat than he could get by grubbing in a month. I intended to supply him with meat, and also to get him to assist my little boy in packing and salting up my bears. He had never seen a bear killed in his life. I told him I had six killed then, and my dogs were hard after another. He went off to his little cabin, which was a short distance in the brush, and his wife was very anxious he should go with me. So we started and went to where I had left my three bears, and made a camp. We then gathered my meat, and salted and scaffold it, as I had done the other. Night now came on, but no word from my dogs yet. I afterwards found they had treed the bear about five miles off, near to a man's house, and had barked at it the whole enduring night. Poor fellows! many a time they looked for me, and wondered why I didn't come, for they know'd there was no mistake in me, and I know'd they were as good as ever fluttered. In the morning, as soon as it was light enough to see, the man took his gun and went to them, and shot the bear and killed it. My dogs, however, wouldn't have anything to say to this stranger; so they left him, and came early in the morning back to me.

We got our breakfast and cut out again, and we killed four large and very fat bears that day. We hunted out the week, and in that time we killed seventeen, all of them first rate. When we closed our hunt, I gave the man over a thousand weight of fine, fat bear-meat, which pleased him mightily, and made him feel as rich as a Jew. I saw him the next fall, and he told me he had plenty of meat to do him the whole year from his week's hunt. My son and me now went home. This was the week between Christmas and New Year, that we made this hunt.

When I got home, one of my neighbors was out of meat, and wanted me to go back, and let him go with me, to take another hunt. I couldn't refuse; but I told him I was afraid the bear had taken to house by that time, for after they get very fat in the fall and early part of the winter, they go into their holes, in large hollow trees, or into hollow logs, or their cane-houses, or the harricanes; and lie there till spring, like frozen snakes. And one thing about this will seem mighty strange to many people. From about the first of January to about the last of April, these varments lie in their holes altogether. In all that time they have no food to eat; and yet when they come out, they are not an ounce lighter than when they went to house. I don't know the cause of this, and still I know it is a fact; and I leave it for others who have more learning than myself to account for it. They have not a particle of food with them, but they just lie and suck the bottom of their paw all the time. I have killed many of them in their trees, which enables me to speak positively on this subject. However, my neighbor, whose name was McDaniel, and my little son and me, went on down to the lake to my second camp, where I had killed my seventeen bears the week before, and turned out to hunting. But we hunted hard all day without getting a single start. We had carried but little provisions with us, and the next morning was entirely out of meat. I sent my son about three miles off, to the house of an old friend, to get some. The old gentleman was much pleased to hear I was hunting in those parts, for the year before the bears had killed a great many of his hogs. He was that day killing his bacon hogs, and so he gave my son some meat, and sent word to me that I must come in to his house that evening, that he would have plenty of feed for my dogs, and some accommodations for ourselves; but before my son got back, we had gone out hunting, and in a large cane brake my dogs found a big bear in a cane-house, which he had fixed for his winter-quarters, as they sometimes do.

When my lead dog found him, and raised the yell, all the rest broke to him, but none of them entered his house until we got up. I encouraged my dogs, and they knowed me so well, that I could have made them seize the old serpent himself, with all his horns and heads, and cloven foot and ugliness into the bargain, if he would only have come to light, so that they could have seen him. They bulged in, and in an instant the bear followed them out, and I told my friend to shoot him, as he was mighty wrathy to kill a bear. He did so, and killed him prime. We carried him to our camp, by which time my son had returned; and after we got our dinners we packed up, and cut for the house of my old friend, whose name was Davidson.

We got there, and staid with him that night; and the next morning, having salted up our meat, we left it with him, and started to take a hunt between the Obion lake and the Red foot lake; as there had been a dreadful harricane, which passed between them, and I was sure there must be a heap of bears in the fallen timber. We had gone about five miles without seeing any sign at all; but at length we got on some high cany ridges, and, as we rode along, I saw a hole in a large black oak, and on examining more closely, I discovered that a bear had clomb the tree. I could see his tracks going up, but none coming down, and so I was sure he was in there. A person who is acquainted with bear-hunting, can tell easy enough when the varment is in the hollow; for as they go up they don't slip a bit, but as they come down they make long scratches with their nails.

My friend was a little ahead of me, but I called him back, and told him there was a bear in that tree, and I must have him out. So we lit from our horses, and I found a small tree which I thought I could fall so as to lodge against my bear tree, and we fell to work chopping it with our tomahawks. I intended, when we lodged the tree against the other, to let my little son go up, and look into the hole, for he could climb like a squirrel. We had chopp'd on a little time and stopp'd to rest, when I heard my dogs barking mighty severe at some distance from us, and I told my friend I knowed they had a bear; for it is the nature of a dog, when he finds you are hunting bears, to hunt for nothing else; he becomes fond of the meat, and considers other game as "not worth a notice," as old Johnson said of the devil.

We concluded to leave our tree a bit, and went to my dogs, and when we got there, sure enough they had an eternal great big fat bear up a tree, just ready for shooting. My friend again petitioned me for liberty to shoot this one also. I had a little rather not, as the bear was so big, but I couldn't refuse; and so he blazed away, and down came the old fellow like some great log had fell. I now missed one of my dogs, the same that I before spoke of as having treed the bear by himself sometime before, when I had started the three in the cane brake. I told my friend that my missing dog had a bear somewhere, just as sure as fate; so I left them to butcher the one we had just killed, and I went up on a piece of high ground to listen for my dog. I heard him barking with all his might some distance off, and I pushed ahead for him. My other dogs hearing him broke to him, and when I got there, sure enough again he had another bear ready treed; if he hadn't, I wish I may be shot. I fired on him, and brought him down; and then went back, and help'd finish butchering the one at which I had left my friend. We then packed both to our tree where we had left my boy. By this time, the little fellow had cut the tree down that we intended to lodge, but it fell the wrong way; he had then feather'd in on the big tree, to cut that, and had found that it was nothing but a shell on the outside, and all doted in the middle, as too many of our big men are in these days, having only an outside appearance. My friend and my son cut away on it, and I went off about a hundred yards with my dogs to keep them from running under the tree when it should fall. On looking back at the hole, I saw the bear's head out of it, looking down at them as they were cutting. I hollered to them to look up, and they did so; and McDaniel catched up his gun, but by this time the bear was out, and coming down the tree. He fired at it, and as soon as it touched the ground the dogs were all round it, and they had a roll-and-tumble fight to the foot of the hill, where they stopp'd him. I ran up, and putting my gun against the bear, fired and killed him. We had now three, and so we made our scaffold and salted them up.

In the morning I left my son at the camp, and we started on towards the harricane; and when we had went about a mile, we started a very large bear, but we got along mighty slow on account of the cracks in the earth occasioned by the earthquakes. We, however, made out to keep in hearing of the dogs for about three miles, and then we come to the harricane. Here we had to quit our horses, as old Nick himself couldn't have got through it without sneaking it along in the form that he put on, to make a fool of our old grandmother Eve. By this time several of my dogs had got tired and come back; but we went ahead on foot for some little time in the harricane, when we met a bear coming straight to us, and not more than twenty or thirty yards off. I started my tired dogs after him, and McDaniel pursued them, and I went on to where my other dogs were. I had seen the track of the bear they were after, and I knowed he was a screamer. I followed on to about the middle of the harricane, but my dogs pursued him so close, that they made him climb an old stump about twenty feet high. I got in shooting distance of him and fired, but I was all over in such a flutter from fatigue and running, that I couldn't hold steady; but, however, I broke his shoulder, and he fell. I run up and loaded my gun as quick as possible, and shot him again and killed him. When I went to take out my knife to butcher him, I found I had lost it in coming through the harricane. The vines and briers was so thick that I would sometimes have to get down and crawl like a varment to get through at all; and a vine had, as I supposed, caught in the handle and pulled it out. While I was standing and studying what to do, my friend came to me. He had followed my trail through the harricane, and had found my knife, which was might good news to me; as a hunter hates the worst in the world to lose a good dog, or any part of his hunting tools. I now left McDaniel to butcher the bear, and I went after our horses, and brought them as near as the nature of the case would allow. I then took our bags, and went back to where he was; and when we had skinned the bear, we flecced off the fat and carried it to our horses at several loads. We then packed it up on our horses, and had a heavy pack of it on each one. We now started and went on till about sunset, when I concluded we must be near our camp; so I hollered and my son answered me, and we moved on in the direction to the camp. We had gone but a little way when I heard my dogs make a warm start again; and I jumped down from my horse and gave him up to my friend, and told him I would follow them. He went on to the camp, and I went ahead after my dogs with all my might for a considerable distance, till at last night came on. The woods were very rough and hilly, and all covered over with cane.

I now was compelled to move on more slowly; and was frequently falling over logs, and into the cracks made by the earthquakes, so that I was very much afraid I would break my gun. However, I went on about three miles, when I came to a good big creek, which I waded. It was very cold, and the creek was about knee-deep; but I felt no great inconvenience from it just then, as I was all over wet with sweat from running, and I felt hot enough. After I got over this creek and out of the cane, which was very thick on all our creeks, I listened for my dogs. I found they had either treed or brought the bear to a stop, as they continued barking in the same place. I pushed on as near in the direction of the noise as I could, till I found the hill was too steep for me to climb, and so I backed and went down the creek some distance, till I came to a hollow, and then took up that, till I came to a place where I could climb up the hill. It was mighty dark, and was difficult to see my way, or anything else. When I got up the hill, I found I had passed the dogs; and so I turned and went to them. I found, when I got there, they had treed the bear in a large forked poplar, and it was setting in the fork.

I could see the lump, but not plain enough to shoot with any certainty, as there was no moonlight; and so I set in to hunting for some dry brush to make me a light; but I could find none, though I could find that the ground was torn mightily to pieces by the cracks.

At last I thought I could shoot by guess, and kill him; so I pointed as near the lump as I could, and fired away. But the bear didn't come, he only clumb up higher, and got out on a limb, which helped me to see him better. I now loaded up again and fired, but this time he didn't move at all. I commenced loading for a third fire, but the first thing I knowed, the bear was down among my dogs, and they were fighting all around me. I had my big butcher in my belt, and I had a pair of dressed buckskin breeches on. So I took out my knife, and stood, determined, if he should get hold of me, to defend myself in the best way I could. I stood there for some time, and could now and then see a white dog I had, but the rest of them, and the bear, which were dark colored, I couldn't see at all, it was so miserable dark. They still fought around me, and sometimes within three feet of me; but, at last, the bear got down into one of the cracks that the earthquakes had made in the ground, about four feet deep, and I could tell the biting end of him by the hollering of my dogs. So I took my gun and pushed the muzzle of it about, till I thought I had it against the main part of his body, and fired; but it happened to be only the fleshy part of his foreleg. With this he jumped out of the crack, and he and the dogs had another hard fight around me, as before. At last, however, they forced him back into the crack again, as he was when I had shot.

I had laid down my gun in the dark, and I now began to hunt for it; and, while hunting, I got hold of a pole, and I concluded I would punch him awhile with that. I did so, and when I would punch him, the dogs would jump in on him, when he would bite them badly, and they would jump out again. I concluded, as he would take punching so patiently, it might be that he would lie still enough for me to get down in the crack, and feel slowly along till I could find the right place to give him a dig with my butcher. So I got down, and my dogs got in before him and kept his head towards them, till I got along easily up to him; and placing my hand on his rump, felt for his shoulder, just behind which I intended to stick him. I made a lunge with my long knife, and fortunately stuck him right through the heart, at which he just sank down, and I crawled out in a hurry. In a little time my dogs all come out too, and seemed satisfied, which was the way they always had of telling me that they had finished him.

I suffered very much that night with cold, as my leather breeches, and everything else I had on, was wet and frozen. But I managed to get my bear out of this crack after several hard trials, and so I butchered him and laid down to try to sleep. But my fire was very bad, and I couldn't find anything that would burn well to make it any better; and so I concluded I should freeze, if I didn't warm myself in some way by exercise. So I got up and hollered awhile, and then I would just jump up and down with all my might, and throw myself into all sorts of motions. But all this wouldn't do; for my blood was now getting cold, and the chills coming all over me. I was so tired, too, that I could hardly walk; but I thought I would do the best I could to save my life, and then, if I died, nobody would be to blame. So I went to a tree about two feet through, and not a limb on it for thirty feet, and I would climb up to the limbs, and then lock my arms together around it, and slide down to the bottom again. This would make the insides of my legs and arms feel mighty warm and good. I continued this till daylight in the morning, and how often I clumb up my tree and slid down I don't know, but I reckon at least a hundred times.

In the morning I got my bear hung up so as to be safe, and then set out to hunt for my camp. I found it after awhile, and McDaniel and my son were very much rejoiced to see me get back, for they were about to give me up for lost. We got our breakfasts, and then secured our meat by building a high scaffold, and covering it over. We had no fear of its spoiling, for the weather was so cold that it couldn't.

We now started after my other bear, which had caused

me so much trouble and suffering; and before we got him, we got a start after another, and took him also. We went on the creek I had crossed the night before, and camped, and then went to where my bear was that I had killed in the crack. When we examined the place, McDaniel said he wouldn't have gone into it, as I did, for all the bears in the woods.

We then took the meat down to our camp and salted it, and also the last one we had killed; intending in the morning, to make a hunt in the harricane again.

We prepared for resting that night, and I can assure the reader I was in need of it. We had laid down by our fire, and about ten o'clock there came a most terrible earthquake, which shook the earth so, that we were rocked about like we had been in a cradle. We were very much alarmed; for though we were accustomed to feel earthquakes, we were not right in the region which had been torn to pieces by them in 1812, and we thought it might take a notion and swallow us up, like the big fish did Jonah.

In the morning we packed up and moved to the harricane, where we made another camp, and turned out that evening and killed a very large bear, which made eight we had now killed in this hunt.

The next morning we entered the harricane again, and in a little or no time my dogs were in full cry. We pursued them, and soon came to a thick cane-brake, in which they had stopp'd their bear. We got up close to him, as the cane was so thick that we couldn't see more than a few feet. Here I made my friend hold the cane a little open with his gun till I shot the bear, which was a mighty large one. I killed him dead in his tracks. We got him out and butchered him, and in a little time started another and killed him, which now made ten we had killed; and we knowed we couldn't pack any more home, as we had only five horses along; therefore we returned to the camp and salted up all our meat, to be ready for a start homeward next morning.

The morning came, and we packed our horses with the meat, and had as much as they could possibly carry, and sure enough cut out for home. It was about thirty miles, and we reached home the second day. I had now accommodated my neighbor with meat enough to do him, and had killed in all, up to that time, fifty-eight bears, during the fall and winter.

As soon as the time come for them to quit their houses and come out again in the spring, I took a notion to hunt a little more, and in about one month I killed forty-seven more, which made one hundred and five bears which I had killed in less than one year from that time.

PART II

The Missouri
and Beyond

1808-1870

12

JOHN COLTER:

The Strong and the Fleet

John Colter (c. 1775–1813), the first of the great mountain men, is one of the legendary figures of the West: a man who was fascinated by danger; a man who traveled alone and on foot over vast stretches of uncharted wilderness; a man, most of all, who ran like the wind. Born in Virginia and raised mostly in Kentucky, Colter was described by a fellow trapper as being about five feet, ten inches tall and having "an open . . . and pleasing countenance of the Daniel Boone stamp." He is first heard of in Louisville in October 1803, when his name was added to the list of recruits for the Lewis and Clark expedition. The two pathfinders mention his name frequently in their journals, and they relied on him to undertake the most hazardous missions. Granted a discharge on the return journey, Colter remained in the mountains, hunting and trapping through the winter of 1806–1807. On his way back to civilization in the spring he met an expedition of the Missouri Fur Company and was persuaded to return to the mountains with them.

Colter spent the next three years in the Rockies. Carrying only a thirty-pound pack, his gun, and some ammunition, he traveled alone among the headwaters of the Missouri—up and down the Wind River, the Bighorn, the Yellowstone—looking for beaver and trying to bring the Indians in to trade. During his wanderings he became the first white man to see the Teton Range and what is now Yellowstone Park, reports of whose geysers and boiling springs would long be dismissed as tall tales by skeptics back in the States.

It was in the spring of 1808, near the Three Forks of the Missouri River, a region rich in beaver but guarded by hostile Blackfeet, that Colter's most famous adventure took place: his swift-footed escape from the Indians. A number of other close calls finally convinced him to quit the mountains, and in May 1810 he came paddling down the Missouri to St. Louis, where he related his adventures to, among others, an English botanist named John Bradbury. Colter married a young woman named Sally and settled down on a farm, where he died a few years later, apparently of jaundice. His story, printed as a footnote in Bradbury's Travels, *was later immortalized in Washington Irving's* Astoria.

This man came to St. Louis in May, 1810, in a small canoe, from the head waters of the Missouri, a distance of three thousand miles, which he traversed in thirty days. I saw him on his arrival, and received from him an account of his adventures after he had separated from Lewis and Clarke's party: one of these, from its singularity, I shall relate. On the arrival of the party on the head waters of the Missouri, Colter, observing an appearance of abundance of beaver being there, he got permission to remain and hunt for some time, which he did in company with a man of the name of Dixon, who had traversed the immense tract of country from St. Louis to the head waters of the Missouri alone. Soon after he separated from Dixon, and *trapped in* company with a hunter named Potts; and aware of the

From *Travels in the Interior of America*, by John Bradbury, second edition, 1819. Reprinted in Reuben Gold Thwaites, ed., *Early Western Travels*, vol. 5 (Cleveland; Arthur H. Clark Co., 1904), pp. 44–47.

hostility of the Blackfeet Indians, one of whom had been killed by Lewis, they set their traps at night, and took them up early in the morning, remaining concealed during the day. They were examining their traps early one morning, in a creek about six miles from that branch of the Missouri called Jefferson's Fork, and were ascending in a canoe, when they suddenly heard a great noise, resembling the trampling of animals; but they could not ascertain the fact, as the high perpendicular banks on each side of the river impeded their view. Colter immediately pronounced it to be occasioned by Indians, and advised an instant retreat; but was accused of cowardice by Potts, who insisted that the noise was caused by buffaloes, and they proceeded on. In a few minutes afterwards their doubts were removed, by a party of Indians making their appearance on both sides of the creek, to the amount of five or six hundred, who beckoned them to come ashore. As retreat was now impossible, Colter turned the head of the canoe to the shore; and at the moment of its touching, an Indian seized the rifle belonging to Potts; but Colter, who is a remarkably strong man, immediately retook it, and handed it to Potts, who remained in the canoe, and on receiving it pushed off into the river. He had scarcely quitted the shore when an arrow was shot at him, and he cried out, "*Colter, I am wounded.*" Colter remonstrated with him on the folly of attempting to escape, and urged him to come ashore. Instead of complying, he instantly levelled his rifle at an Indian, and shot him dead on the spot. This conduct, situated as he was, may appear to have been an act of madness; but it was doubtless the effect of sudden, but sound reasoning; for if taken alive, he must have expected to be tortured to death, according to their custom. He was instantly pierced with arrows so numerous, that, to use the language of Colter, "*he was made a riddle of.*" They now seized Colter, stripped him entirely naked, and began to consult on the manner in which he should be put to death. They were first inclined to set him up as a mark to shoot at; but the chief interfered, and seizing him by the shoulder, asked him if he could run fast? Colter, who had been some time amongst the Kee-kat-sa, or Crow Indians, had in a considerable degree acquired the Blackfoot language, and was also well acquainted with Indian customs. He knew that he had now to run for his life, with the dreadful odds of five or six hundred against him, and those armed Indians; therefore cunningly replied that he was a very bad runner, although he was considered by the hunters as remarkably swift. The chief now commanded the party to remain stationary, and led Colter out on the prairie three or four hundred yards, and released him, bidding him *to save himself if he could.* At that instant the horrid war whoop sounded in the ears of poor Colter, who, urged with the hope of preserving life, ran with a speed at which he was himself surprised. He proceeded towards the Jefferson Fork, having to traverse a plain six miles in breadth, abounding with the prickly pear, on which he was every instant treading with his naked feet. He ran nearly half way across the plain before he ventured to look over his shoulder, when he perceived that the Indians were very much scattered, and that he had gained ground to a considerable distance from the main body; but one Indian, who carried a spear, was much before all the rest, and not more than a hundred yards from him. A faint gleam of hope now cheered the heart of Colter: he derived confidence from the belief that escape was within the bounds of possibility; but that confidence was nearly being fatal to him, for he exerted himself to such a degree, that the blood gushed from his nostrils, and soon almost covered the fore part of his body. He had now arrived within a mile of the river, when he distinctly heard the appalling sound of footsteps behind him, and every instant expected to feel the spear of his pursuer. Again he turned his head, and saw the savage not twenty yards from him. Determined if possible to avoid the expected blow, he suddenly stopped, turned round, and spread out his arms. The Indian, surprised by the suddenness of the action, and perhaps at the bloody appearance of Colter, also attempted to stop; but exhausted with running, he fell whilst endeavouring to throw his spear, which stuck in the ground, and broke in his hand. Colter instantly snatched up the pointed part, with which he pinned him to the earth, and then continued his flight. The foremost of the Indians, on arriving at the place, stopped till others came up to join them, when they set up a hideous yell. Every moment of this time was improved by Colter, who, although fainting and exhausted, succeeded in gaining the skirting of the cotton wood trees, on the borders of the fork, through which he ran, and plunged into the river. Fortunately for him, a little below this place there was an island, against the upper point of which a raft of drift timber had lodged. He dived under the raft, and after several efforts, got his head above water amongst the trunks of trees, covered over with smaller wood to the depth of several feet. Scarcely had he secured himself, when the Indians arrived on the river, screeching and yelling, as Colter expressed it, "like so many devils." They were frequently on the raft during the day, and were seen through the chinks by Colter, who was congratulating himself on his escape, until the idea arose that they might set the raft on fire. In horrible suspense he remained until night, when hearing no more of the Indians, he dived from under the raft, and swam silently down the river to a considerable distance, when he landed, and travelled all night. Although happy in having escaped from the Indians, his situation was still dreadful: he was completely naked, under a burning sun; the soles of his feet were entirely filled with the thorns of the prickly pear; he was hungry, and had no means of killing game, although he saw abundance around him, and was at least seven days journey from Lisa's Fort, on the Bighorn branch of the Roche Jaune River. These were circumstances under which almost any man but an American hunter would have despaired. He arrived at the fort in seven days, having subsisted on a root much esteemed by the Indians of the Missouri, now known by naturalists as *psoralea esculenta*.

13

JAMES CLYMAN:

Witness to History

The career of James Clyman (1791–1881) as trapper, guide, and pioneer settler spans the history of America's westward movement from the wilderness edge of Virginia in the 1790s to the fertile valleys of California and Oregon in the 1840s and 1850s. Besides having his own full share of adventures, Clyman was a witness and chronicler of many of the great events of that movement.

A Virginian, lean and rangy, with dark blue eyes and a gentle manner, Clyman had moved with his parents first to Pennsylvania, then to the Ohio frontier, where he served as a mounted ranger in the Indian campaigns of 1812. Later, he drifted westward and in the spring of 1823 found himself in St. Louis, where William Ashley was recruiting men for his second expedition to the Rocky Mountain fur country. Ashley's fur ventures were the training ground for some of the most celebrated of the mountainmen, including Jedediah Smith, Thomas Fitzpatrick, Hugh Glass, Jim Bridger, Jim Beckwourth (all of whom are represented in this volume), and William and Milton

179

Sublette, as well as Clyman himself, who signed on as a clerk. That first summer Clyman barely escaped with his life when Ashley's party was attacked by Arikaras on the Upper Missouri. A few months later he was with Smith and Fitzpatrick on their historic crossing of the Great South Pass, which opened the way through the mountains to the western fur country and which soon became the principle route to Oregon and California for thousands of emigrants. Not long afterward Clyman proved his skill as a woodsman when, becoming separated from his companions, he walked from the Sweetwater River back to Fort Atkinson, near the mouth of the Platte—a distance of 600 miles across a harsh and hostile wilderness.

Clyman was one of the few mountainmen to survive not only Indian attacks, drunken brawls, and grizzly bears, but also the strain imposed on a man's mind and body by constant exposure to danger, to a poor diet, to bad weather, and to frequent hunger and thirst. After his retirement from the fur trade in 1827, he settled for a time in Illinois and Wisconsin, where he served as a militiaman in the Black Hawk War. Heading west again in the 1840s, he became the leader of emigrant trains bound for Oregon and California. His forty years of wandering ended abruptly with his marriage to the daughter of a California emigrant, at Napa, in 1849. There he bought a ranch, where he lived until his death, one month short of his ninetieth birthday. Clyman's reminiscences, which he compiled from his diaries during the later part of his life, are among the most valuable sources of the history of the early Western frontier.

Haveing been imployed in Public Surveys in the state of Illinois through the winter of 1823 [1822] and the early part of 24 [23] I came to St Louis about the first of February to ricieve pay for past services and rimaining there Some days I heard a report that General William H Ashly was engageing men for a Trip to the mouth of the Yellow Stone river   I

From "James Clyman, His Diaries and Reminiscences," Charles L. Camp, ed., *California Historical Society Quarterly*, vol. 4 (San Francisco, 1925), pp. 110–116, 122–123, 130, 132–139. Reprinted by permission.

made enquiry as to what was the object but found no person who seemed to possess the desired infor-mation finding whare Ashleys dwelling was I called on him the same evening Several Gentlemen being present he invited me to call again on a certain evening which I did he then gave a lenthy account of game found in that Region Deer, elk Bear and Buffalo but to crown all immence Quantities of Beaver whose skins ware verry valuable sell-ing from $5 to 8$ per pound at that time in St Louis and the men he wished to engage ware to [be] huters trappers and traders for furs and peltrees my curiosity now being satis-fied St Louis being a fine place for Spending money I did not leave immediately not having spent all my funds I loitered about without employment

Haveing fomed a Slight acquaintance with Mr Ashley we occasionly passed each other on the streets at length one day Meeting him he told me he had been looking for me a few days back and enquired as to my employment I informed him that I was entirely unemployed he said he wished then that I would assist him ingageing men for his Rockey mountain epedition and he wished me to call at his house in the evening which I accordingly did getting in-structions as to whare I would most probably find men willing to engage which [were to be] found in grog Shops and other sinks of degredation he rented a house & fur-nished it with provisions Bread from to Bakers—pork plenty, which the men had to cook for themselves

On the 8th [10th] of March 1824 [1823] all things ready we shoved off from the shore fired a swivel which was answered by a Shout form the shore which we returned with a will and porceed up stream under sail

A discription of our crew I cannt give but Fallstafs Bat-tallion was genteel in comparison I think we had about seventy all told Two Keel Boats with crews of French some St Louis gumboes as they ware called

We proceeded slowly up the Misourie River under sail wen winds ware favourable and towline when not Towing or what was then calld cordell is a slow and tedious method of assending swift waters

It is done by the men walking on the shore and hawling the Boat by a long cord   Nothing of importance came under wiew for some months except loosing men who left us from time to time & engaging a few new men of a much better appearance than those we lost   The Missourie is a monotinous crooked stream with large cottonwood forest trees on one side and small young groth on the other with a bare Sand Barr intervening   I will state one circumstanc only which will show something of the character of Missourie Boats men

The winds are occasionally very strong and when head winds prevail we ware forced to lay by   this circumstanc happened. once before we left the Settlements   the men went out gunning and that night came in with plenty of game Eggs Fowls Turkeys and what not   Haveing a fire on shore they dressed cooked and eat untill midnight being care full to burn all the fragments   the wind still Blowing in the morning several Neighbours came in hunting for poultry   liberty was given to search the boats but they found nothing and left   the wind abateing somewhat the cord was got out amd pulling around a bend the wind became a farir sailing breeze and [the sails] wa[r]e ordred unfurled when out droped pigs and poultry in abundance

A man was ordred to Jump in the skiff and pick up the pigs and poultry

Ariveing at Council Bluffs we m[a]de several exchanges (8) eight or Ten of our men enlisting and 2 or 3 of the Soldier whose [terms of enlistment] was nearly expired engageing with us   The officers being verry liberal furnished us with a Quantity of vegetables   here we leave the last appearance of civilization and [enter] fully Indian country game becomeing more plenty we furnished ourselvs with meat daily

But I pass on to the arickaree villages whare we met with our defeat   on ariveing in sight of the villages the barr in front was lined with squaws packing up water thinking to have to stand a siege

For a better understanding it is necessay that I state tha[t] the Missourie furr company have established a small

trading house . . . some (60) or (80) miles below the arric-
kree villages the winter previous to our assent and the arrickarees haveing taken some Sioux squaws prisoners previously one of these Squaws got away from them and made
for this trading post and they persuing come near overtaking her in sight of the post   the men in the house ran out
and fired on the Pesueing arrickarees killing (2) others so
that Rees considered war was fully declared bctwen them
and the whites   But General Asley thought he could make
them understand that his [company] was not resposable for
Injuries done by the Missourie fur company But the Rees
could not make the distiction   they however agreed to
recieve pay for thier loss but the geeneral would make them
a present but would not pay the Misourie fur companies
damages

After one days talk they agreed to open trade on the
sand bar in fron of the village but the onley article of Trade
they wantd was ammunition   For feare of a difficulty, the
boats ware kept at anchor in the streame, and the skiffs
were used for communications Betteen the boats and the
shore.   we obtained twenty horses in three d[a]ys trading,
but in doing this we gave them a fine supply of Powder and
ball which on (the) fourth day wee found out to [our]
Sorrow

In the night of the third day Several of our men without
permition went and remained in the village amongst
them   our Interperter Mr [Edward] Rose   about midnight
he came runing into camp & informed us that one of our
men . . . was killed in the village and war was declared in
earnest   We had no Military organization dicipline or
Subordination   Several advised to cross over the river at
once but thought best to wait untill day light But General
Ashley our imployer Thought best to wait till morning and
go into the village and demand the body of our comrade
and his Murderer   Ashley being the most interested his
advice prevailed   We laid on our arms e[x]pecting an attact
as their was a continual Hubbub in the village

At length morning appeared every thing still
undecided   finally one shot was fired into our camp the

distance being however to great for certain aim   Shortly firing became Quite general we seeing nothing to fire at   Here let me give a Short discription of an Indian City or village as it is usually caled   Picture to your self (50) or (100) large potatoe holes as they are usuly caled in the west (10) to (15) feet in diameter and 8 to 10 feet high in the center covered on the outside with small willow brush then a layer of coarse grass a coat of earth over all a hole in one side for a door and another in the top to let out the smoke a small fire in the center *all Told*   The continual wars between them and Sioux had caused them to picket in their place   You will easely prceive that we had little else to do than to Stand on a bear sand barr and be shot at, at long range   Their being seven or Eigh hundred guns in village and we having the day previously furnished them with abundance of Powder and Ball   [There were] many calls for the boats to come ashore and take us on board but no prayers or threats had the [slightest effect] the Boats men being completely Parylized   Several men being wounded a skiff was brought ashore   all rushed for the Skiff and came near sinking it but it went the boat full of men and water the shot still coming thicker and the aim better we making a brest work of our horses they nerly all being killed   the skiffs having taken sevarl loads on Board the boats at length the shot coming thicker and faster one of the skiffs was leg go   the men clambering on Boad let the skiff float off in their great eaganess to conceal themselves from the rapid fire of the enemy   I seeing no hopes of Skiffs or boats comeing ashore left my hiding place behind a dead hors, ran up stream a short distance to get the advantage of the current and concieving myself to be a tolerable strong swimer stuck the muzzle of my rifle in [my] belt the lock ove my head with all my clothes on but not having made suffi-cien calculation for the strong current was carried passed the boat within a few feet of the same   one Mr Thomas Eddie [saw me] but the shot coming thick he did not ven-ture from behin the cargo Box and so could not reach me with a setting pole which [he] held in his hands   K[n]owing now or at (least) thinking that I had the river to swim my first aim was to rid myself of all my encumbraces and my Rifle was the greatest   in my attempt to draw it over my head it sliped down the lock ketching in my belt   comeing to the surface to breathe I found it hindred worse than it did at first   making one more effort I turned the lock side ways and it sliped through which gave me some relief but still finding myself to much encumbred I next unbucled my belt and let go my Pistols   still continue- ing to disengage my self I next let go my Ball Pouch and finally one Sleeve of my Hunting shirt which was buckskin and held an immence weight of water when rising to the surface I heard the voice of encoragemnt saying hold on Clyman I will soon relieve you   This [from] Reed Gibson who had swam in and caught the skiff the men had let go afloat and was but a few rods from me   I was so much exausted that he had to haul me into the skiff wh[ere] I lay for a moment to cacth breath when I arose to take the only remaining ore when Gibson caled oh, god I am shot and fell forward in the skiff   I encouraged him and [said] Perhaps not fatally give a few pulls more and we will be out of reach   he raised and gave sevreral more strokes with the oar using it as a paddle when [he] co[m]plained of feeling faint when he fell forward again and I took his plac in the sterm and shoved it across to the East shore whare we landed   I hauled the skiff up on the shore and told Gibson to remain in the Skiff and I would go upon the high land whare I could see if any danger beset us thair. After getting up on the river bank and looking around I Discovered sevral Indian in the water swimming over [some] of whoom ware nearly across the stream   I spoke to Gibson telling him of the circumstance   he mearly said save yourself Clyman and pay no attention to me as I am a dead man and they can get nothing of me but my Scalp   My first Idea was to get in the skiff and meet them in the water and brain them with the oar   But on second look I conconcluded there ware to many of them and they ware too near the shore   then I looked for some place to hide But there being onley a scant row of brush along the shore I concluded to take to the open Pararie and run for life   by this time

Gibson had scrambled up the bank and stood by my side and said   run Clyman but if you escape write to my friends in Virginia and tell them what has become of me   I [ran] for the open Prarie and Gibson for the brush to hide   at first I started a little distance down the river but fearing that I might be headed in some bend I steered directly for the open Prarie and looking Back I saw three Inians mount the bank being intirely divested of garments excepting a belt aroun the waist containing a Knife and Tomahawk and Bows and arrows in their [hands]   they made but little halt and started after me   one to the right the other to the left while the third took direct after me   I took direct for the rising ground I think about three miles of(f)   there being no chanc for dodging the ground being smooth and level   but haveing the start of some 20 or 30 rods we had appearantle an even race for about one hour when I began to have the palpitation of the heart and I found my man was gaining on me   I had now arived at a moderately roling ground and for the first time turned a hill out of sight   I turned to the right and found a hole was[h]ed in the earth some 3 feet long 1½ feet wide and Pehaps 2 feet deep with weeds and grass perhaps one foot high surrounding it into this hole I droped and persuer immediatle hove in sight and passed me about fifty yards distant both my right an left hand persuers haveing fallen cosiderably in the rear and particularly the one on my right here fortune favoured me for my direct persuer soon passed over some uneven ground got out of sight when I arose and talking to the right stnuck into a low ground which covered me and following it soon came into a moderately steep ravin   in all this time I gained breath and I did not see my persuers until I gained the top of the ridge over a Quarter of a mile from my friend   when I gained this elevation I turned around [and saw] the three standing near togather   I made them a low bow with both my hand and thanked god for my present Safety and diliveranc

But I did not remain long here   wishing to put the gratest possible distance between me and the Arrickarees I still continued Southward over a smoothe roling ground   But what ware my reflection being at least Three Hundred miles from any assistanc unarmed and u[n]provided with any sort of means of precureing a subsistance not even a pocket Knife I began to feel after passing So many dangers that my pro[s]pects ware still verry slim,   mounting some high land I saw ahed of me the river and Quite a grove of timber and being verry thirsty I made for the water intending to take a good rest in the timber   I took one drink of water and setting down on a drift log a few minuits I chanced to look [at] the [river] and here came the boats floating down the stream   the [men] watcing along the shores saw me about as soon as I saw them   the boat was laid in and I got aboard

I spoke of my friend Gibson whe[n] I was informed he was on board   I immediately wen[t] to the cabin whare he lay but he did not recognize me being in the agonies of Death the shot having passed through his bowels   I could not refrain from weeping over him who lost his lifee but saved mine   he did not live but an hour or so and we buried him that evening the onley one of (12) [13] that ware killed at the arrickarees   Eleven being left on the sand bar and their Scalps taken for the squaws to sing and dance over

Before meeting with this defeat I think few men had Stronger Ideas of their bravery and disregard of fear than I had but standing on a bear and open sand barr to be shot at from bihind a picketed Indian village was more than I had contacted for and some what cooled my courage   before leaving the grave of my friend Gibson that [day and] before I had an oppertunity of writeing to his friends I forgot his post office and so never have written   We fell down a few miles and lay by several day to wait and [see] if any more men had escaped the but[c]hery when on the third or fourth day Jack Larisson came to us naked as when he was born and the skin peeling off of him from the effects of the sun   he was wounded a ball passing through the fleshy part of one thigh and ldging in the other   the ball was easily exticated and in a few days he was hobbling around   Larrisson had lain between two dead horses untill the boats left and he saw no other chance of escape but to

swim the river   then divesting himself of all his clothing
he took the water   the Indians came running and firing at
his head but [he] escaped without further injury   the
wound Before mentioned he had recieved in the early part
of the battle if it can be called Battle   supposing no more
men had survived the slaughte[r] we again droped down
the river. . . .

[Unwilling to lose any more men or supplies in further
encounters with the Arikaras, General Ashley abandoned
the traditional Missouri River route to the Rocky Mountain
beaver country. Instead, he purchased horses from the
Sioux and dispatched his men overland, across the arid
plains of South Dakota. Clyman was assigned to the party
lead by twenty-four-year-old Jedediah Smith—a party that
also included young William Sublette and Thomas Fitzpatrick. After struggling through the ashen wastes of the Badlands, the party found itself in the rugged canyons of the
Black Hills, near the South Fork of the Cheyenne River.]

. . . [O]ne evening late gowing d[o]wn a small stream
we came into a Kenyon and pushed ouselves down so far
that [that] our horses had no room to turn   while looking
for a way out it became dark   by unpacking and leading
our animals down over Slipery rocks three of us got down to
a n[i]ce open glade whare we killed a Buffaloe and fared
Sumpiously that night while the rest of the Company remained in the Kenyon without room to lie down   we now
found it would not do to follow down any stream in these
mountains as we ware shure to meet with rocky inaccessible places   So with great exertion we again assended to the
top of a ridge and ware Quite lucky in gitting a main devide
which led us a considerable distance before [we] had to
desend again   but this portion of the mountain furnished
our horses with no food and they began to be verry poor
and weak so we left 3 men and five horses behind to recruit
while the rest of us proceded on there being some sighn of
Beaver in the vicinity and hoping to soon find more where
we Might all Stop for a time   The Crow Indians being our
place of destination a half Breed by the name of Rose who
spoke the crow tongue was dispached ahead to find the

Crows and try to induce some of them to come to our assistance we to travel directly west as near as circumstances would permit supposing we ware on the waters of Powder River we ought to be within the bounds of the Crow country continueing five days travel since leaveing our given out horses and likewise Since Rose left us late in the afternoon while passing through a Brushy bottom a large Grssely came down the vally we being in single file men on foot leding pack horses he struck us about the center then turning ran paralel to our line Captain Smith being in the advanc he ran to the open ground and as he immerged from the thicket he and the bear met face to face Grissly did not hesitate a moment but sprung on the Captain taking him by the head first pitc[h]ing sprawling on the earth he gave him a grab by the middle fortunately cat[c]hing by the ball pouch and Butcher K[n]ife which he broke but breaking several of his ribs and cutting his head badly none of us having any sugical Knowledge what was to be done one Said come take hold and he wuld say why not you so it went around I asked the Captain what was best he said one or 2 [go] for water and if you have a needle and threat git it out and sew up my wounds around my head which was bleeding freely I got a pair of scissors and cut off his hair and then began my first Job of d(r)essing wounds upon examination I [found] the bear had taken nearly all his head in his capcious mouth close to his left eye on one side and clos to his right ear on the other and laid the skull bare to near the crown of the head leaving a white streak whare his teeth passed one of his ears was torn from his head out to the outer rim after stitching all the other wounds in the best way I was capabl and according to the captains directions the ear being the last I told him I could do nothing for his Eare O you must try to stich up some way or other said he then I put in my needle stiching it through and through and over and over laying the lacerated parts togather as nice as I could with my hands water was found in about ame mille when we all moved down and encamped the captain being able to mount his horse and ride to camp whare we pitched a tent the onley one we had and made him as comfortable as circumstances would permit   this gave us a lisson on the charcter of the grissly Baare which we did not forget. . . .

. . . [I]n February [1824] we made an efort to cross the mountains north of the wind River [ra]nge but found the snow too deep and had to return and take a Southern course east of the wind river range which is here the main Rockey mountans and the main dividing ridge betwen the Atlantic and Pacific. . . .

We . . . now moved over a low ridge and Struck on Sweet Water Since assertained to be a tributary of the Platte river it was cold and clear the evening that we encamped on Sweet water many of [the] South sides of the hills ware bare of Snow   Buffalo scarce and rattions limited   some time in the night the wind arose to a hericane direct from the north and we had [to] Keep awake and hold on to our blankets and robes to keep them from flying away   in the morning we gathered a large pile of dry pine logs and fixed up our blankets against the wind but the back current brought all the smoke and ashes into our faces   in fifteen or twenty minuets after taking down our Screen ou[r] fire blew intirely away and left us the wood but no fire   we then cleared away the snow under the lea of a clump of willows   fixed ourselves as comfortable as circumstances would permit   laid to sleep the wind still blowing all day and night without abatement   the next morning several of us wrapt ourselves in our robes and attempted to take some exercise following down the stream   it became confined in a narrow Kenyon   under the points of some rocks we would be partly secure from the cold blast   toward evening my companion Mr Branch Saw a mountain sheep on the rocks allmost perpedicular over us and fired at him   had the good luck to hit him when he came tumbling down to our feet   we soon prepared him and packed him to camp whare efforts were made to broil small pieces but soon gave it up the wind still keeping up such a continual blast as to prevent even a starving mountaneer from satisfying his hunger   we all took to our blankets again it being the only way to keep from perishing the blast being so

strong and cold   Late in the night however the lull came on
and being awake I arose and found it Quite comfortable   I
struck up a fire and commenced cooking and eating by
broiling thin slices of meat   after a short time my comrades
began to arise and we talked cooked eat the remainder of
the night   in the morning we started out in various directions some to look for game and some to look for more
comfortable Quarters our prsent camp being close to the
East foot of the wind River mountain and on a low divide
directly south of the Wind rever vally having a full sweep
for the North Wind [which] Caused as such [an]
uncomfortab[l]e time   Two pa[r]ties proceeded one in
Quest of game the other for a camping ground   I went
down the sweet water some four or five miles to whare the
Kenyon opened out into Quite a valley and found plenty of
dry aspin wood in a small grove at the Lower end of the
Kenyon and likewise plenty of Mountain Sheep on the cliffs
which bounded the stream one of which I had the luck to
kill and which I Buried in a snowdrift   the next morning
we packed up and moved down to the Aspin grove whare
we remained some two or three weeks Subsisting on
Mountain sheep   on our way to our new camp we ware
overtaken by one of the heaviest falls of snow that I ever
witnessed with but verry slight wind   the snow came
down in one perfect sheet but fortunately it did not las[t]
but a short time and we made our camp in good season   as
I before said we did not leave this camp untill the Mountain
Sheep began to get scarce and wild and before leaving we
here made a cash of Powder Lead and several other articles
supposed to be not needed in our Springs hunt and it was
here likewise understood that should circumstances at any
time seperate us we would meet at this place and at (and) all
event we would all met here again or at some navigable
point on the stream below at or by the first [of] June according to our recording on leaving sweet water w struck in a
south westerly direction this being some of the last days of
February I think in 1825 [1824]   our stock of dried meat
being verry scant we soon run out entirely—no game to be
found   It appears this winter was extremely dry and cold

one fourth of the g[r]round on those ridges south of
Sweetwater being entirely bare from the effect of strong
west winds which carried the snow over to the East and
south sides of the ridges about sixth morning out Mr
Sublette and myself ware in the advance looking out for
game a few antelope had been see[n] the evening
previous   as light snow falling we came on the fresh track
of a buffalo and supposing he could not be far off we started
full speed after him   in running about a mile we came in
sight of him laying down   the animal being thick a[nd]
hevy it [was] difficult to hit a vital part when he is laying
down   we consulted as to the surest way [of] disabling him
and came to the concusion that I fire at the rump and if
posible breake his coupling while Sublett would fire at his
Shoulder and disable him in forward parts so we [a]greed
Sublett counting one two three while we both drew aim
and both pull trigger at the word fire when both of our rifles
went of simutan[eo]u[sly] and both effected what we desired the animal struling to rise but could not   Sublett
beat me in reloading and approached and shot him in the
head Just as the company came in sight on a hight of land
when they all raised a Shout of Delight at [the] sight many
not having tasted food for four days & none of us from two
to three   now you may suppose we had a happy time in
butchering . . .

Our company coming up we butchered our meat in
short order many of the men eating large slices raw   we
packed up our meat & traveled on untill in the afternoon in
hopes of finding water but did not succeed but finding
large clumps of sage brush we camped all eaving & part of
the night   continuing on we found we had crossed the
main ridge [South Pass] of the Rocky mountain in the month
of January [February] 15 days without water or only such as
we got from melting snow our horses eating snow and
living fairly when beaver ground was found   although we
struck Sandy [River] about noon some of the men went
immediately   to   cutting   the   ice   with   thier
Tomahauks   called out frose to the bottom   I walked
down they had got down the length of thier arms and was

about to give it up   I pulled out one of my pistols and fired
in to the hole   up came the water plentifull for man &
horse   there being a small growth of willows along the
stream we had wood & water plenty but our supply of meat
had given out   passed down the stream   one[e] day in the
eavning a buffalo was killed and we were all happy for the
present   this stream and one other we passd and on the
20th of February we reached Green river where I had the
luck to kill two wild geese   here Captain Smith with seven
men left us he going farther south   we left to trap on the
branches of the stream as soon as the ice gave way   in a few
day(s) wild geese became plenty on thawy & Springy
places   the ice giving way we found beaver plenty and we
commenced trapping   We found a small family of diggers
or Shoshone Indians on our trapping ground whom we
feed with the overplus of Beaver   the snow disapearing
our diggar friends moved off without our knowledge of
when or where and when they had gone our horses runing
loose on[e] night they all disapeared and we were unable to
find them or in what direction they had gone   we continued trapping on foot with fair success for about six
weeks when the 10th of June was drawing close and we had
promised all who were alive to meet at our cash on Sweet
Water   accordingly we cashed traps & furs hung our saddle & horse equipments on trees & set out for Sweet
water   the same day about noon on turning the point of a
ridge we meet face to face with five & six indians mounted
on some of our horses   preparing to take possession of as
many horses each on[e] taking hold of a lariet and ordering
our friens to dismount but after a short consultation we
decided to go with them to thier camp about one mile up a
steep mountain where we found six lodges 18 men with a
large supply of squaws & children & our old acquaintences
that we had fed with the fat of Beaver while the earth was
thickly covered with snow   we made our camp on rising
ground in easy gunshot of thier village   all our horses wer
given up but one and we concluded this one was hid in the
mountain so we caught one of the men tied him fast told
them we intended to kill him if our horse was not given

back which soon brought him   we gave them a few presents and left for our old camp   dug up our cashe cut down our saddles and again started for Sweet water   this brought us to the 15th of June   no sight of Smith or his paryt   remaining here a few days Fitzpatrick & myself mounted & fowling [following] down stream some 15 miles we concluded the stream was unna[vi]gable it beeing generally broad & Shallow and all our bagga[g]e would have to be packed to some navigable point below where I would be found waiting my comrades who would not be more than three or four days in the rear   I moved slowly down stream three days to the mouth where it enters the North Platt   Sweetwater is generally bare of all kind of timber but here near the mouth grew a small thick clump of willoes   in this I cut a lodging place and geathered some driftwood for a fire which I was just preparing to strike fire I heard human voices on the stream below   carfuly watching I saw a number of Indians advance up along the opisite side of the stream being here about 4 rods wide   they come up & all stoped on the other side   there being a lot of dry wood they soon raised 4 or 5 fires   turned loose or tithered all their horses thier being 22 Indians and 30 horses   I did not feel myself perfectly safe with so large number a war party in my rear vacinity   recoclecting that for ½ mile back the country was bare & sandy the moon a few days before the full I could be trased as easly as if it had been snow so I walked backward across the sandy reagon out to a narrow rocky ridge & following along the same to where the creek broke through it I crossed over to the east side and climbing a high point of rocks I had a fair vew of my disagreeable neighbors at about 40 rods distance   some of them lay down and slept while some others kept up the fire   about midnight they all arose collected up thier horses   too of the horses crossed over the creek   two Indians on horse back folowed after when a shout was raised & eight or ten mounted went to assist hunting the fugitives   after an hours ride backward & farword they gave up & all started of north   I crawled down from my pearch & caught a few moments of cool feverish sleep.   next day I surveyed the

canyon [Devil's Gate] through which the river passes fear-
fuly swift without any perpendicular fall   while on one of
the high cliffs I discovered about 20 Ind[ians] approach the
stream right where I had left a bout halfhour before all on
foot   they soon mad a small raft of driftwood on which
they piled their war equipments & clothes swam the
stream and went South   I returned to my observatory
on Sweetwater I remained in this vacinity eleven
days heard nothing of my party began to get
lonsome   examened my store of amuniton found I had
plenty of Powder but only eleven bullets reconitering all the
curcumstances in my mind I thought if I spent a week in
trying to find my old companions & should not be lucky
enough to meet with them I would not have balls enough to
take me to civilisation & not knowing whither I was on Platt
or the Arkansas on the 12th day in the afternoon I left my
look out at the mouth of Sweetwater and proceeded down
stream knowing that civil[iz]ation could be reached
Eastward   the days were quite warm & I had to keep near
the water nothing occured for several day worth
mentioning   at length I found a bull boat lying drifted up
on a sand bar and the marks of a large Indian ranch on the
main shore   I knew by the boat some white men had
[been] here for the Indians never made such boats   this
gave me a fient hope of meeting some white men in this
Indian world   but continuing down stream several days I
saw several persons running Buffalow on the hills on the
other side of the river but to far to tell who they were   Great
herds of Buffalo were drivin across the river right around
me   I shot one and dried some meat   remained here two
days in hopes of meeting some human beeing   even a
friendly Indian would be a relief to my solitude but no
person appearing I moved off down stream   some two or
three days after [this] I came into a grove of large old
cottonwoods where a number of village Martins were
nesting   I laied down in the shade and enjoyed their twit-
tering for some hours   it reminded me of home &
civilisation   I saw a number of wild horses on the [prairie?]
and I thought I would like to ride   there is what hunters

call "creasing"; this is done by shooting the animal through
the neck close above the main bone   this stuns them for a
minute or more   The next buffalo I killed I made a
halter,   I was forced to keep near the watter for there were
no springs or streams on the plain.   A fine black stallion
came down to drink and beeing in close gun shot I fired   as
soon as he had gained the main bank he fell & I ran up &
haltered him but he never moved for his neck was broken
so I missed my wild ride   still continuing my journy at
length I came to a large recent lodge trail crossing the
stream   I thought it would be plesent to communicate
with humans even though it were Indians so I plunged into
the stream and crossed over   the water was only breast
deep any where   the villiag was about two miles out in the
hills   on my approach to them I did not attract thier attention until within a few rods of thier lodges when a lot of
men & boys came running up to me yelling most hidously
when one man ran up & snatched my butcher knife and
waved it across my breast   I thought this a bravado so
bared my breast for the fated streike & this perhaps saved
my life for he immediatly commensed taking such things as
suited him others taking my blankets then all my balls
firesteel & flint   another untied my powder into a rag
when one or two cam rapedly up on horseback   then they
all left one of the mounted me[n] talking very loud &
rapidly   then he ordered me to mount behing him which I
was glad to do   he took me to his lodge and gave me to
understand that I must not roam around any for some of
them were bad and would kill me   I remained in his lodge
all night and after the morning meal he had three horses
broght   he & his son each mounted one and told me to
mount the other   he rode forward his son in the rear   we
rode basck over the river & about two miles on the trail
where I dismounted and went on a foot again   they sitting
on thier horses watched me untill I had passed over half
mile when they returned,   my hair had not been cut since I
left St Louis   I lost my hat at the defeat of the Arickrees and
had been bareheaded ever since   my hair was quite
long   my friend had beged for my hair the morning before

we left his lodge   I had granted his request so he barbered
me with a dull butcher knife   before leaving me he made
me understand he loved me that he had saved my lief and
wanted the hair for a memento of me   as soon as my
friends were fairly out of sight I left the trail fearing some
unfriendly Indian   the grass was thick and tall which
made it hard to brake through so I frequently took ridges
which led me from my course   the second day in the afternoon I came to a pool of water under an oak
tree   drank   sat down under the shade a short time   ate a
few grains of parched corn (which my friends had given
me) when I heard a growling of some animals near by   I
advanced a few steps and saw two Badgers fighting   I
aimed at one but my gun missd fire   they started off   I
geathered some bones (horse brobly)   ran after & killed
both   I struck fire with my gunlock   skined & roasted
them   made a bundle of grass & willow bark.   it rained all
the later part of the night but I started early in the morning
the wet grass beeing more pleasant to travel than the
dry   it continu[ed] showery for several days   the mos-
quitos be uncommonly bad   I could not sleep and it got so
damp I could not obtain fire and I had to swim several
rivers   at last I struck a trail that seamed to lead in the right
direction which I determined to follow to its extreeam
end   on the second day in the afternoon I got so sleepy &
nervous that it was with difficulity I kept the trail   a
number of times I tumbled down asleep but a quick nervous gerk would bring me to my feet again   in one of these
fits I started up on the trail traveled some 40 rods when I
hapened to notise I was going back the way I had
come   turning right around I went on for some time with
my head down when raisin my eyes with great surprise I
saw the stars & stripe waving over Fort Leavenworth
[Atkinson]   I swoned emmediatly   how long I lay uncon-
cious I do not know I was so overpowered with joy   The
stars & stripes came so unexpected that I was completly
overcome being on decending ground I sat contemplating
the scene   I made several attemps to raise but as often fell
back for the want of strength to stand   after some minnites

I began to breathe easier but certainly no man ever enjoyed the sight of our flag better than I did   I walked on down to the fort   there beeing no guard on duty I by axident came to the door of Captain Rileys quarters where a waiter brought out the Captain who conducted me to General Leavenworth who assigned me a company & gave me a writen introduction to the setttelers where I got credit for a change of clothing some shoes & a soldiers cap   I remained here receiving rashions as a soldier for ten days when to my surprise Mr Fitspatrick Mr Stone & Mr Brench arived in a more pitible state if possible than myself.   Fitspatrick went back to the cashe after leaving me   they opened the cashe found the powder somwhat damp spread it out to dry got all ready to pack up when Smith and party arived   the day being quite warm the snow melted on the mountains and raised the water & they came to the conclusion to build a boat there & Fitspatrick Stone & Branch to get the furs down the best way the could   Captain Smith to take charge of all the hunting & traping and to remain in the country the season   so acordingly they made a skin boat & Captain coming down on horsback to bring me back again, (but I was off surveying the canyon)   he saw where the Indians had been where I had cut my lodge in the willows and not finding me came to the conclusion the Indians had killed me so made that report

the three men hauld the boat down stream untill it was nearly worn out and the water still falling so they cashed the furs on Indipendence rock and ran down into the Canyon   thier boat filled & they lost two of thier guns & all of thier balls   they broke the Brass mounting of the gun with rocks bent it into balls with which they killed a few buffalo,   the Skin boat I saw on the sand bar was made by four men . . . who crossed over from the mouth of the Bighorn thier winter camp and landing on the shore walked up into the valliage which proved to be Arickaree   two of them escaped but the other two were killed   this [tribe] afterward proved to be the same people I saw runing buffalo   by axident I escaped from them   the camp I waided the river to meet were Pownees and here too I bearly saved my scalp but lost my hair

14

HUGH GLASS:

The Will to Endure

We do not know when Hugh Glass was born or when he died, but the saga of this man, who literally crawled back to life and civilization after being mauled by a grizzly bear and left for dead by his companions, ranks with John Colter's run as one of the legendary survival stories of the Far West. First related by Glass himself and repeated around countless campfires, the tale has been celebrated in newspaper accounts, in histories, in novels, in John G. Niedhardt's epic poem, The Song of Hugh Glass *and, more recently, in the movies* (Man of the Wilderness).*

As a fellow mountainman said of Glass: "In point of adventures, dangers, and narrow escapes, and capacity for endurance, and the sufferings which befell him, this man was preeminent." The man who spoke those words of praise, a trapper and hunter named George C. Yount, had talked with Glass in the winter of 1828–1829, at the Bear River rendezvous, near the Great Salt Lake. According to Yount, Glass had started life as a sailor, but was soon overtaken by a sequence of disasters and near-escapes of the kind that seemed to plague him all his life. Captured by pirates under the notorious Jean Lafitte, Glass was forced to join the pirate band. He managed to slip away one night on the coast of Texas, only to fall into the hands of the Pawnees. The Indians were about to burn him at the stake when Glass's cool bravery in the face of death persuaded them to spare him. Some months later, while his captors were visiting St. Louis, Glass made his escape. There, in the spring of 1823, he joined General William Ashley's second fur-trading expedition up the Missouri River. He was among those wounded in the battle with the Arikaras, but his wounds apparently were not too serious for by the end of the summer he was on his way to the mouth of the Yellowstone with the party of Ashley's partner, Major Andrew Henry. It was on this journey that Glass had his nearly fatal encounter with a grizzly bear. The episode and its heroic sequel, together with Glass's subsequent adventures, are related here in what is probably the best of the early accounts: George Yount's reminiscences as dictated to a friend.

As Major Henry pressed onwards towards the Yellow Stone, constrained to use great caution, he had struck a tributary of the Missouri & was following its channel, where the Buffalo & the Buffalo-berries were found abundant & proved convenient for food—But the band must keep together, as they were liable, at any moment, to be assailed, by the Pickarees [Arikaras] in ambush—He accordingly selected two distinguished hunters, one of which was Allen, of Mohave notoriety, & a bosom friend of Yount's, to precede the party, from a half a mile to a mile, in order to kill meat for food—

Glass, as was usual, could not be kept, in obedience to orders, with the band, but persevered to thread his way alone through the bushes and chapparel—As the two hunters were wending their way, up the River, Allen discovered Glass dodging along in the forest alone & said to his companion, "there look at that fellow, Glass; see him foolishly exposing his life—I wish some Grizzly Bear would

pounce upon him & teach him a lesson of obedience to
orders, & to keep in his place—He is ever off, scouting in
the bushes & exposing his life & himself to dangers"—

Glass disappeared in the chapperel, & within half an
hour his screams were heard—The two hunters hastened to
his relief & discovered a huge Grizy Bear, with two
Cubs—The monster had seized him, torn the flesh from the
lower part of the body, & from the lower limbs—He also
had his neck shockingly torn, even to the degree that an
aperture appeared to have been made into the windpipe, &
his breath to exude at the side of his neck—It is not probable however that any aperture was made into the
windpipe—Blood flowed freely, but fortunately no bone
was broken—& his hands & arms were not disabled—

The whole party were soon there, the monster & her
cubs were slain, & the victim cared for in the best degree
possible, under existing circumstances—A convenient
hand litter was prepared & the sufferer carried by his
humane fellow-trappers from day to day—He retained all
his faculties but those of speech & locomotion—Too feeble
to walk, or help himself at all, his comrads every moment
waited his death—Day by day they ministered to his
wants, & no one counted it any hardship—

Among those rude & rough trappers of the wilderness,
fellow feeling & devotion to eachothers wants is a remarkable & universal feature or characteristic—It is admirable &
worthy the imitation of even the highest grade of civilized
men—We have remarked it at every step in the investiga-
tion, which, in preparing this work, has devolved on
us—

After having thus carried Glass six days, it became
necessary for the party to croud their journey, as the season
for trapping was fast transpiring—Major Henry therefore
offered four hundred Dolls to any two of his men, who
would volunteer to remain until he should die, decently
bury him & then press on their way to overtake the main
body—One man & a boy volunteered to remain [according
to tradition the man was named Fitzgerald and the boy was
Jim Bridger, then nineteen years old]—They did so, & the

party urged forward towards the Yellow Stone—

The two waited several days, & he still lived—No change was apparent,—They dressed his wounds daily & fed & nourished him with water from the spring & such light food as he could swallow—Still he was speechless but could use his hands—Both his lower limbs were quite disabled—As he lay by the spring, Buffalo berries hung in clusters & in great profusion over him & around his bed, which was made soft with dry leaves & two blankets—

Quite discouraged & impatient for his death, as there remained no hope of his recovery, the two resolved to leave him there to die alone in the wilderness—They took from him his knife, camp kettle & Rifle, laid him smoothely on his blankets, & left him thus to die a lingering death, or be torn in pieces by the ferocious wild beasts & to be seen no more till they should meet him at the dread tribunal of eternal judgment—

He could hear their every word, but could not speak nor move his body—His arms he could use—& he stretched them out imploringly, but in vain—They departed & silence reigned around him—Oppressed with grief & his hard fate, he soon became delirious—Visions of benevolent beings appeared. Around him were numerous friendly faces, smiling encouragement & exhorting him not to despond, & assuring him that all would be well at last—He declared to Yount that he was never alone, by day or by night—

He could reach the water & take it to his mouth in the hollow of his hand, & could pluck the berries from the bushes to eat as he might need—One morning, after several weeks, he found by his side a huge Rattlesnake—With a small stone he slew the reptile, jambed off its head & cast it from him—Having laid the dead serpant by his side he jambed off small parts from time to time, & bruised it thoroughly & moistened it with water from the spring & made of it a grateful food on which he fed from day to day—

At length the wolves came & took from under him his Blankets, & having dragged them some distance, tore them in pieces—,Thus he was left solely on his bed of leaves—In this condition he must have lain many weeks how many he could never tell—Meantime the two, the man & boy, false to their trust, came up with Major Henry & the party, & reported that Glass had died & they had decently buried his remains, & brot his effects with them, his gun, knife & Camp kettle, & received the promised reward for their fidelity, Four Hundred Dollars—

After a long period, his strength began to revive, & he crawled a few rods, & laid himself down again during several days—Then again he resumed his journey, every day increasing his distance some rods—after many long & tedious days, & even weeks—he found himself upon his feet & began to walk—Soon he could travel nearly a mile in a day This distance he even increased daily more & more—Thus covered with wounds, which would frequently bleed, & require much attention, he urged his journey, through a howling wilderness, a distance of more than Two Hundred miles, to the nearest trading post—

Often by the way he would find the decaying carcases of Buffalos, which, wounded by the hunter, or some more powerful animal, had died—From these he gained nourishing food, by pounding out the marrow from the bones, & eating it seasoned with Buffalo-berries & moistened with limped water from the brooks & springs—With sharp stones he would dig from the earth nourishing roots, which he had learned to discriminate while sojourning with the Paunees—

At this trading post he passed the winter, as Autumn had worn away, & the cold season had overtaken him there—During the bracing season of winter, his strength was rapidly restored—As the following spring opened, he found himself again a well man, able to resume his journey to rejoin Major Henry & his band of trappers—Fortunately as he was about to depart, an express party arrived, on its way to carry orders to Major Henry, at his post on the Yellow Stone, & Glass joined this party to accompany them to Henry's Fort—

This journey was to Glass no more than a season of pastime & pleasure—Days, weeks & even months of journying were as nothing, after the scenes of the previous Summer & Autumn—He knew no fatigure but after a day's travel, could leap and frolic, like the young fawn—On reaching Major Henry's encampment, the reader can better imagine than the writer describe the scene as he rode up to his old party of fellow trappers—One without, on seeing Glass ride up ran in to report to Major H. & the rest that Glass had arrived—

Impossible! Glass had been dead and buried more than a year & one of those who buried his remains was present—But Glass entered, told his story & recapitulated his wrongs & sufferings & asked for his Camp kettle & his Rifle—The Major replied by bringing the *recreant boy* before him—His Camp Kettle was there, but the false and dastardly man had gone with Glass's Rifle to Council Bluff—To the boy Glass addressed himself after the following manner—"Go, my boy—I leave you to the punishment of your own conscience & your God—If they forgive you, then be happy—I have nothing to say to you—but, dont forget hereafter that truth & fidelity are too valuable to be trifled with"—

He had still to mourn the loss of his Rifle, which he valued above all price—During this year Glass remained to trap with the party with which he had left St. Louis under Major H.—At the opening of the following Spring, he accompanied this party to trap again on Plat River;—where they were remarkably successful & accumulated an immense amount of furs—

It then became necessary to send an Express, with a freight of furs, down the Platt River, & thence to Ashly at St. Louis—Glass & four others volunteered for this hazardous enterprize—One of the four was Dutton; the individual who gave to Yount the balance of Glass' adventurous life, & the particulars of his tragical death—Up to the *present date* Glass told to Yount all which we have here written & Allen confirmed the truth of it all

As this Express Expedition was descending Platt River, in Boats made of Buffalo skins & fully freighted, they made the shore upon the prarie, where they found a very numerous body of Indians, which they mistook to be Pawness, but who proved to be Pickarees—These two nations speak nearly the same language, & were often mistaken one for the other—The savages manifested great cordiality & friendship—At that time the Pawness were in friendly alliance with the whites, but the Pickarees were dealy hostile—

This error proved fatal in the following manner—As the expedition approached the shore, a multitude of the savages met them with great cordiality, invited them into their wigwams & spread a feast before them—All except Dutton left their Rifles in their boats; he carried his with him—While eating some words were dropped which led Glass to suspect the error, & he said to one near him—"these are Pickarees"—The Chief understanding him, replied, "No, Pawnees we"—Glass ran & the rest followed him—But, on reaching their Boats, the guns were all missing—& the savages were close in pursuit—

The party rowed hastily across the River, & fled—The savages swam after them & a running fight ensued—They did not pursue Dutton for fear of his Rifle—but he looking behind, saw all his fellows, except Glass, killed; & three savages in close pursuit of him as he entered a ledge of rocks—He afterwards saw the savages walking leisurely & sitting upon the rocks, & naturly concluded that they must have slain Glass—

Dutton then bent his course towards a place in the wilderness, where he with the other trappers & with Glass had cached a large supply of provisions & other property—After many days wandering, he reached the near neighborhood of the cache & secreted himself to wait for the darkness of night, before approaching it—

After dark, to his astonishment, he beheld numerous fires lighted in its immediate vicinity, & naturally concluded that a party of savages lay encamped there—He accordingly waited during another day, in a secluded cave of the mountain—But yet the following night the fires appeared again—Thus night after night, those fires appeared, till he was in danger of perishing with hunger—

Atlength at midday, as Dutton lay secreted in his cave, almost famished with thirst, a man passed the mouth of his cave—He crept to the light, & to his astonishment, there was Glass—whom he had supposed to have been slain by the savages, in the ledge of rocks—

Glass had lighted those fires, night after night, in order to deceive the savages, & cause them to suppose that a large company of white men were there encamped—The two then remained & lived sumptuously on the provisions there cached, until well recruited, & then took up their march for Cuncil Bluffs—

At this fort Glass found the recreant individual, who had so cruelly deserted him, when he lay helpless & torn so shockingly by the Grizzly Bear—He also there recovered his favorite Rifle—To the man he only addressed himself as he did to the boy—"Go, false man, & answer to your own conscience & to your God;—I have suffered enough in all reason by your perfidy—You was well paid to have remained with me until I should be able to walk—You promised to do so—or to wait my death & decently bury my remains—I heard the bargain—Your shameful perfidy & heartless cruelty - - - - but enough—Again I say, settle the matter with your own conscience & your God" "Give me my favorite Rifle"—

It is remarkable to observe how highly these men of the wilderness value their firearms—No amount of money can purchase one of them—Next to his own heart's blood, the trapper's Rifle is the dearest object to him on earth—Yount has slept with it by his side more than forty years & solemnly avers that if it be not near him, sleep loses its refreshment & the world is desolate—nothing can supply the lack of it, & all the luxuries of the world are vanity without it—

After leaving Council Bluffs Glass encountered another adventure similar to the last described & was the sole surviver of the whole party of trappers, with the exception of one, & this one reached the identical trading post, to which Glass had crawled two hundred miles, after having been torn by the monster Bear, & two days after to the astonish-

ment of all in came Glass, having wandered more than
three hundred miles, with no other weapon than a sheath
knife, & subsisted on berries & the carcases of deceased
Buffalos—

At the Fort a purse of Three Hundred Dolls was bestowed upon him & with this money he travelled to the
extremely western settlements on the Missouri & became a
partner in an enterprize for tading in New Mexico—But the
same passion for travelling alone never forsook him, & he
would never encamp with his fellows, but always miles
distant roaming solitary & sleeping in silent loneliness—
Often he would not be seen by his fellow travellers during many weeks, & yet he always knew where to find them,
& could at any time fly to their aid when danger
threatened—

After a year's labor with but indifferent success, he
found himself at Toas on the borders of New Mexico, where
Provost, a merchant of some distinction, employed him to
conduct a band of trappers into the territory of the
Eutaus—At that time the Snakes & Eutaus were engaged in
a very sanguinary war; & all white people who were found
among either of those savages, were regarded by the other
as their enemies & slain or made prisoners without
mercy—

The whole of this band, while trapping in the Eutau
country, were fallen upon by the Snakes & his escape then
was hardly less remarkable than those before related—They
were descending a river in canoes, & leisurely trapping for
Beaver with great success—In their canoes they had very
many carcases of the animal, form which they had taken the
pelts, & the choice bits for food—At noon day, they discovered a solitary squaw upon the shore, busily employed in
digging roots—

She did not discover them, & one proposed to land &
give her some caracasses of beaver—The boat glided toward the shore so still as hardly to occasion a ripple upon
the water—So soon as they made the land, three of them
hastily ran up the bank, each with a carcas in his hand,
towards the squaw—On a sudden as she saw them she sat

up an unearthly screm—One huge savage was lying a
sleep, a few yards beyond her, who, on awaking, hastily let
fly an arrow, which pierced one of the trappers quite
through the lungs

Others came flocking over the hills & arrows filled the
air—The one first shot was mortally wounded, & could not
survive more than a few moments—The rest betook themselves to their boats, & pulled out into the stream beyond
the reach of the arrows—As the savage ran up hastily to take
the scalp of the wounded man, he levelled as he lay & shot
the villian dead at his feet—

The wounded one now called to his fellows in the Boats,
& begged them to return & reload his Rifle & leave him
there to die, his refle by his side—Glass complied, & pulled
toward the shore, charged the dying man's gun & had only
time to lay it thus by his side, when showers of arrows flew
thick around him—

The poor dying brother begged him not to move his
body for it was torture; & Glass turned to flee to his boat, &
at the moment was struck in the back by an arrow, which
broke & left the point bedded deep near the spine—He
reached his boat & the expiring fellow cried aloud, "leave
me & consult your own safety—I can live but few moments,
but if breath & strength remain I will yet kill one of
them"—The party pulled lustily out into the River, where
they sat & saw the tawny host come down upon the dying
brother—The sharp crack of his Rifle was heard, & one
savage fell near the ill fated trapper, & in an instant he was
torn in pieces & his sufferings ended—

The party sailed fast down the river & escaped—But
Glass, after all was the greatest sufferer—This the reader
will readily believe when told the fact which not only Yount
but other credible witnesses can attest, that he travelled
through the Wilderness *Seven Hundred Miles* with that
arrow in his inflamed back and then submitted to be laid
upon his face & endure the cutting of the missel from his
flesh swolen & inflamed to an astonishing degree—Yount
well knew the hardy trapper who performed this awful
operation with a razor

Of the above narration the writer entertains no doubt whatever—It is no fiction, neither is it exaggerated—All must admit that there was in this brawny trapper a fortitude & a capacity for endurance such as rarely falls to the lot of mortal man—And such a series of adventures, dangers & sufferings has rarely fallen to the lot of humanity—

But we now approach the termination of his very remarkable career—After remaining at Tous many months, while his wound was healing, & his bodily health & strength recuperating, Glass again embarked with a party of trappers, far up the Yellow Stone, near its source; to remain there during a year & gather furs to be sold to the American Fur company, & also to hunt during the winter months—

It was a cold & dreary winter in those bleak regions—The party erected for themselves huts of logs, from which they sallied out to return at evening, or frequently & be screened from the frequent storms—One pleasant day [believed to be in the early spring of 1833] Glass, with two others, proposed to cross upon the ice to an Island & there erect for themselves a temporary abode, where to remain a few days, & return at intervals to the main encampment—

All being made ready, two having taken upon their backs their load of provisions & implements to start, the third having casually omitted some trifling preparation, proposed to them not to wait, but proceed & he would follow their footprints in the snow; & soon overtake them—The two accordingly took up their journey not at all apprehending danger—The distance to the Island was but a few miles, & no savages had for a long time molested, or even visited them—

The third was soon ready, & followed not more than a mile behind—It was easy to trace them as they travelled on snowshoes—Just before he reached the Island, to his astonishment, there lay one of his comrades weltering in his blood, an arrow having passed quite through his body—No savage was near, nor any sound or appearance of man or beast—

Resolved to know the worst, he laid down his burden &

ran hastily forward—Soon however he realized the whole—Within a hundred yards, there lay the body of poor Glass, pierced through & through with arrows, his life extinct, & his blood melting the untrodden snow still warm & quivering—No savage had approached them, nor was any footprint near—But the deed was done—

The whole party were hastily in pursuit but the savages [probably Blackfeet] were gone beyond the reach of their pursuers, & none could avenge the death of those two favorites of the camp—That was a day of mourning—The remains of poor Glass there interred in the lonely wilderness—He had his failings—But his fellow trappers bear testimony to his honor, integrity & fidelity—He could be relied on—& no man would fly more swiftly, nor contribute more freely to the relief of a suffering fellow man than he—

15

JAMES OHIO PATTIE:
Opening the Southwest Trail

*James Ohio Pattie (1804–c. 1850), who ranks with Jedediah
Smith (see Selection 17), as one of the most notable figures in the
history of the Southwest frontier, was born the son and grand-
son of frontiersmen. His grandfather was one of the founders of
Kentucky, a woodsman who fought under George Rogers Clark
during the Revolution. His father, Sylvester Pattie, had moved
to the Missouri frontier before the War of 1812, and when the
country began filling up he headed West again, up the Missouri
River, beyond the line of settlement. James Ohio inherited his
family's hatred of towns and their love of wandering and adventure. When his mother died and his father decided to try a career
in the mountain fur trade, young Pattie, scarcely out of his
teens, begged to be taken along. Sylvester agreed and, in the
summer of 1824, father and son joined a trading caravan bound
for Santa Fe. It was one of the first trading expeditions to the
Southwest, for the hostility of the Spanish authorities in New
Mexico had long discouraged American traders from venturing
in that direction. Now, more favorable reports were being re-*

ceived, and the untapped source of beaver pelts was beginning to attract American merchants and trappers.

The Patties rambled through the Southwest for six years, hunting, trapping, mining copper, exploring the harsh lands of New Mexico and Arizona, and opening new trails for later travelers. They won and lost fortunes, and endured an incredible series of mishaps and disasters. On one occasion James Ohio escaped a nightime Indian attack unscathed, though his blanket was shot full of arrows. Setting off for the Pacific coast in the fall of 1827, not many months after Jedediah Smith had made his way back from California, father and son nearly perished of thirst while trying to cross the lower California desert. They were rescued by friendly Indians, only to be thrown in jail by the Mexicans as a warning to other trespassers. There, sick and exhausted, the elder Pattie died. James Ohio was eventually freed during a smallpox epidemic when he offered to vaccinate the Mexicans and Indians. Traveling up and down California and into Mexico, he at last managed to make his way back to the United States, where he published his Unheard of Hardships and Dangers *in 1831. Thereafter he passed into obscurity, but he is believed to have joined the California gold rush in 1849 and to have died in a snowstorm in the Sierras.*

Pattie's account of his adventures, though often confused as to dates and events, and doubtless embellished for the sake of a good yarn, remains nonetheless a classic of frontier literature. It presents a graphic picture of the life of the mountainman, the country through which he traveled, and the culture of the Southwest tribes. The following excerpt begins in Santa Fe in mid-November, 1824, shortly after the Patties arrival in New Mexico and shortly after James Ohio had won the gratitude of the Mexican governor by rescuing his daughter, Jacova, from a band of Comanches.

At eight the following morning we received a license, allowing us to trap in different parts of the country. We were now divided into small parties. Mr. [Bernard] Pratte [a

From *The Personal Narrative of James O. Pattie* . . . , edited by Timothy Flint (Cincinnati, 1831). Reprinted in Reuben Gold Thwaites, ed., *Early Western Travels*, vol. 18 (Cleveland: Arthur H. Clark Company, 1905), pp. 84–111.

St. Louis trader] added three to our original number, they making the company, to which my father and myself belonged, seven. On the 22d, we set off. Our course lay down the del Norte [Rio Grande] to the Helay [Gila], a river never before explored by white people. We left our goods with a merchant, until we should return in the spring. Our whole day's journey lay over a handsome plain covered with herds of the different domestic animals. We reached Picacheh a small town in the evening. . . .

On the 27th, we arrived at the residence of Jacova and her father. It was a large and even magnificent building. We remained here until the 30th, receiving the utmost attention and kindness. At our departure, the kind old governor pressed a great many presents on us; but we refused all, except a horse for each one of us, some flour and dried meat.

Seven hunters coming up with us, who were going in our direction, we concluded to travel with them, as our united strength would better enable us to contend with the hostile Indians, through whose country our course lay. We made our way slowly, descending the river bank, until we reached the last town or settlement in this part of the province, called Socoro. The population of the part of the country, through which we travelled was entirely confined to a chain of settlements along the bottoms of the del Norte, and those of some of the rivers, which empty into it. I did not see, during the whole of this journey, an enclosed field, and not even a garden.

After remaining one day here, in order to recruit our horses, we resumed our course down the river, Dec. 3d. The bottoms, through which we now passed, were thinly timbered, and the only growth was cotton-wood and willow. We saw great numbers of bears, deer and turkeys. A bear having chased one of our men into the camp, we killed it.

On the 7th we left the del Norte, and took a direct course for the Copper mines [at Santa Rita, about a hundred miles west, hear the head waters of the Gila River]. We next travelled from the river over a mountainous country four days, at the expiration of which time we reached this point of our destination. We were here for one night, and I had not leisure to examine the mode, in which the copper was manufactured. In the morning we hired two Spanish servants to accompany us; and taking a north-west course pursued our journey, until we reached the Helay on the 14th. We found the country the greater part of the two last days hilly and somwhat barren with a growth of pine, live oak, *pinion*, cedar and some small trees, of which I did not know the name. We caught thirty beavers, the first night we encamped on this river. The next morning, accompanied by another man, I began to ascend the bank of the stream to explore, and ascertain if beaver were to be found still higher, leaving the remainder of the party to trap slowly up, until they should meet us on our return. We threw a pack over our shoulders, containing a part of the beavers, we had killed, as we made our way on foot. The first day we were fatigued by the difficulty of getting through the high grass, which covered the heavily timbered bottom. In the evening we arrived at the foot of the mountains, that shut in the river on both sides, and encamped. We saw during the day several bears, but did not disturb them, as they showed no ill feeling towards us.

On the morning of the 13th we started early, and crossed the river, here a beautiful clear stream about thirty yards in width, running over a rocky bottom, and filled with fish. We made but little advance this day, as bluffs came in so close to the river, as to compel us to cross it thirty-six times. We were obliged to scramble along under the cliffs, sometimes upon our hands and knees, through a thick tangle of grape-vines and under-brush. Added to the unpleasantness of this mode of getting along in itself, we did not know, but the next moment would bring us face to face with a bear, which might accost us suddenly. We were rejoiced, when this rough ground gave place again to the level bottom. At night we reached a point, where the river forked, and encamped on the point between the forks. We found here a boiling spring so near the main stream, that the fish caught in the one might be thrown in the other without leaving the spot, where it was taken. In six minutes it would be thoroughly cooked.

The following morning my companion and myself separated, agreeing to meet after four days at this spring. We were each to ascend a fork of the river. The banks of that which fell to my lot, were very brushy, and frequented by numbers of bears, of whom I felt fearful, as I had never before travelled alone in the woods. I walked on with caution until night, and encamped near a pile of drift wood, which I set on fire, thinking thus to frighten any animals that might approach during the night. I placed a spit, with a turkey I had killed upon it, before the fire to roast. After I had eaten my supper I laid down by the side of a log with my gun by my side. I did not fall asleep for some time. I was aroused from slumber by a noise in the leaves, and raising my head saw a panther stretched on the log by which I was lying, within six feet of me. I raised my gun gently to my face, and shot it in the head. Then springing to my feet, I ran about ten steps, and stopped to reload my gun, not knowing if I had killed the panther or not. Before I finished loading my gun, I heard the discharge of one on the other fork, as I concluded, the two running parallel with each other, separated only by a narrow ridge. A second discharge quickly followed the first, which led me to suppose, that my comrade was attacked by Indians.

I immediately set out and reached the hot spring by day break, where I found my associate also. The report of my gun had awakened him, when he saw a bear standing upon its hind feet within a few yards of him growling. He fired his gun, then his pistol, and retreated, thinking, with regard to me, as I had with regard to him, that I was attacked by Indians. Our conclusion now was, to ascend one of the forks in company, and then cross over, and descend the other. In consequence we resumed the course, I had taken the preceding day. We made two day's journey, without beaver enough to recompense us for our trouble, and then crossed to the east fork, trapping as we went, until we again reached the main stream. Some distance below this, we met those of our party we had left behind, with the exception of the seven, who joined us on the del Norte. They had deserted the expedition, and set off upon their return down the river. We now all hastened to overtake them, but it was to no purpose. They still kept in advance, trapping clean as they went, so that we even found it difficult to catch enough to eat.

Finding it impossible to come up with them, we ceased to urge our poor horses, as they were much jaded, and tender footed beside, and travelled slowly, catching what beaver we could, and killing some deer, although the latter were scarce, owing, probably to the season of the year. The river here was beautiful, running between banks covered with tall cotton-woods and willows. This bottom extended back a mile on each side. Beyond rose high and rather barren hills.

On the 20th we came to a point, where the river entered a cavern between two mountains. We were compelled to return upon our steps, until we found a low gap in the mountains. We were three day's crossing, and the travelling was both fatiguing and difficult. We found nothing to kill.

On the 23rd we came upon the river, where it emptied into a beautiful plain. We set our traps, but to no purpose, for the beavers were all caught, or alarmed. The river here pursues a west course. We travelled slowly, using every effort to kill something to eat, but without success.

On the morning of the 26th we concluded, that we must kill a horse, as we had eaten nothing for four day's and a half, except the small portion or a hare caught by my dogs, which fell to the lot of each of a party of seven. Before we obtained this, we had become weak in body and mind, complaining, and desponding of our success in search of beaver. Desirous of returning to some settlement, my father encouraged our party to eat some of the horses, and pursue our journey. We were all reluctant to begin to partake of the horse-flesh; and the actual thing without bread of salt was as bad as the anticipation of it. We were somewhat strengthened, however, and hastened on, while our supply lasted, in the hope of either overtaking those in advance of us, or finding another stream yet undiscovered by trappers.

The latter desire was gratified the first of January, 1825. The stream, we discovered, carried as much water as the

Helay, heading north. We called it the river St. Francisco.*
After travelling up its banks about four miles, we encamped, and set all our traps, and killed a couple of fat
turkies. In the morning we examined our traps, and found
in them 37 beavers! This success restored our spirits instan-
taneously. Exhilarating prospects now opened before us,
and we pushed on with animation. The banks of this river
are for the most part incapable of cultivation being in many
places formed of high and rugged mountains. Upon these
we saw multitudes of mountain sheep. These animals are
not found on level ground, being there slow of foot, but on
these cliffs and rocks they are so nimble and expert in
jumping from point to point, that no dog of wolf can overtake them. One of them that we killed had the largest horns,
that I ever saw on animals of any description. One of them
would hold a gallon of water. Their meat tastes like our
mutton. Their hair is short like a deer's, though fine. The
French call them the *gros cornes,* from the size of their horns
which curl around their ears, like our domestic sheep.
These animals are about the size of a large deer. We traced
this river to its head, but not without great difficulty, as the
cliffs in many places came so near the water's edge, that we
were compelled to cross points of the mountain, which
fatigued both ourselves and our horses exceedingly.

The right hand fork of this river, and the left of the Helay
head in the same mountains, which is covered with snow,
and divides its waters from those of Red river. We finished
our trapping on this river, on the 14th. We had caught the
very considerable number of 250 beavers, and had used
and preserved most of the meat, we had killed. On the 19th
we arrived on the river Helay, encamped, and buried our
furs in a secure position, as we intended to return home by
this route.

On the 20th we began to descend the Helay, hoping to
find in our descent another beaver stream emptying into it.
We had abandoned the hope of rejoining the hunters, that
had left us, and been the occasion of our being compelled to

*The present name of this stream, one of the initial forks of the Gila. The confluence
is in Arizona, a few miles over the New Mexican border.—THWAITES.

feed upon horse flesh. No better was to be expected of us, than that we should take leave to imprecate many a curse upon their heads; and that they might experience no better fate, than to fall into the hands of the savages, or be torn in pieces by the white [grizzly] bears.* At the same time, so ready are the hearts of mountain hunters to relent, that I have not a doubt that each man of us would have risqued his life to save any one of them from the very fate, we imprecated upon them.

In fact, on the night of the 22d, four of them, actually half starved, arrived at our camp, declaring, that they had eaten nothing for five days. Nothwithstanding our recent curses bestowed upon them, we received them as brothers. They related that the Indians had assaulted and defeated them, robbing them of all their horses, and killing one of their number. Next day the remaining two came in, one of them severely wounded in the head by an Indian arrow. They remained with us two days, during which we attempted to induce them to lead us against the Indians, who had robbed them, that we might assist them to recover what had been robbed from them. No persuasion would induce them to this course. They insisted at the same time, that if we attempted to go on by ourselves, we should share the same fate, which had befallen them.

On the morning of the 25th, we gave them three horses, and as much dried meat as would last them to the mines, distant about 150 miles. Fully impressed, that the Indians would massacre us, they took such a farewell of us, as if never expecting to see us again.

In the evening of the same day, although the weather threatened a storm, we packed up, and began to descend the river. We encamped this night in a huge cavern in the midst of the rocks. About night it began to blow a tempest, and to snow fast. Our horses became impatient under the pelting of the storm, broke their ropes, and disappeared. In the morning, the earth was covered with snow, four or five

---

*The yellow-brown fur of the grizzly bear frequently turns silver-gray at the tips. often to such an extent that the animal looks white.—ED.

inches deep. One of our companions accompanied me to search for our horses. We soon came upon their trail, and followed it, until it crossed the river. We found it on the opposite side, and pursued it up a creek, that empties into the Helay on the north shore. We passed a cave at the foot of the cliffs. As its mouth I remarked, that the bushes were beaten down, as though some animal had been browsing upon them. I was aware, that a bear had entered the cave. We collected some pine knots, split them with our tomahawks, and kindled torches, with which I proposed to my companion, that we should enter the cave together, and shoot the bear. He gave me a decided refusal, notwithstanding I reminded him, that I had, more than once, stood by him in a similar adventure; and notwithstanding I made him sensible, that a bear in a den is by no means so formidable, as when ranging freely in the woods. Finding it impossible to prevail on him to accompany me, I lashed my torch to a stick, and placed it parallel with the gun barrel, so as that I could see the sights on it, and entered the cave. I advanced cautiously onward about twenty yards, seeing nothing. On a sudden the bear reared himself erect within seven feet of me, and began to growl, and gnash his teeth. I levelled my gun and shot him between the eyes, and began to retreat. Whatever light it may throw upon my courage, I admit, that I was in such a hurry, as to stumble, and extinguish my light. The growling and struggling of the bear did not at all contribute to allay my apprehensions. On the contrary, I was in such haste to get out of the dark place, thinking the bear just at my heels, that I fell several times on the rocks, by which I cut my limbs, and lost my gun. When I reached the light, my companion declared, and I can believe it, that I was as pale as a corpse. It was some time, before I could summon sufficient courage to re-enter the cavern for my gun. But having re-kindled my light, and borrowed my companion's gun, I entered the cavern again, advanced and listened. All was silent, and I advanced still further, and found my gun, near where I had shot the bear. Here again I paused and listened. I then advanced onward a few strides, where to my great joy I found the animal dead. I returned, and brought my companion in with me. We attempted to drag the carcass from the den, but so great was the size, that we found ourselves wholly unable. We went out, found our horses, and returned to camp for assistance. My father severely reprimanded me for venturing to attack such a dangerous animal in its den, when the failure to kill it outright by the first shot, would have been sure to be followed by my death.

Four of us were detached to the den. We were soon enabled to drag the bear to the light, and by the aid of our beast to take it to camp. It was both the largest and whitest bear I ever saw. The best proof, I can give, of the size and fatness is, that we extracted ten gallons of oil from it. The meat we dried, and put the oil in a trough, which we secured in a deep crevice of a cliff, beyond the reach of animals of prey. We were sensible that it would prove a treasure to us on our return.

On the 28th we resumed our journey, and pushed down the stream to reach a point on the river, where trapping had not been practised. On the 30th, we reached this point, and found the man, that the Indians had killed. They had cut him in quarters, after the fashion of butchers. His head, with the hat on, was stuck on a stake. It was full of the arrows, which they had probably discharged into it, as they had danced around it. We gathered up the parts of the body, and buried them.

At this point we commenced setting our traps. We found the river skirted with very wide bottoms, thick-set with the musquito [mesquite] trees, which bear a pod in the shape of a bean, which is exceedingly sweet. It constitutes one of the chief articles of Indian subsistence; and they contrive to prepare from it a very palatable kind of bread, of which we all became very fond. The wild animals also feed upon this pod.

On the 31st we moved our camp ten miles. On the way we noted many fresh traces of Indians, and killed a bear, that attacked us. The river pursues a west course amidst high mountains on each side. We trapped slowly onward, still descending the river, and unmolested by the Indians.

On the 8th of February, we reached the mouth of a small river entering the Helay on the north shore. Here we unexpectedly came upon a small party of Indians, that fled at the sight of us, in such consternation and hurry, as to leave all their effects, which consisted of a quantity of the bread mentioned above, and some robes made of rabbit skins. Still more; they left a small child. The child was old enough to distinguish us from its own people, for it opened its little throat, and screamed so lustily, that we feared it would have fits. The poor thing meanwhile made its best efforts to fly from us. We neither plundered nor molested their little store. We bound the child in such a manner, that it could not stray away, and get lost, aware, that after they deemed us sufficiently far off, the parents would return, and take the child away. We thence ascended the small river about four miles, and encamped. For fear of surpize, and apprehending the return of the savages, that had fled from us, and perhaps in greater force, we secured our camp with a small breast-work. We discovered very little encouragement in regard to our trapping pursuit, for we noted few signs of beavers on this stream. The night passed without bringing us an disturbance. In the morning two of us returned to the Indian camp. The Indians had re-visited it, and removed every thing of value, and what gave us great satisfaction, their child. In proof, that the feelings of human nature are the same every where, and that the language of kindness is a universal one; in token of their gratitude, as we understood it, they had suspended a package on a kind of stick, which they had stuck erect. Availing ourselves of their offer, we examined the present, and found it to contain a large dressed buck skin, an article, which we greatly needed for moccasins, of which some of us were in pressing want. On the same stick we tied a red handkerchief by way of some return.

We thence continued to travel up this stream four days in succession, with very little incident to diversify our march. We found the banks of this river plentifully timbered with trees of various species, and the land fine for cultivation. On the morning of the 13th, we returned to the

Helay, and found on our way, that the Indians had taken the handkerchief, we had left, though none of them had shown any disposition, as we had hoped, to visit us. We named the stream we had left, the deserted fork, on account of having found it destitute of beavers. We thence resumed our course down the Helay, which continues to flow through a most beautiful country. Warned by the frequent traces of fresh Indian foot-prints, we every night adopted the expedient of enclosing our horses in a pen, feeding them with cotton-wood bark, which we found much better for them than grass. . . .

March 3d, we trapped along down a small stream, that empties into the Helay on the south side, having its head in a south west direction. It being very remarkable for the number of its beavers, we gave it the name of Beaver river. At this place we collected 200 skins; and on the 10th continued to descend the Helay, until the 20th, when we turned back with as much fur, as our beasts could pack. . . . On the 25th we returned to Beaver river, and dug up the furs that we had buried, or cashed, as the phrase is, and concluded to ascend it, trapping towards its head, whence we purposed to cross over to the Helay above the mountains, where we had suffered so much in crossing. About six miles up the stream, we stopped to set our traps, three being selected to remain behind in the camp to dry the skins, my father to make a pen for the horses, and I to guard them, while they were turned loose to feed in the grass. We had pitched our camp near the bank of the river, in a thick grove of timber, extending about a hundred yards in width. Behind the timber was a narrow plain of about the same width, and still further on was a high hill, to which I repaired, to watch my horses, and descry whatever might pass in the distance. Immediately back of the hill I discovered a small lake, by the noise made by the ducks and geese in it. Looking more attentively, I remarked what gave me much more satisfaction, that is to say, three beaver lodges. I returned, and made my father acquainted with my discovery. The party despatched to set traps had returned. My father informed them of my discovery, and told them to set traps in the little lake. As we passed towards the lake, we observed the horses and mules all crowded together. At first we concluded that they collected together in this way, because they had fed enough. We soon discovered, that it was owing to another cause. I had put down my gun, and stepped into the water, to prepare a bed for my trap, while the others were busy in preparing theirs. Instantly the Indians raised a yell, and the quick report of guns ensued. This noise was almost drowned in the fierce shouts that followed, succeeded by a shower of arrows falling among us like hail. As we ran for the camp leaving all the horses in their power, we saw six Indians stealthily following our trail, as though they were tracking a deer. They occasionally stopped, raised themselves, and surveyed every thing around them. We concealed ourselves behind a large cotton-wood tree, and waited until they came within a hundred yards of us. Each of us selected a separate Indian for a mark, and our signal to fire together was to be a whistle. The sign was given, and we fired together. My mark fell dead, and my companions' severely wounded. The other Indians seized their dead and wounded companions, and fled.

We now rejoined our company, who were busily occupied in dodging the arrows, that came in a shower from the summit of the hill, where I had stationed myself to watch our horses. Discovering that they were too far from us, to be reached by our bullets, we retreated to the timber, in hopes to draw them down to the plain. But they had had too ample proofs of our being marksmen, to think of returning down to our level, and were satisfied to remain yelling, and letting fly their arrows at random. We found cause both for regret and joy; regret, that our horses were in their power, and joy, that their unprovoked attack had been defeated with loss to themselves, and none to us.

At length they ceased yelling, and disappeared. . . .

In the morning of the 26th, we despatched two of our men to bring our traps and furs. We had no longer any way of conveying them with us, for the Indians had taken all our horses. We, however, in the late contest, had taken four of their's, left behind in the haste of their retreat. As our companions were returning to camp with the traps, which they had taken up to bury, they discovered the Indians, sliding along insidiously towards our camp. We were all engaged in eating our breakfast in entire confidence. Our men cried out to us, that the enemy was close upon us. We sprang to our arms. The Indians instantly fled to the top of the hill, which we had named battlehill. In a few minutes they were all paraded on the horses and mules stolen from us. . . . We accordingly faced them, and fired upon them, which induced them to clear themselves most expeditiously.

We proceeded to bury our furs; and having packed our four horses with provisions and two traps, we commenced our march. Having travelled about ten miles, we encamped in a thicket without kindling a fire, and kept a strict guard all night. Next morning we made an early march, still along the banks of the river. Its banks are still plentifully timbered with cotton-wood and willow. The bottoms on each side afford a fine soil for cultivation. From these bottoms the hills rise to an enormous height, and their summits are covered with perpetual snow. . . . A species of tree, which I had never seen before, here arrested my attention. It grows to the height of forty or fifty feet. The top is cone shaped, and almost without foliage. The bark resembles that of the prickly pear; and the body is covered with thorns. I have seen some three feet in diameter at the root, and throwing up twelve distinct shafts.*

On the 29th, we made our last encampment on this river, intending to return to it no more, except for our furs. We set our two traps for the last time, and caught a beaver in each.—We skinned the animals, and prepared the skins to hold water, through fear, that we might find none on our unknown route through the mountains to the Helay, from which we judged ourselves distant two hundred miles. Our provisions were all spoiled. We had nothing to carry with us to satisfy hunger, but the bodies of the two beavers

*This is apparently the giant cactus.—THWAITES.

which we had caught, the night before. We had nothing to sustain us in this disconsolate march, but our trust in providence; for we could not but forsee hunger, fatigue and pain, as the inevitable attendants upon our journey. To increase the depression of our spirits, our moccasins were worn out, our feet sore and tender, and the route full of sharp rocks. . . .

[After an arduous march eastward, traveling sometimes for days without food or water, the Patties, weary and emaciated, arrived back at the copper mines on April 29.]

The Spaniards seemed exceedingly rejoiced, and welcomed us home, as though we were of their own nation, religion and kindred. They assured us, that they had no expectation ever to see us again. The superintendent of the mines, especially, who appeared to me a gentleman of the highest order, received us with particular kindness, and supplied all our pressing wants. Here we remained, to rest and recruit ourselves, until the 2d of May. My father then advised me to travel to Santa Fe, to get some of our goods, and purchase a new supply of horses, with which to return, and bring in our furs. I had a horse, which we had taken from the Indians, shod with copper shoes, and in company with four of my companions, and the superintendent of the mines, I started for Santa Fe. . . .

We arrived at the house of the governor on the 12th. Jacova, his daughter, received us with the utmost affection; and shed tears on observing me so ill; as I was in fact reduced by starvation and fatigue, to skin and bone. Beings in a more wretched plight she could not often have an opportunity to see. My hair hung matted and uncombed. My head was surmounted with an old straw hat. My legs were fitted with leather leggins, and my body arrayed in a leather hunting shirt, and no want of dirt about any part of the whole. My companions did not shame me, in comparison, by being better clad. But all these repulsive circumstances notwithstanding, we were welcomed by the governor and Jacova, as kindly, as if we had been clad in a manner worthy of their establishment.

We rested ourselves here three days. . . . I once more

dressed myself decently, and spared to my companions all my clothes that fitted them. We all had our hair trimmed. All this had much improved our appearance. . . .

On the 18th we arrived at Santa Fe. . . . I took a part of my goods, and started back to the mines on the 21st. None of my companions were willing to accompany me on account of the great apprehended danger from the Indians between this place and the mines. In consequence, I hired a man to go with me, and having purchased what horses I wanted, we two travelled on in company. . . .

We arrived at the mines the first day of June, having experienced no molestation from the Indians. We continued here, making arrangements for our expedition to bring in the furs, until the 6th. The good natured commander gave us provisions to last us to the point where our furs were buried, and back again. Still more, he armed ten of his laborers, and detached them to accompany us. The company consisted of four Americans, the man hired at Santa Fe, and the commander's ten men, fifteen in all.

We left the mines on the 7th, and reached Battle-hill on Beaver river on the 22d. I need not attempt to describe my feelings, for no description could paint them, when I found the furs all gone, and perceived that the Indians had discovered them and taken them away. All that, for which we had hazarded ourselves, and suffered every thing but death, was gone. The whole fruit of our long, toilsome and dangerous expedition was lost, and all my golden hopes of prosperity and comfort vanished like a dream. I tried to convince myself, that repining was of no use, and we started for the river San Francisco on the 29th. Here we found the small quantity buried there, our whole compensation for a year's toil, misery and danger. We met no Indians either going or returning.

16

JAMES P. BECKWOURTH:

Squaw-Man

The frontier trapper and trader often found it was good policy to get himself adopted by an Indian tribe. For one thing, it gave him a distinct advantage over rival traders if he had a powerful chief for an adopted father or a chief's daughter for a wife. Such an alliance also offered security against treachery from hostile factions of the tribe, as well as bringing the comforts and pleasures of family life to men who lived far from friends and relations of their own race. James Beckwourth (1798–1867) carried this policy further than most, winning a slew of Indian maidens and even becoming a full-fledged chief of the Crow tribe. Born in Virginia to a mulatto mother and a white father, his color and features closely resembled those of an Indian. His family moved to St. Louis, where young Beckwourth's highly active imagination must have been stirred by tales of life on the great plains, for in 1823 he hired on as a groom in William Ashley's fur trading expedition up the Missouri River—in a party which also included Jedediah Smith and Thomas Fitzpatrick (see Selections 17 and 21). Not long after, he began his career as *trader, hunter, squaw-man, and warrior among the Indians, abandoning white society altogether from about 1826 to about 1833. He later served with Stephen Kearny in the war with Mexico and joined the Colorado gold rush in 1859. He died in Denver about`1867.*

There was many an ego on the frontier that could have matched Beckwourth's for sheer bombast, and many a tale told around the campfire was no doubt as exciting as his. Beckwourth only differed from the rest in that he committed his stories to print. Consequently his name survives while not a trace is left of most of his contemporaries. The Life and Adventures of James P. Beckwourth, "written from his own dictation" by T. D. Bonner and published in New York in1856, was attacked as the work "of a charming liar" who borrowed the adventures of others and made them his own. Another writer, comparing Beckwourth's account of the 1823 expedition with Ashley's narrative, found Beckwourth "singularly reliable." But however authentic Beckwourth's stories may or may not be, they are typical enough—even in their strutting bravado—to present a representative portrait of the hunter of the plains.

We spent the summer months at our leisure, trading with the Indians, hunting, sporting, and preparing for the fall harvest of beaver. We made acquaintance with several of the Black Feet, who came to the post to trade. One of their chiefs invited Mr. Sublet to establish a branch post in their country, telling him that they had many people and horses, and plenty of beaver, and if his goods were to be obtained they would trade considerably; his being so far off prevented his people coming to Mr. Sublet's camp.

The Indian appearing sincere, and there being a prospect of opening a profitable trade, Sublet proposed to establish a post among the Black Feet if any of the men were willing to risk their scalps in attending it. I offered to go, although I was well aware the tribe knew that I had contrib-

From *The Life and Adventures of James P. Beckwourth, Mountaineer, Scout, and Pioneer, and Chief of the Crow Nation Indians,* Written from his own Dictation by T. D. Bonner (New York: Harper and Brothers, 1856), pp. 113–120, 144–150, 153–155m 183–177m 198–199.

uted to the destruction of a number of their braves, but, to the Indian, the greater the brave, the higher their respect for him, even though an enemy. So, taking my boy Baptiste and one man with me, we packed up and started for Beaver River, which is a branch of the Missouri, and in the heart of the Black Foot country.

On our arrival, the Indians manifested great appearance of friendship, and were highly pleased at having a trading-post so conveniently at hand. I soon rose to be a great man among them, and the chief offered me his daughter for a wife. Considering this an alliance that would guarantee my life as well as enlarge my trade, I accepted his offer, and, without any superfluous ceremony, became son-in-law to *As-as-to*, the head chief of the Black Feet. *As-as-to*, interpreted, means heavy shield. To me the alliance was more *offensive* than defensive, but *thrift* was my object more than hymeneal enjoyments. Trade prospered greatly. I purchased beaver and horses at my own price. Many times I bought a fine beaver-skin for a butcher-knife or a plug of tobacco.

After a residence among them of a few days, I had slight difficulty in my family affairs. A party of Indians came into camp one day, bringing with them three white men's scalps. The sight of them made my blood boil with rage; but there was no help for it, so I determined to wait with patience my day of revenge. In accordance with their custom, a scalp-dance was held, at which there was much additional rejoicing.

My *wife* came to me with the information that her people were rejoicing, and that she wished to join them in the dance.

I replied, "No; these scalps belonged to my people; my heart is crying for their death; you must not rejoice when my heart cries; you must not dance when I mourn."

She then went out, as I supposed, satisfied. My two white friends, having a great curiosity to witness the performance, were looking out upon the scene. I reproved them for wishing to witness the savage rejoicings over the fall of white men who had probably belonged to our own company.

One of them answered, "Well, your wife is the best dancer of the whole party; she out-dances them all."

This was a sting which pierced my very heart. Taking my battle-axe, and forcing myself into the ring, I watched my opportunity, and struck my disobedient wife a heavy blow in the head with the side of my battle-axe, which dropped her as if a ball had pierced her heart.

I dragged her through the crowd, and left her; I then went back to my tent.

This act was performed in such a bold manner, under the very noses of hundreds of them, that they were thunderstruck, and for a moment remained motionless with surprise. When I entered the tent, I said to my companions, "There, now, you had better prepare to hold on to your own scalps, since you take so much interest in a celebration over those of your murdered brethren." Their countenances turned ashy pale, expecting instant death.

By this time the whole Indian camp was in a blaze. "Kill him! kill him! burn him! burn him!" was shouted throughout the camp in their own language, which I plainly understood. I was collected, for I knew they could kill me but once.

Soon I heard the voice of my father-in-law crying, in a tone which sounded above all, "Stop! hold! hold! warriors! listen to your chief."

All was hushed in an instant, and he continued: "Warriors! I am the loser of a daughter, and her brothers have lost a sister; you have lost nothing. She was the wife of the trader; I gave her to him. When your wives disobey your commands, you kill them; that is your right. That thing disobeyed her husband; he told her not to dance; she disobeyed him; she had no ears; he killed her, and he did right. He did as you all would have done, and you shall neither kill nor harm him for it. I promised the white chief that, if he would send a trader to my people, I would protect him and return him unharmed; this I must do, and he shall not be hurt here. Warriors! wait till you meet him in battle, or, perhaps, in his own camp, then kill him; but here his life is sacred. What if we kill them all, and take what they have? It will last but a few suns; we shall then want more.

Whom do we get sach-o-pach (powder) from? We get it from the whites; and when we have expended what we have, we must do without, or go to them for more. When we have no powder, can we fight our enemies with plenty? If we kill these three men, whom I have given the word of a chief to protect, the white chief will send us no more, but his braves will revenge the death of their brothers. No, no; you shall not harm them here. They have eaten of our meat, and drunk of our water; they have also smoked with us. When they have sold their goods, let them return in peace."

At this time there were a great many Flat Heads at the Black Foot camp, as they were at peace with each other. After the speech of my father-in-law, a great brave of the Flat Heads, called Bad Hand, replied, "Hey! you are yourself again; you talk well; you talk like *As-as-to* again. We are now at peace; if you had killed these men, we should have made war on you again; we should have raised the battle-axe, never to have buried it. These whites are ours, and the Flat Heads would have revenged their deaths if they had been killed in your camp."

The chief then made a loud and long harangue, after which all became quiet. *As-as-to* next came to my camp and said, "My son, you have done right; that woman I gave you had no sense; her ears were stopped up; she would not hearken to you, and you had a right to kill her. But I have another daughter, who is younger than she was. She is more beautiful; she has good sense and good ears. You may have her in the place of the bad one; she will hearken to all you say to her."

"Well," thought I, "this is getting married again before I have even had time to *mourn*."

But I replied, "Very well, my father, I will accept of your kind offer," well knowing, at the same time, that to refuse him would be to offend, as he would suppose that I disdained his generosity.

My second wife was brought to me. I found her, as her father had represented, far more intelligent and far prettier than her other sister, and I was really proud of the change. I now possessed one that many a warrior had performed deeds of bloody valor to obtain; for it is a high honor to get the daughter of a great chief to wife, and many a bold warrior has sacrificed his life in seeking to attain such a prize.

During the night, while I and my wife were quietly reposing, some person crawled into our couch, sobbing most bitterly. Angry at the intrusion, I asked who was there.

"Me," answered a voice, which, although well-nigh stifled with bitter sobs, I recognized as that of my other wife, whom every one had supposed dead. After lying outside the lodge senseless for some hours, she had recovered and groped her way to my bed.

"Go away," I said, "You have no business here; I have a new wife now, one who has sense."

"I will not go away," she replied; "my ears are open now. I was a fool not to hearken to my husband's words when his heart was crying, but now I have good sense, and will always hearken to your words."

It did really seem as if her heart was broken, and she kept her position until morning. I thought myself now well supplied with wives, having *two* more than I cared to have; but I deemed it hardly worth while to complain, as I should soon leave the camp, wives and all.

It is a universal adage, "When you are among Romans, do as the Romans do." I conformed to the customs of a people really pagan, but who regarded themselves both enlightened and powerful. I was risking my life for gold, that I might return one day with plenty, to share with her I tenderly loved. My body was among the Indians, but my mind was far away from them and their bloody deeds. Experience has revealed to me that civilized man can accustom himself to any mode of life when pelf is the governing principle—that power which dominates through all the ramifications of social life, and gives expression to the universal instinct of self-interest. . . .

[Among the Crows Beckwourth's reputation as a warrior soars after he defeats a party of their enemies, the Cheyenne. As a joke, Beckwourth's friend Greenwood

convinces the Crows that Beckwourth is really a long-lost
son of their tribe, captured by the Cheyennes when he was
a child. At the first opportunity the Crows joyfully welcome
him back to the fold.]

The same evening Captain Bridger and myself started
out with our traps, intending to be gone three or four days.
We followed up a small stream until it forked, when Bridger
proposed that I should take one fork and he the other, and
the one who had set his traps first should cross the hill
which separated the two streams and rejoin the other. Thus
we parted, expecting to meet again in a few hours. I continued my course up the stream in pursuit of beaver villages
until I found myself among an innumerable drove of
horses, and I could plainly see they were not wild ones.

The horses were guarded by several of their Indian
owners, or horse-guards, as they term them, who had discovered me long before I saw them. I could hear their
signals to each other, and in a few moments I was surrounded by them, and escape was impossible. I resigned
myself to my fate: if they were enemies, I knew they could
kill me but once, and to attempt to defend myself would
entail inevitable death. I took the chances between death
and mercy; I surrendered my gun, traps, and what else I
had, and was marched to camp under a strong escort of
horse-guards. I felt very sure that my guards were Crows,
therefore I did not feel greatly alarmed at my situation. On
arriving at their village, I was ushered into the chief's
lodge, where there were several old men and women,
whom I conceived to be members of the family. My capture
was known throughout the village in five minutes, and
hundreds gathered around the lodge to get a sight of the
prisoner. In the crowd were some who had talked to
Greenwood a few weeks before. They at once exclaimed,
"That is the lost Crow, the great brave who has killed so
many of our enemies. He is our brother."

This threw the whole village in commotion; old and
young were impatient to obtain a sight of the "great brave."
Orders were immediately given to summon all the old
women taken by the Shi-ans at the time of their captivity so

many winters past, who had suffered the loss of a son at that time. The lodge was cleared for the *examining committee,* and the old women, breathless with excitement, their eyes wild and protruding, and their nostrils dilated, arrived in squads, until the lodge was filled to overflowing. I believe never was mortal gazed at with such intense and sustained interest as I was on that occasion. Arms and legs were critically scrutinized. My face next passed the ordeal; then my neck, back, breast, and all parts of my body, even down to my feet, which did not escape the examination of these anxious matrons, in their endeavors to discover some mark or peculiarity whereby to recognize their brave son.

At length one old woman, after having scanned my visage with the utmost intentness, came forward and said, "If this is my son, he has a mole over one of his eyes."

My eyelids were immediately pulled down to the utmost stretch of their elasticity, when, sure enough, she discovered a mole just over my left eye!

"Then, and oh then!" such shouts of joy as were uttered by that honest-hearted woman were seldom before heard, while all in the crowd took part in her rejoicing. It was uncultivated joy, but not the less heartfelt and intense. It was a joy which a mother can only experience when she recovers a son whom she had supposed dead in his earliest days. She has mourned him silently through weary nights and busy days for the long space of twenty years; suddenly he presents himself before her in robust manhood, and graced with the highest name an Indian can appreciate. It is but nature, either in the savage breast or civilized, that hails such a return with overwhelming joy, and feels the mother's undying affection awakened beyond all control.

All the other claimants resigning their pretensions, I was fairly carried along by the excited crowd to the lodge of the "Big Bowl," who was my father. The news of my having proved to be the son of Mrs. Big Bowl flew through the village with the speed of lightning, and, on my arrival at the paternal lodge, I found it filled with all degrees of my newly-discovered relatives, who welcomed me nearly to death. They seized me in their arms and hugged me, and my face positively burned with the enraptured kisses of my numerous fair sisters, with a long host of cousins, aunts, and other more remote kindred. All these welcoming ladies as firmly believed in my identity with the lost one as they believed in the existence of the Great Spirit.

My father knew me to be his son; told all the Crows that the dead was alive again, and the lost one was found. He knew it was fact; Greenwood had said so, and the words of Greenwood were true; his tongue was not crooked—he would not lie. He also had told him that his son was a great brave among the white men; that his arm was strong; that the Black Feet quailed before his rifle and battle-axe; that his lodge was full of their scalps which his knife had taken; that they must rally around me to support and protect me; and that his long-lost son would be a strong breastwork to their nation, and he would teach them how to defeat their enemies.

They all promised that they would do as his words had indicated.

My unmarried sisters were four in number, very pretty, intelligent young women. They, as soon as the departure of the crowd would admit, took off my old leggins, and moccasins, and other garments, and supplied their place with new ones, most beautifully ornamented according to their very last fashion. My sisters were very ingenious in such work, and they wellnigh quarreled among themselves for the privilege of dressing me. When my toilet was finished to their satisfaction, I could compare in elegance with the most popular warrior of the tribe when in full costume. They also prepared me a bed, not so high as Haman's gallows certainly, but just as high as the lodge would admit. This was also a token of their esteem and sisterly affection.

While conversing to the extent of my ability with my father in the evening, and affording him full information respecting the white people, their great cities, their numbers, their power, their opulence, he suddenly demanded of me if I wanted a wife; thinking, no doubt, that, if he got me married, I should lose all discontent, and forgo any wish of returning to the whites.

I assented, of course.

"Very well," said he, "you shall have a pretty wife and a good one."

Away he strode to the lodge of one of the greatest braves, and asked one of his daughters of him to bestow upon his son, who the chief must have heard was also a great brave. The consent of the parent was readily given. The name of my prospective father-in-law was Black-lodge. He had three very pretty daughters, whose names were Still-water, Blackfish, and Three-roads.

Even the untutored daughters of the wild woods need a little time to prepare for such an important event, but long and tedious courtships are unknown among them.

The ensuing day the three daughters were brought to my father's lodge by their father, and I was requested to take my choice. "Still-water" was the eldest, and I liked her name; if it was emblematic of her disposition, she was the woman I should prefer. "Still-water," accordingly, was my choice. They were all superbly attired in garments which must have cost them months of labor, which garments the young women ever keep in readiness against such an interesting occasion as the present.

The acceptance of my wife was the completion of the ceremony, and I was again a married man, as sacredly in their eyes as if the Holy Christian Church had fastened the irrevocable knot upon us.

Among the Indians, the daughter receives no patrimony on her wedding-day, and her mother and father never pass a word with the son-in-law after—a custom religiously observed among them, though for what reason I never learned. The other relatives are under no such restraint.

My brothers made me a present of twenty as fine horses as any in the nation—all trained war-horses. I was also presented with all the arms and instruments requisite for an Indian campaign.

My wife's deportment coincided with her name; she would have reflected honor upon many a civilized household. She was affectionate, obedient, gentle, cheerful, and, apparently, quite happy. No domestic thunder-storms, no curtain-lectures ever disturbed the serenity of our connubial lodge. I speedily formed acquaintance with all my immediate neighbors, and the Morning Star (which was the name conferred upon me on my recognition as the lost son) was soon a companion to all the young warriors in the village. No power on earth could have shaken their faith in my positive identity with the lost son. Nature seemed to prompt the old woman to recognize me as her missing child, and all my new relatives placed implicit faith in the genuineness of her discovery. Greenwood had spoken it, "and his tongue was not crooked." What could I do under the circumstances? Even if I should deny my Crow origin, they would not believe me. How could I dash with an unwelcome and incredible explanation all the joy that had been manifested on my return—the cordial welcome, the rapturous embraces of those who hailed me as a son and a brother, the exuberant joy of the whole nation for the return of a long-lost Crow, who, stolen when a child, had returned in the strength of maturity, graced with the name of a great brave, and the generous strife I had occasioned in their endeavors to accord me the warmest welcome? I could not find it in my heart to undeceive these unsuspecting people and tear myself away from their untutored caresses.

Thus I commenced my Indian life with the Crows. I said to myself, "I can trap in their streams unmolested, and derive more profit under their protection than if among my own men, exposed incessantly to assassination and alarm." I therefore resolved to abide with them, to guard my secret, to do my best in their company, and in assisting them to subdue their enemies. . . .

After fêting for about ten days among my new neighbors, I joined a small war-party of about forty men, embodied for the ostensible purpose of capturing horses, but actually to kill their enemies. After advancing for three days, we fell in with a party of eleven of the Blood Indians, a band of the Black Foot tribe, immemorial enemies of the Crows. Our chief ordered a charge upon them. I advanced directly upon their line, and had struck down my man before the others came up. The others, after making a furious advance, that threatened annihilation to our few foes, curveted aside in Indian fashion, thus losing the effect of a first onset. I corrected this unwarlike custom. On this occasion, seeing me engaged hand to hand with the enemy's whole force, they immediately came to my assistance, and the opposing party were quickly dispatched. I despoiled my victim of his gun, lance, war-club, bow, and quiver of arrows. Now I was the greatest man in the party, for I had killed the first warrior. We then painted our faces black (their mode of announcing victory), and rode back to the village, bearing eleven scalps. We entered the village singing and shouting, the crowds blocking up our way so that it was with difficulty we could get along. My wife met me at some distance from our lodge, and to her I gave my greatest trophy, the gun. My pretty sisters next presenting themselves for some share of the spoils, I gave them what remained, and they returned to their lodge singing and dancing all the way. Their delight was unbounded in their new-found relative, who had drawn the first blood. My companions told how I had charged direct upon the enemy, how I struck down the first Indian at a blow, what strength there was in my arm, and a great deal more in my commendation. Again I was lionized and fêted. Relatives I had not seen before now advanced and made my acquaintance. I was feasted by all the sachems and great braves of the village until their kindness nearly fatigued me to death, and I was glad to retire to my lodge to seek a season of quietude.

It was a custom rigidly observed by the Crows, when a son had drawn the first blood of the enemy, for the father to distribute all his property among the village, always largely recollecting his own kin in the proposed distribution. I saw that my achievement had ruined my poor old father. He seemed contented, however, to sacrifice his worldly goods to the prowess of his illustrious son. It was the Crows' religion, and he was thoroughly orthodox. Another traditional memento was to paint a chief's coat with an image of the sun, and hang that, together with a scarlet blanket, in the top of a tree, as an offering to the Great Spirit, to propitiate him to continue his favorable regards.

Several small bands of the village had a grand dance after the victory, each band by itself. I watched them for some time, to see which band or clique contained the most active men. Having singled one, I broke into the ring, and joined the performance with great heartiness. Then their shouts arose, "The great brave, the Antelope, has joined our band!" and their dancing increased in vehemence, and their singing became more hilarious. By the act of joining their clique I becme incorporated with their number.

A feud now broke out, which had been long brewing, between two different parties in our village, one of which worshiped foxes, and the other worshiped dodgs. The warriors of the latter party were called Dog Soldiers, of which I was the leader; the other party was led by Red Eyes. The quarrel originated about the prowess of the respective parties, and was fostered by Red Eyes, on the part of the rival company, and by Yellow Belly (in Indian A-re-she-res), a man in my company. This A-re-she-res was as brave an Indian as ever trod the plain, but he was also a very bad Indian—that is, he was disagreeable in his manners, and very insulting in his conversation.

Red Eyes was equally brave, but of a different disposition. His was a reserved pride; the braggadocio of A-re-she-res offended him. This rivalry developed into an open rupture, and the pipe-men were obliged to interfere to prevent open hostilities. At length it was proposed, in order to cement a final peace between the two warriors, that each should select from his own party a certain number of men, and go and wage common war against some enemy—the question of bravery to be decided by the number of scalps brought in on each side.

Red Eyes accordingly chose from his party eighteen of the best men, himself making the nineteenth—men who would suffer death rather than show their backs to the enemy. A-re-she-res, with his accustomed fanfaronade, said, "I can beat that party with less men; I will only take sixteen men, and bring in more scalps than they."

He came to me and said, "Enemy of Horses, I want you to go with me and die with me. It is of no use for you to stay with this people; they are not brave any longer. Come with me, and we will enter the spirit land together, where the inhabitants are all brave. There is better hunting ground in the country of the Great Spirit. Come!"

I replied I would rather not go on such an errand. I have women to live for, and defend against the enemies of the Crows; that when I fought I wished to destroy the enemy and preserve my own life. "That," said I, "is bravery and prudence combined."

"Ah!" answered he, "you a leader of the Dog Soldiers, and refuse to go! There are prettier women in the land of the Great Spirit than any of your squaws, and game in much greater abundance. I care nothing about my life: I am ready to go to the land of the Great Spirit. You must go with me; perhaps your medicine will save not only yourself, but all of us. If so, it will be so much the better."

I, not wishing to be thought cowardly, especially by A-re-she-res, at length consented to accompany him, on the condition that he would stifle all harsh feeling against our brethren, and, let our expedition result as it would, accept the decision in good faith, and never refer to the past.

"It is well," he said; "let it be as your words speak."

The two parties started on different routes to the Cheyenne country. I regarded it as a foolhardy enterprise, but if it resulted in the establishment of peace, I was contented to take part in it, at whatever personal sacrifice. We used every precaution against a surprise, and A-re-she-res willingly adapted his movements to my counsel; for, though he was as brave as a lion, and fought with the utmost desperation, he was very inconsiderate of consequences, and had no power of calculating present combinations to come at a desired result.

After traveling about twenty days, we arrived at a considerable elevation, from whence we could see, at some distance on the prairie, about thirty of the enemy engaged in killing buffalo. We could also see their village at a distance of three miles.

"There is an opportunity," said A-re-she-res; "now let us charge these Indians in the open prairie."

"No, no," I replied; "there are too many of them; the Cheyennes are brave warriors; if you wish to carry home their scalps, we must get into their path and waylay them; by that means we shall kill many of them, and run less risk of our own lives. We shall gain more honor by preserving the lives of our warriors, and taking back the scalps of the enemy, than by sacrificing our lives in a rash and inconsiderate charge."

"Your words are true," said he, "and we will do as you say."

"Then," added I, "turn your robes the hair side out, and follow me."

We wound our way down the trail through which they must necessarily pass to reach their village, and kept on until we reached a place where there were three gullies worn by the passage of the water. Through the centre gully the trail passed, thus leaving a formidable position on each side, in which an ambuscade had ample concealment. I divided my party, giving the command of one division to A-re-she-res. We took our stations in the ditches on each side the trail, though not exactly opposite to each other. I directed the opposite party not to fire a gun until they should hear ours, and then each man to take the enemy in the order of precedence. The unsuspecting Cheyennes, as soon as they had finished butchering and dressing the buffalo, began to approach us in parties of from three to eight or ten, their horses loaded with meat, which they were bearing to the village. When there were about a dozen abreast of my party, I made a signal to fire, and nine Cheyennes fell before our balls, and eight before those of A-re-she-res's party. Some few of the enemy who had passed on, hearing the guns, returned to see what the matter was, and three of them became victims to our bullets. We all rushed from our hiding-places then, and some fell to scalping the prostrate foe, and some to cutting the lashings of the meat in order to secure the horses, the remainder keeping the surviving enemy at bay. Having taken twenty scalps, we sprang upon the horses we had freed from their packs, and retreated precipitately, for the enemy was coming in sight in great numbers.

We made direct for the timber, and, leaving our horses, took refuge in a rocky place in the mountain, where we considered ourselves protected for a while from their attacks. To storm us in front they had to advance right in the face of our bullets, and to reach us in the rear they had to take a circuitous route of several miles round the base of the mountain. The enemy evinced the utmost bravery, as they made repeated assaults right up to the fortification that sheltered us. Their bullets showered around us without injury, but we could bring down one man at every discharge. To scalp them, however, was out of the question.

During the combat a great Cheyenne brave, named Leg-in-the-Water, charged directly into our midst, and aimed a deadly thrust with his lance at one of our braves. The warrior assailed instantly shivered the weapon with his battle-axe, and inflicted a ghastly wound in his assailant's shoulder with a second blow. He managed to escape, leaving his horse dead in our midst.

By this time we were encompassed with the enemy, which induced the belief in our minds that retreat would be the safest course. None of our party was wounded except A-re-she-res, who had his arm broken with a bullet between the shoulder and elbow. He made light of the wound, only regretting that he could no longer discharge his gun; but he wielded his battle-axe with his left hand as well as ever.

When night came on we evacuated our fortress, unperceived by our enemies. They, deeming our escape impossible, were quietly resting, intending to assault us with their whole force in the morning, and take our scalps at all hazards. Moving with the stealth of a cat, we proceeded along the summit of a rocky cliff until we came to a cleft or ravine, through which we descended from the bluff to the bottom, which was covered with a heavy growth of timber. We then hastened home, arriving there on the twenty-eight day from the time we left.

They had given us over for lost; but when they saw us returning with twenty scalps, and only one of our party hurt, their grief gave way to admiration, and we were hailed with shouts of applause.

Our rival party, under Red Eyes, had returned five or six days previously, bringing with them seventeen scalps, obtained at the loss of one man. Our party was declared the victor, since we had taken the greatest number of scalps, with the weaker party, and without loss of life, thus excelling our rivals in three several points. Red Eyes cheerfully acknowledged himself beaten, good feeling was restored, and the subject of each other's bravery was never after discussed.

We had still another advantage, inasmuch as we could dance, a celebration they were deprived of, as they had lost a warrior; they, however, joined our party, and wanted nothing in heartiness to render our dance sufficiently boisterous to suffice for the purpose of both. . . .

I trust that the reader does not suppose that I waded through these scenes of carnage and desolation without some serious reflections on the matter. Disgusted at the repeated acts of cruelty I witnessed, I often resolved to leave these wild children of the forest and return to civilized life; but before I could act upon my decision, another scene of strife would occur, and the Enemy of Horses was always the first sought for by the tribe. I had been uniformly successful so far; and how I had escaped, while scores of warriors had been stricken down at my side, was more than I could understand. I was well aware that many of my friends knew of the life I was leading, and I almost feared to think of the opinions they must form of my character. But, in justification, it may be urged that the Crows had never shed the blood of the white man during my stay in their camp, and I did not intend they ever should, if I could raise a voice to prevent it. They were constantly at war with tribes who coveted the scalps of the white man, but the Crows were uniformly faithful in their obligations to my race, and would rather serve than injure their white brethren without any consideration of profit.

In addition to this, Self-interest would whisper her counsel. I knew I could acquire the riches of Croesus if I could but dispose of the valuable stock of pelty I had the means of accumulating. I required but an object in view to turn the attention of the Indians to the thousands of traps that were laid to rust. I would occasionally use arguments to turn them from their unprofitable life, and engage them in peaceful industry. But I found the Indian would be Indian still, in spite of my efforts to improve him.

17

JEDEDIAH SMITH:
Survival in the Desert

Among the trappers and explorers of the West, Jedediah Strong Smith (1798–1831) was a man apart. A land-borne Odysseus, relentlessly driven to travel where no white man had traveled before, his epic journeys carried him over thousands of miles of unknown wilderness. During his nine short years in the mountains he became the first white American to travel overland to California, the first explorer of the Great Basin, the first to travel by land from San Diego to the mouth of the Columbia, and the first to discover the South Pass in Wyoming, the great gateway to the Far West. Smith was also a skilled leader of tough mountainmen. Yet he remained a civilized and deeply religious man. He neither smoked nor chewed nor swore, and he seldom drank. He would no sooner be parted from his Bible than from his rifle.

Born in Bainbridge, New York, Smith stayed home just long enough to acquire a reasonable amount of learning. Lured westward by dreams of adventure in the wilderness, he signed on as a member of the first expedition of the Rocky Mountain

Fur Company in 1822 and eventually became a partner in the firm. Remaining in the mountains until his death nine years later, he survived massacres, starvation, deserts, raging torrents, blizzards, and grizzly bears. Among his greatest achievements was his overland journey through the Southwest to California. Setting out from the Salt Lake rendezvous in the fall of 1826 at the head of a column of seventeen men, he blazed a trail southward through the Utah and Nevada wilderness, made a grueling march across the Mojave desert, and eventually reached the Pacific Coast—to the astonishment of the Spanish authorities. Suspected of being spies, the bearded hunters were threatened with imprisonment but were finally permitted to travel back across the mountains. Leaving most of his men behind to hunt, Smith and two others struggled over the snowbound Sierras and across the Nevada and Utah desert, almost dying of thirst before reaching the Salt Lake rendezvous. A month later Smith was retracing his steps through the Southwest, intent on relieving his hunting party and exploring the Oregon coast. Ahead were desert marches and Indian attacks that took the lives of most of his companions. But Smith survived long enough to retire from the mountains in 1830. He had grown rich in the fur trade, but he was too restless to settle down and a year later he entered the Sante Fe trade. In May 1831, while out scouting for water, he was ambushed and killed by Comanches near the Cimarron River in southwestern Kansas.

Smith's contributions to the opening of the West were long forgotten, and credit for his discoveries went to other men. Only in the present century, when many of his journals and letters were found, has Smith's achievement begun to be recognized. In the following letter, written on July 27, 1827, upon his return to the Salt Lake rendezvous, Smith summarizes his first trip to California and the torturous return journey across the Utah desert. The letter is addressed to General William Clark, the Superintendent of Indian Affairs in St. Louis who, some twenty years before, had explored the northern route to the Pacific with his partner, Meriweather Lewis. Shortly after its receipt by Clark, Smith's letter was published in a St. Louis newspaper.

From the *Missouri Republican*, October 11, 1827. Reprinted in *The Ashley-Smith Explorations*, Harrison C. Dale, ed. (Cleveland: Arthur H. Clark Co., 1941), pp. 182–190.

Sir, My situation in this country has enabled me to collect information respecting a section of the country which has hitherto been measurably veiled in obscurity to the citizens of the United States. I allude to the country s.w. of the Great Lake west of the Rocky mountains.

I started about the 22d of august 1826, from the Great Salt lake, with a party of fifteen men, for the purpose of exploring the country s.w. which was entirely unknown to me, and of which I could collect no satisfactory information from the Indians who inhabit this country on its n.e. borders.

My general course on leaving the Salt lake was s.w. and w. Passing the Little Uta lake and ascending Ashley's river [probably the Sevier], which empties into the Little Uta lake. From this lake I found no more signs of buffalo; there are a few antelope and mountain sheep, and an abundance of black tailed hares. On Ashley's river, I found a nation of Indians who call themselves *Sampatch*; they were friendly disposed towards us. I passed over a range of mountains running s.e. and n.w. and struck a river running s.w. which I called Adams river, in compliment to our president. [This was probably the Muddy River, which flows into Meadow Valley Wash, near what is now Caliente, in Southeastern Nevada]. The water is of a muddy cast, and is a little brackish. The country is mountainous to east; towards the west there are sandy plains and detached rocky hills.

Passing down this river some distance, I fell in with a nation of Indians who call themselves *Pa-Ulches* [Paiutes] (those Indians as well as those last mentioned, wear rabbit skin robes) who raise some little corn and pumpkins. The country is nearly destitute of game of any description, except a few hares. Here (about ten days march down it) the river turns to the south east. On the s.w. side of the river there is a cave, the entrance of which is about 10 or 15 feet high, and 5 or 6 feet in width; after descending about 15 feet, a room opens out from 25 to 30 in length and 15 to 20 feet in width; the roof, sides and floor are solid rock salt, a sample of which I send you, with some other articles which will be hereafter described. I here found a kind of plant of the prickly pear kind, which I called the cabbage pear, the largest of which grows about two feet and a half high and 1½ feet in diameter; upon examination I found it to be nearly of the substance of a turnip, altho' by no means palatable; its form was similar to that of an egg, being smaller at the ground and top than in the middle; it is covered with pricks similar to the prickly pear with which you are acquainted.

There are here also a number of shrubs and small trees with which I was not acquainted previous to my route there, and which I cannot at present describe satisfactorily, as it would take more space than I can here allot.

The *Pa Ulches* have a number of marble pipes, one of which I obtained and send you, altho' it has been broken since I have had it in my possession; they told me there was a quantity of the same material in their country. I also obtained of them a knife of flint, which I send you, but it has likewise been broken by accident.

I followed Adams river two days further to where it empties into the Seedskeeder [the Colorado] a south east course. I crossed the Seedskeeder, and went down it four days a south east course; I here found the country remarkably barren, rocky, and mountainous; there are a good many rapids in the river, but at this place a valley opens out about 5 to 15 miles in width, which on the river banks is timbered and fertile. I here found a nation of Indians who call themselves *Ammuchabas* [the Mojaves]; they cultivate the soil, and raise corn, beans, pumpkins, watermelons and muskmelons in abundance, and also a little wheat and cotton. I was now nearly destitute of horses, and had learned what it was to do without food; I therefore remained there fifteen days and recruited my men, and I was enabled also to exchange my horses and purchase a few more of a few runaway Indians who stole some horses of the Spaniards. I here got information of the Spanish country (the Californias) and obtained two guides, recrossed the Seedskadeer, which I afterwards found emptied into the Gulf of California about 80 miles from this place by the name of the Collarado. . . .

I travelled a west course fifteen days over a country of complete barrens, generally travelling from morning until night without water. I crossed a salt plain [the Mojave Desert] about 20 miles long and 8 wide; on the surface was a crust of beautiful white salt, quite thin. Under this surface there is a layer of salt from a half to one and a half inches in depth; between this and the upper layer there is about four inches of yellowish sand.

On my arrival in the province of Upper California, I was looked upon with suspicion, and was compelled to appear in presence of the governor of the Californias residing at San Diego, where, by the assistance of some American gentlemen (especially Captain W. H. Cunningham, of the ship Courier from Boston) I was enabled to obtain permission to return with my men the route I came, and purchased such supplies as I stood in want of. The governor would not allow me to trade up the sea coast towards Bodaga. I returned to my party and purchased such articles as were necessary, and went eastward of the Spanish settlements on the route I had come in. I then steered my course N.W. keeping from 150 miles to 200 miles from the sea coast. A very high range of mountains [the Sierra Nevada] lay on the east. After travelling three hundred miles in that direction through a country somewhat fertile, in which there was a great many Indians, mostly naked and destitute of arms, with the exception of a few bows and arrows and what is very singular amongst Indians, they cut their hair to the length of three inches; they proved to be friendly; their manner of living is on fish, roots, acorns and grass.

On my arrival at the river [probably the Stanislaus] which I named the *Wimmul-che* (named after a tribe of Indians which resides on it, of that name) I found a few beaver, and elk, deer, and antelope in abundance. I here made a small hunt, and attempted to take my party across the [mountain] which I before mentioned, and which I called *Mount Joseph*, to come on and join my partners at the Great Salt lake. I found the snow so deep on Mount Joseph that I could not cross my horses, five of which starved to death; I was compelled therefore to return to the valley which I had left, and there, leaving my party, I started with two men, seven horses and provisions for ourselves, and started on the 20th of may, and succeeded in crossing it in eight days, having lost only two horses and one mule. I found the snow on the top of this mountain from 4 to 8 feet deep, but it was so consolidated by the heat of the sun that my horses only sunk from half a foot to one foot deep.

After travelling twenty days from the east side of Mount Joseph, I struck the s.w. corner of the Great Salt lake, travelling over a country completely barren and destitute of game. We frequently travelled without water sometimes for two days over sandy deserts, where there was no sign of vegetation and when we found water in some of the rocky hills, we most generally found some Indians who appeared the most miserable of the human race having nothing to subsist on (nor any clothing) except grass seed, grasshoppers, etc. When we arrived at the Salt lake, we had but one horse and one mule remaining, which were so feeble and poor that they could scarce carry the little camp equipage which I had along; the balance of my horses I was compelled to eat as they gave out.

The company are now starting, and therefore must close my commmunication. Yours respectfully,

(signed) Jedediah S. Smith, of the firm of Smith, Jackson and Sublette.

18

BILL WILLIAMS:

Knowing When to Quit

Of all the eccentric characters that roamed the Western mountains in the 1820s and 1830s, one of the more quirky and colorful
was a gaunt, red-haired, red-bearded fellow called "Old Bill"
Williams (d. 1849). Wobbly of gait, awkward in the saddle,
standing six feet one in height, he had a face like the Badlands,
spoke an outlandish jargon, and wore a fantastic getup of
buckskins, beads, and feathers. He was a shrewd hunter and
woodsman, well practiced in the arts of self-preservation, and
among men known for their independent spirit he was more
stubbornly independent than most. Having little use for even
the primitive society of the frontier settlements, he would come
riding in at the end of a season's hunt and stay just long enough
to collect his earnings and spend every penny in one tremendous
spree. Then, rid of the burden in his pockets, he would head for
the mountains again, a free man.

Kentucky born, like so many of his compatriots in the Rockies, William Sherley Williams apparently started out as an
itinerant Methodist preacher in Missouri. In 1825 he joined a

*surveying party that was setting out to mark the Santa Fe Trail,
and in the next year began trapping in the Gila River country of
New Mexico and Arizona. For a time he lived among the Hopi
Indians, learning their language and teaching them Christian-
ity. But he soon turned to hunting and trapping full time,
spending the next twenty-two years roaming the West from
Missouri to the Pacific, from Texas to the Columbia River. He
was a member of Joe Walker's expedition to California in 1832
(see Selection 22), and he served as a guide on John C. Fremont's
disastrous expedition of 1848, when eleven men died of cold and
starvation near the headwaters of the Rio Grande, in southwestern Colorado. A few weeks later, toward the end of March
1849, while trying to recover some of the party's lost property,
Williams and a companion were ambushed and killed by Indians, probably the Utes. His name survives today in Bill Williams Mountain and the Bill Williams River, both in Arizona,
and in the Williams River Mountains and the Bill Williams Fork
of the Colorado River in Colorado.*

*Although Williams neither wrote nor dictated his memoirs, a
good portrait by a contemporary is found in* Life in the Far
West *(1840), a dramatic narrative by a young English adventurer named George Frederick Ruxton. Ruxton's record of Williams' colorful dialect was quickly adopted by fiction writers as
the standard jargon of the mountainmen. La Bonté and Killbuck
were the fictionalized heroes of Ruxton's narrative.*

La Bonté was at this time one of a band of eight trappers,
whose hunting ground was about the head waters of the
Yellow Stone, which we have before said is in the country
of the Blackfeet. With him were Killbuck, Meek, Marcelline, and three others; and the leader of the party was Bill
Williams, that old "hard case" who had spent forty years
and more in the mountains, until he had become as tough
as the parflèche soles of his mocassins. They were all good
men and true, expert hunters, and well-trained moun-

From "Life in the Far West," by George Frederick Ruxton. *Blackwood's Edinburgh
Magazine*, September 1848, pp. 294–299.

taineers. After having trapped all the streams they were acquainted with, it was determined to strike into the mountains, at a point where old Williams affirmed, from the "run" of the hills, there must be plenty of water, although not one of the party had before explored the country, or knew any thing of its nature, or of the likelihood of its affording game for themselves or pasture for their animals. However, they packed their peltry, and put out for the land in view—a lofty peak, dimly seen above the more regular summit of the chain, being their landmark.

For the first day or two their route lay between two ridges of mountains, and by following the little valley which skirted a creek, they kept on level ground, and saved their animals considerable labour and fatigue. Williams always rode ahead, his body bent over his saddle-horn, across which rested a long heavy rifle, his keen gray eyes peering from under the slouched brim of a flexible felt-hat, black and shining with grease. His buckskin hunting-shirt, bedaubed until it had the appearance of polished leather, hung in folds over his bony carcass; his nether extremities being clothed in pantaloons of the same material (with scattered fringes down the outside of the leg—which ornaments, however, had been pretty well thinned to supply "wangs" for mending mocassins or pack-saddles), which, shrunk with wet, clung tightly to his long, spare, sinewy legs. His feet were thrust into a pair of Mexican stirrups made of wood, and as big as coal-scuttles; and iron spurs of incredible proportions, with tinkling drops attached to the rowels, were fastened to his heel—a bead-worked strap, four inches broad, securing them over the instep. In the shoulder-belt which sustained his powder-horn and bullet-pouch, were fastened the various instruments essential to one pursuing his mode of life. An awl, with deer-horn handle, and the point defended by a case of cherry-wood carved by his own hand, hung at the back of the belt, side by side with a worm for cleaning the rifle; and under this was a squat and quaint-looking bullet mould, the handles guarded by strips of buckskin to save his fingers from burning while running balls, having for its companion a little bottle made from the point of an antelope's horn, scraped transparent, which contained the "medicine" used in baiting the traps. The old coon's face was sharp and thin, a long nose and chin hob-nobbing each other; and his head was always bent forward, giving him the appearance of being hump-backed. He *appeared* to look neither to the right nor left, but, in fact, his little twinkling eye was everywhere. He looked at no one he was addressing, always seeming to be thinking of something else than the subject of his discourse, speaking in a whining, thin, cracked voice, and in a tone that left the hearer in doubt whether he was laughing or crying. On the present occasion he had joined this band, and naturally assumed the leadership (for Bill ever refused to go in harness), in opposition to his usual practice, which was to hunt alone. His character was well known. Acquainted with every inch of the Far West, and with all the Indian tribes who inhabited it, he never failed to outwit his Red enemies, and generally made his appearance at the rendezvous, from his solitary expeditions, with galore of beaver, when numerous bands of trappers dropped in on foot, having been despoiled of their packs and animals by the very Indians through the midst of whom old Williams had contrived to pass unseen and unmolested. On occasions when he had been in company with others, and attacked by Indians, Bill invariably fought manfully, and with all the coolness that perfect indifference to death or danger could give, but always "on his own hook." His rifle cracked away merrily, and never spoke in vain; and in a charge—if ever it came to that—his keen-edged butcherknife tickled the fleece of many a Blackfoot. But at the same time, if he saw that discretion was the better part of valour, and affairs wore so cloudy an aspect as to render retreat advisable, he would first express his opinion in curt terms, and decisively, and, charging up his rifle, would take himself off, and "cache"* so effectually that to search for him was utterly useless. Thus, when with a large party of trappers, when any thing occurred which gave him

*Hide—from *cacher*.—RUXTON.

a hint that trouble was coming, or more Indians were about than he considered good for his animals, Bill was wont to exclaim—

"Do 'ee hyar now, boys, thar's sign about? this hoss feels like caching"; and, without more words, and stoically deaf to all remonstrances, he would forthwith proceed to pack his animals, talking the while to an old, crop-eared, raw-boned Nez-percé pony, his own particular saddle-horse, who, in dogged temper and iron hardiness, was a worthy companion of his self-willed master. This beast, as Bill seized his apishamore to lay upon its galled back, would express displeasure by humping its back and shaking its withers with a wincing motion, that always excited the ire of the old trapper; and no sooner had he laid the apishamore smoothly on the chafed skin, than a wriggle of the animal shook it off.

"Do 'ee hyar now, you darned crittur!" he would whine out, "can't 'ee keep quiet your old fleece now? Isn't this old coon putting out to save 'ee from the darned Injuns now, do 'ee hyar?" And then, continuing his work, and taking no notice of his comrades, who stood by bantering the eccentric trapper, he would soliloquise—"Do 'ee hyar now? This niggur sees sign ahead—he does; he'll be afoot afore long, if he don't keep his eye skinned—*he* will. *Injuns* is all about, they ar': Blackfoot at that. Can't come round this child— they can't, wagh!" And at last, his pack animals securely tied to the tail of his horse, he would mount, and throwing the rifle across the horn of his saddle, and without noticing his companions would drive the jingling spurs into his horse's gaunt sides, and muttering, "Can't come round this child—they can't!" would ride away; and nothing more would be seen or heard of him perhaps for months, when they would not unfrequently, themselves bereft of animals in the scrape he had foreseen, find him located in some solitary valley, in his lonely camp, with his animals securely picketed around, and his peltries safe.

However, if he took it into his head to keep company with a party, all felt perfectly secure under his charge. His iron frame defied fatigue, and, at night, his love for himself and his own animals was sufficient guarantee that the camp would be well guarded. As he rode ahead, his spurs jingling, and thumping the sides of his old horse at every step, he managed, with admirable dexterity, to take advantage of the best line of country to follow—avoiding the gullies and cañons and broken ground which would otherwise have impeded his advance. This tact appeared instinctive, for he looked neither right nor left, whilst continuing a course as straight as possible at the foot of the mountains. In selecting a camping site, he displayed equal skill: wood, water, and grass began to fill his thoughts towards sundown, and when these three requisites for a camping ground presented themselves, old Bill sprang from his saddle, unpacked his animals in a twinkling, and hobbled them, struck fire and ignited a few chips (leaving the rest to pack in the wood), lit his pipe, and enjoyed himself. On one occasion, when passing through the valley, they had come upon a band of fine buffalo cows, and shortly after camping, two of the party rode in with a good supply of fat fleece. One of the party was a "greenhorn" on his first hunt, and, fresh from a fort on Platte, was as yet uninitiated in the mysteries of mountain cooking. Bill, lazily smoking his pipe, called to him, as he happened to be nearest, to butcher off a piece of meat and put it in his pot. Markhead seized the fleece, and commenced innocently carving off a huge ration, when a gasping roar from the old trapper caused him to drop his knife.

"Ti-yah," growled Bill, "do 'ee hyar, now, you darned greenhorn, do 'ee spile fat cow like that whar you was raised? Them doin's won't shine in this crowd, boy, do 'e hyar, darn you? What! butcher meat across the grain! why, whar'll the blood be goin' to, you precious Spaniard? Down the grain I say," he continued in a severe tone of rebuke, "and let your flaps be long, or out the juice'll run slick—do 'ee hyar, now?" But this heretical error nearly cost the old trapper his appetite, and all night long he grumbled his horror at seeing "fat cow spiled in that fashion."

When two or three days' journey brought them to the end of the valley, and they commenced the passage of the mountain, their march was obstructed by all kinds of obstacles; although they had chosen what appeared to be a gap in the chain, and what was in fact the only practicable passage in that vicinity. They followed the cañon of a branch of the Yellow Stone, where it entered the mountain; but from this point it became a torrent, and it was only by dint of incredible exertions that they reached the summit of the ridge. Game was exceedingly scarce in the vicinity, and they suffered extremely from hunger, having, on more than one occasion, recourse to the parflêche soles of their mocassins to allay its pangs. Old Bill, however, never grumbled! He chewed away at his shoes with relish even, and as long as he had a pipeful of tobacco in his pouch, was a happy man. Starvation was as yet far off, for all their animals were in existence; but as they were in a country where it was difficult to procure a remount, each trapper hesitated to sacrifice one of his horses to his appetite.

From the summit of the ridge, Bill recognised the country on the opposite side to that whence they had just ascended as familiar to him, and pronounced it to be full of beaver, as well as abounding in the less desirable commodity of Indians. This was the valley lying about the lakes now called Eustis and Biddle, in which are many thermal and mineral springs, well known to the trappers by the names of the Soda, Beer, and Brimstone Springs, and regarded by them, with no little awe and curiosity, as being the breathing places of his Satanic majesty—considered, moreover, to be the "biggest kind" of "Medicine" to be found in the mountains. If truth be told, old Bill hardly relished the idea of entering the country, which he pronounced to be of "bad medicine" notoriety, but nevertheless agreed to guide them to the best trapping ground.

One day they reached a creek full of beaver signs, and determined to halt here and establish their headquarters, while they trapped in the neighbourhood. We must here observe, that at this period—which was one of considerable rivalry amongst the various trading companies in the Indian country—the Indians, having become possessed of arms and ammunition in great quantities, had grown unusually daring and persevering in their attacks on the white hunters who passed through their country, and consequently the trappers were compelled to roam about in larger bands for mutual protection, which, although it made them less liable to open attack, yet rendered it more difficult for them to pursue their calling without being discovered; for, where one or two men might pass unseen, the broad trail of large party, with its animals, was not likely to escape the sharp eyes of the cunning savages.

They had scarcely encamped when the old leader, who had sallied out a short distance from camp to reconnoitre the neighbourhood, returned with an Indian mocassin in his hand, and informed his companions that its late owner and others were about.

"Do 'ee hyar now, boys, thar's *Injuns* knocking round, and Blackfoot at that; but thar's plenty of beaver, too, and this child means trapping any how."

His companions were anxious to leave such dangerous vicinity; but the old fellow, contrary to his usual caution, determined to remain where he was—saying that there were Indians all over the country for that matter; and as they had determined to hunt here, he had made up his mind too—which was conclusive, and all agreed to stop where they were, in spite of the Indians. La Bonte killed a couple of mountain sheep close to camp, and they feasted rarely on the fat mutton that night, and were unmolested by marauding Blackfeet.

The next morning, leaving two of their number in camp, they started in parties of two, to hunt for beaver sign and set their traps. Markhead paired with one Batiste, Killbuck and La Bonte formed another couple, Meek and Marcelline another; two Canadians trapped together, and Bill Williams and another remained to guard the camp; but this last, leaving Bill mending his mocassins, started off to kill a mountain sheep, a band of which animals was visible.

Markhead and his companion, the first couple on the list, followed a creek, which entered that on which they had encamped, about ten miles distant. Beaver sign was abundant, and they had set eight traps, when Markhead came suddenly upon fresh Indian sign, where squaws had passed through the shrubbery on the banks of the stream to procure water, as he knew from observing a large stone placed by them in the stream, on which to stand to enable them to dip their kettles in the deepest water. Beckoning to his companion to follow, and cocking his rifle, he carefully pushed aside the bushes and noiselessly proceeded up the bank, when, creeping on hands and knees, he gained the top, and, looking from his hiding-place, descried three Indian huts standing on a little plateau near the creek. Smoke curled from the roofs of branches, but the skin doors were carefully closed, so that he was unable to distinguish the number of the inmates. At a little distance, however, he observed two or three squaws gathering wood, with the usual attendance of curs, whose acuteness in detecting the scent of strangers was much to be dreaded.

Markhead was a rash and daring young fellow, caring no more for Indians than he did for prairie dogs, and acting ever on the spur of the moment, and as his inclination dictated, regardless of consequences. He at once determined to enter the lodges, and attack the enemy, should any be there; and the other trapper was fain to join him in the enterprise. The lodges proved empty, but the fires were still burning and meat cooking upon them, to which the hungry hunters did ample justice, besides helping themselves to whatever goods and chattels, in the shape of leather and mocassins, took their fancy.

Gathering their spoil into a bundle, they sought their horses, which they had left tied under cover of the timber on the banks of the creek; and, mounting, took the back trail, to pick up their traps and remove from so dangerous a neighbourhood. They were approaching the spot where the first trap was set, a thick growth of ash and quaking-ash concealing the stream, when Markhead, who was riding ahead, observed the bushes agitated, as if some animal was making its way through them. He instantly stopped his horse, and his companion rode to his side, to inquire the cause of this abrupt halt. They were within a few yards of the belt of shrubs which skirted the stream; and before

Markhead had time to reply, a dozen swarthy heads and shoulders suddenly protruded from the leafy screen, and as many rifle-barrels and arrows were pointing at their breasts. Before the trappers had time to turn their horses and fly, a cloud of smoke burst from the thicket almost in their faces. Batiste, pierced with several balls, fell dead from his horse, and Markhead felt himself severely wounded. However, he struck the spurs into his horse; and as some half-score Blackfeet jumped with loud cries from their cover, he discharged his rifle amongst them, and galloped off, a volley of balls and arrows whistling after him. He drew no bit until he reined up at the camp-fire, where he found Bill quietly dressing a deer-skin. That worthy looked up from his work; and seeing Markhead's face streaming with blood, and the very unequivocal evidence of an Indian rencontre in the shape of an arrow sticking in his back, he asked,—"Do 'ee feel bad now, boy? Whar away you see them darned Blackfoot?"

"Well, pull this arrow out of my back, and may be I'll feel like telling," answered Markhead.

"Do 'ee hyar now! hold on till I've grained this cussed skin, will 'ee! Did 'ee ever see sich a darned pelt, now? it won't take the smoke any how I fix it." And Markhead was fain to wait the leisure of the imperturable old trapper, before he was eased of his annoying companion.

Old Bill expressed no surprise or grief when informed of the fate of poor Batiste. He said it was "just like greenhorns, runnin' into them cussed Blackfoot;" and observed that the defunct trapper, being only a Vide-poche, was "no account anyhow." Presently Killbuck and La Bonté galloped into camp, with another alarm of Indians. They had also been attacked suddenly by a band of Blackfeet, but, being in a more open country, had got clear off, after killing two of their assailants, whose scalps hung at the horns of their saddles. They had been in a different direction to that where Markhead and his companion had proceeded, and, from the signs they had observed, expressed their belief that the country was alive with Indians. Neither of these men had been wounded. Presently the two Canadians made their appearance on the bluff, galloping with might and maim to camp, and shouting "Indians, Indians," as they came. All being assembled, and a council held, it was determined to abandon the camp and neighbourhood immediately. Old Bill was already packing his animals, and as he pounded the saddle down on the withers of his old Rocinante, he muttered,—"Do 'ee hyar, now! this coon 'ull cache, *he* will." So mounting his horse, and leading his pack mule by a lariat, he bent over his saddle-horn, dug his ponderous rowels into the lank sides of his beast, and, without a word, struck up the bluff and disappeared.

The others, hastily gathering up their packs, and most of them having lost their traps, quickly followed his example, and "put out."

19

JOE MEEK:

A Good Joke and Some Bad Breaks

Whenever the early chroniclers of the Rocky Mountain fur trade mentioned the name of Joe Meek (1810–1875)—and rarely has a name been more inappropriate—it was his jokes and pranks and droll adventures that were remembered as often as his woodcraft, his marksmanship, and his reckless courage. A trusted friend of other adventurers who appear in this volume— Bridger, Carson, and Fitzpatrick—Meek was an exuberant and good-humored fellow, although sometimes foolhardy. There was the time, for instance, that he rapped a bear over the head with a stick to show he had guts, leaping back just in time to avoid its claws.

Born the son of a Virginia planter (or so he claimed in later years), Meek was described by a friend as being "a tall, broad-shouldered, powerful and handsome man." He was full-bearded and dark-eyed, and he had "plenty of animal courage and spirit"—which perhaps made up for what he lacked in learning and social graces. Heading west at eighteen, and joining a trapping expedition in the spring of 1829, he spent the next eleven years in the mountains, trapping, fighting bears and Indians, carousing at the summer rendezvous, and earning a reputation as a skilled mountainman and an amusing companion. In 1840, with the trapping business on the decline, Meek and his friend Robert (Doc) Newell struck out for Oregon with their Indian families, becoming the first to take wagons over the rugged final stretch of the Oregon Trail, and thus opening the way for the steady stream of emigrants that was soon pouring over the mountains. In the new country "Uncle Joe" Meek became a prominent figure in the Americanization movement and served in turn as a sheriff, a legislator, a United States marshal, and a major in the Indian war of 1855–1856. He died on his Hillsboro, Oregon, farm in 1875.

An artful storyteller who loved notoriety, Meek found a willing listener and publicist in the person of Mrs. Frances Fuller Victor, to whom he dictated his autobiography. Although Meek's stories must be taken with a grain of salt, Mrs. Victor's account does capture much of the man's humor and his cool bravery in the face of danger. The first tale is one that Meek liked to call "the story of the three bares."

The first fall [1830] on the Yellowstone, Hawkins and myself were coming up the river in search of camp, when we discovered a very large bar [bear] on the opposite bank. We shot across, and thought we had killed him, fur he laid quite still. As we wanted to take some trophy of our victory to camp, we tied our mules and left our guns, clothes, and everything except our knives and belts, and swum over to whar the bar war. But instead of being dead, as we expected, he sprung up as we come near him, and took after us. Then you ought to have seen two naked men run! It war a race for life, and a close one, too. But we made the river first. The bank war about fifteen feet high above the water, and the river ten or twelve feet deep; but we didn't halt. Overboard we went, the bar after us, and in the stream

From *The River of the West,* by Frances Fuller Victor (San Francisco: R. W. Bliss & Company, 1870), pp. 91–92, 189–194, 246–250.

about as quick as we war. The current war very strong, and the bar war about half way between Hawkins and me. Hawkins was trying to swim down stream faster than the current war carrying the bar, and I was a trying to hold back. You can reckon that I swam! Every moment I felt myself being washed into the yawning jaws of the mighty beast, whose head war up the stream, and his eyes on me. But the current war too strong for him, and swept him along as fast as it did me. All this time, not a long one, we war looking for some place to land where the bar could not overtake us. Hawkins war the first to make the shore, unknown to the bar, whose head war still up stream; and he set up such a whooping and yelling that the bar landed too, but on the opposite side. I made haste to follow Hawkins, who had landed on the side of the river we started from, either by design or good luck: and then we traveled back a mile and more to whar our mules war left—a bar on one side of the river, and *two bares* on the other!

[The following episode occured while Meek was traveling with Jim Bridger's brigade in the Yellowstone country.]

I war trapping on the Rocky Fork of the Yellowstone. I had been out from camp five days; and war solitary and alone, when I war discovered by a war party of Crows. They had the prairie, and I war forced to run for the Creek bottom; but the beaver had throwed the water out and made dams, so that my mule mired down. While I war struggling in the marsh, the Indians came after me, with tremendous yells; firing a random shot now and then, as they closed in on me.

When they war within about two rods of me, I brought old *Sally*, that is my gun, to my face, ready to fire, and then die; for I knew it war death this time, unless Providence interfered to save me: and I didn't think Providence would do it. But the head chief, when he saw the warlike looks of *Sally*, called out to me to put down my gun, and I should live.

Well, I liked to live,—being then in the prime of life; and though it hurt me powerful, I resolved to part with *Sally*. I laid her down. As I did so, the chief picked her up, and one of the braves sprang at me with a spear, and would have run me through, but the chief knocked him down with the butt of my gun. Then they led me forth to the high plain on the south side of the stream. There they called a halt, and I was given in charge of three women, while the warriors formed a ring to smoke and consult. This gave me an opportunity to count them: they numbered one hundred and eighty-seven men, nine boys, and three women.

After a smoke of three long hours, the chief, who war named "The Bold," called me in the ring, and said:

"I have known the whites for a long time, and I know them to be great liars, deserving death; but if *you* will tell the truth, you shall live."

Then I thought to myself, they will fetch the truth out of me, if thar is any in me. But his highness continued:

"Tell me whar are the whites you belong to; and what is your captain's name."

I said "Bridger is my captain's name; or, in the Crow tongue, *Casapy*, the Blanket chief." At this answer the chief seemed lost in thought. At last he asked me—

"How many men has he?"

I thought about telling the truth and living; but I said "forty," which war a tremendous lie; for thar war two hundred and forty. At this answer The Bold laughed:

"We will make them poor," said he; "and you shall live, but they shall die."

I thought to myself, "hardly;" but I said nothing. He then asked me whar I war to meet the camp, and I told him:—and then how many days before the camp would be thar; which I answered truly, for I wanted them to find the camp.

It war now late in the afternoon, and thar war a great bustle, getting ready for the march to meet Bridger. Two big Indians mounted my mule, but the women made me pack moccasins. The spies started first, and after awhile the main party. Seventy warriors traveled ahead of me: I war placed with the women and boys; and after us the balance of the braves. As we traveled along, the women would prod me with sticks, and laugh, and say "Masta Sheela," (which means white man,) "Masta sheela very poor now." The fair sex was very much amused.

We traveled that way till midnight, the two big bucks riding my mule, and I packing moccasins. Then we camped; the Indians in a ring, with me in the centre, to keep me safe. I didn't sleep very well that night. I'd a heap rather been in some other place.

The next morning we started on in the same order as before: and the squaws making fun of me all day; but I kept mightly quiet. When we stopped to cook that evening, I war set to work, and war head cook, and head waiter too. The third and the fourth day it war the same. I felt pretty bad when we struck camp on the last day: for I knew we must be coming near to Bridger, and that if any thing should go wrong, my life would pay the forfeit.

On the afternoon of the fourth day, the spies, who war in advance, looking out from a high hill, made a sign to the main party. In a moment all sat down. Directly they got another sign, and then they got up and moved on. I war as well up in Indian signs as they war; and I knew they had discovered white men. What war worse, I knew they would soon discover that I had been lying to them. All I had to do then war to trust to luck. Soon we came to the top of the hill, which overlooked the Yellowstone, from which I could see the plains below extending as far as the eye could reach, and about three miles off, the camp of my friends. My heart beat double quick about that time; and I once in a while put my hand to my head, to feel if my scalp war thar.

While I war watching our camp, I discovered that the horse guard had seen us, for I knew the sign he would make if he discovered Indians. I thought the camp a splendid sight that evening. It made a powerful show to me, who did not expect ever to see it after that day. And it *war* a fine sight any how, from the hill whar I stood. About two hundred and fifty men, and women and children in great numbers, and about a thousand horses and mules. Then the beautiful plain, and the sinking sun; and the herds of buffalo that could not be numbered; and the cedar hills, covered with elk,—I never saw so fine a sight as all that looked to me then!

When I turned my eyes on that savage Crow band, and saw the chief standing with his hand on his mouth, lost in amazement; and beheld the warriors' tomahawks and spears glittering in the sun, my heart war very little. Directly the chief turned to me with a horrible scowl. Said he:

"I promised that you should live if you told the truth; but you have told me a great lie."

Then the warriors gathered around, with their tomahawks in their hands; but I war showing off very brave, and kept my eyes fixed on the horse-guard who war approaching the hill to drive in the horses. This drew the attention of the chief, and the warriors too. Seeing that the guard war within about two hundred yards of us, the chief turned to me and ordered me to tell him to come up. I pretended to do what he said; but instead of that I howled out to him to stay off, or he would be killed; and to tell Bridger to try to treat with them, and get me away.

As quick as he could he ran to camp, and in a few minutes Bridger appeared, on his large white horse. He came up to within three hundred yards of us, and called out to me, asking who the Indians war. I answered "Crows." He then told me to say to the chief he wished him to send one of his sub-chiefs to smoke with him.

All this time my heart beat terribly hard. I don't know now why they didn't kill me at once; but the head chief seemed overcome with surprise. When I repeated to him what Bridger said, he reflected a moment, and then ordered the second chief, called Little-Gun, to go and smoke with Bridger. But they kept on preparing for war; getting on their paint and feathers, arranging their scalp locks, selecting their arrows, and getting their ammunition ready.

While this war going on, Little-Gun had approached to within about a hundred yards of Bridger; when, according to the Crow laws of war, each war forced to strip himself, and proceed the remaining distance in a state of nudity, and kiss and embrace. While this interesting ceremony war being performed, five of Bridger's men had followed him, keeping in a ravine until they got within shooting distance, when they showed themselves, and cut off the return of Little-Gun, thus making a prisoner of him.

If you think my heart did not jump up when I saw that, you think wrong. I knew it war kill or cure, now. Every Indian snatched a weapon, and fierce threats of war howled against me. But all at once about a hundred of our trappers appeared on the scene. At the same time Bridger called to me, to tell me to propose to the chief to exchange me for Little-Gun. I explained to The Bold what Bridger wanted to do, and he sullenly consented: for, he said, he could not afford to give a chief for one white dog's scalp. I war then allowed to go towards my camp and Little-Gun towards his; and the rescue I hardly hoped for war accomplished.

In the evening the chief, with forty of his braves, visited Bridger and made a treaty of three months They said they war formerly at war with whites; but that they desired to be friendly with them now, so that together they might fight the Blackfeet, who war everybody's enemies. As for me, they returned me my mule, gun, and beaver packs, and said my name should be *Shiam Shaspusia*, for I could out-lie the Crows.

[Asked about how he hunted buffalo, Joe Meek revealed something of the mountainman's attitude toward his comrades and toward death.]

Waal, there is a good deal of sport in runnin' buffalo. When the camp discovered a band, then every man that wanted to run, made haste to catch his buffalo horse. We sometimes went out thirty or forty strong; sometimes two or three, and at other times a large party started on the hunt; the more the merrier. We alway had great bantering about our horses, each man, according to his own account, having the best one.

When we first start we ride slow, so as not to alarm the buffalo. The nearer we come to the band the greater our excitement. The horses seem to feel it too, and are worrying to be off. When we come so near that the band starts, then the word is given, our horses' mettle is up, and away we go!

Thar may be ten thousand in a band. Directly we crowd them so close that nothing can be seen but dust, nor anything heard but the roar of their trampling and bellowing. The hunger now keeps close on their heels to escape being blinded by the dust, which does not rise as high as a man on horseback, for thirty yards behind the animals. As soon as we are close enough the firing begins, and the band is on the run; and a herd of buffalo can run about as fast as a good race-horse. How they *do* thunder along! They give us a pretty sharp race. Take care! Down goes a rider, and away goes his horse with the band. Do you think we stopped to look after the fallen man? Not we. We rather thought that war fun, and if he got killed, why, "he war unlucky, that war all. Plenty more men: couldn't bother about him."

Thar's a fat cow ahead. I force my way through the band to come up with her. The buffalo crowd around so that I have to put my foot on them, now on one side, now the other, to keep them off my horse. It is lively work, I can tell you. A man has to look sharp not to be run down by the band pressing him on; buffalo and horse at the top of their speed.

Look out; thar's a ravine ahead, as you can see by the plunge which the band makes. Hold up! or somebody goes to the devil now. If the band is large it fills the ravine full to the brim, and the hindmost of the herd pass over on top of the foremost. It requires horsemanship not to be carried over without our own consent; but then we mountain-men are *all* good horsemen. Over the ravine we go; but we do it our own way.

We keep up the chase for about four miles, selecting our game as we run, and killing a number of fat cows to each man; some more and some less. When our horses are tired we slacken up, and turn back. We meet the campkeepers with pack-horses. They soon butcher, pack up the meat, and we all return to camp, whar we laugh at each other's mishaps, and eat fat meat: and this constitutes the glory of mountain life. . . .

One time Kit Carson and myself, and a little Frenchman, named Marteau, went to run buffalo on Powder River. When we came in sight of the band it war agreed that Kit and the Frenchman should do the running, and I should stay with the pack animals. The weather war very cold and I didn't like my part of the duty much.

The Frenchman's horse couldn't run; so I lent him mine. Kit rode his own; not a good buffalo horse either. In running, my horse fell with the Frenchman, and nearly killed him. Kit, who couldn't make his horse catch, jumped off, and caught mine, and tried it again. This time he came up with the band, and killed four fat cows.

When I came up with the pack-anmals, I asked Kit how he came by my horse. He explained, and wanted to know if I had seen anything of Marteau: said my horse had fallen with him, and he thought killed him. "You go over the other side of the hill, and see," said Kit.

"What'll I do with him if he is dead?" said I.

"Can't you pack him to camp?"

"Pack hell" said I; "I should rather pack a load of meat."

"Waal," said Kit, "I'll butcher, if you'll go over and see, anyhow."

So I went over, and found the dead man leaning his head on his hand, and groaning; for he war pretty bad hurt. I got him on his horse, though, after a while, and took him back to whar Kit war at work. We soon finished the butchering job, and started back to camp with our wounded Frenchman, and three loads of fat meat.

"You were not very compassionate toward each other, in the mountains?" [Meek's interviewer asked at this point.]

"That war not our business. We had no time for such things. Besides, live men war what we wanted; dead ones war of no account."

20

ZENAS LEONARD:

Snowbound in the Rockies

*One of the best accounts of the everyday life of the trapper in
the Far West, ranking second only to Osborne Russell's* Journal,
is the Narrative of Zenas Leonard, *first published in 1839.
Leonard (1809–1857), who was born in Clearfield, Pennsylvania, spent the early part of his life working on his father's
farm. Little is known of his personality or his appearance, but
the life of a farmer must have irked him considerably, for the day
he turned twenty-one he threw down the hoe and headed for St.
Louis, determined to become a trapper. In the spring of 1831 he
was taken on as a clerk by a company of trappers and traders
then leaving for the Rocky Mountains. During the journey the
party twice nearly starved and Leonard himself came within a
hair's-breadth of being killed by Indians. The following year he
was at the summer rendezvous at Pierre's Hole, in Idaho, where
he took part in the famous battle against the Blackfeet that was
recorded (from Leonard's and other accounts) in Washington
Irving's* Bonneville.
  In 1833 Leonard joined Captain Joe Walker's expedition

273

down the Humboldt River to the Pacific, thus helping to open that important overland route to California and probably becoming one of the first white men to see the Yosemite Valley. He spent another year in the mountains and then in 1835 returned to Pennsylvania, where constant demands by friends that he retell his adventures finally persuaded him to write them down. But life in Pennsylvania seemed to appeal to him less than ever, for he stayed in Clearfield just long enough to see his Narrative *published in the local newspaper, and then returned to the West. Eventually he settled in Sibley, Missouri, where he lived as a trader until his death.*

The accuracy of Leonard's Narrative *leaves much to be desired, particularly with regard to incidents and dates, since part of his journals were either lost or stolen and he was often forced to rely on memory alone. Nevertheless, he presents a vivid picture of the trapper's life and his accounts of struggling to survive in the wilderness are some of the most exciting to be found. The following selection describes Leonard's first trip to the mountains in 1831, and the hardships and dangers he and his companions encountered on the way.*

The Company under the command of Captains Gant and Blackwell, left St. Louis on the 24th of April, 1831. Each man was furnished with the necessary equipments for the expedition—such as traps, guns, &c.; also horses and goods of various descriptions, to trade with the Indians for furs and Buffaloe robes. We continued our journey in a western direction, in the state of Missouri, on the south side of the Missouri river, through a country thinly inhabited by the whites and friendly Indians, until we arrived at Fort Osage the extreme point of the white settlement. Here we remained several days and purchased and packed up a sufficiency of provision, as we then thought; for our subsistance through the wilderness to what is called the Buffaloe country; a distance of about 200 miles. From thence we

From *The Adventures of Zenas Leonard, Fur Tader and Tapper,* 1831–1836 (1839). Reprinted by W. F. Wagner, ed. (Cleveland: 1904), pp. 59–81.

proceeded up the Missouri until we arrived at the mouth of the Kansas river, where we again tarried two or three days, for the purpose of trading some goods to the Kansas Indians for corn, moccasins, &c. . . .

From thence we proceeded on our journey up the river. We found the country here beautiful indeed—abounding with the most delightful prairies, with here & there a small brook, winding its way to the river, the margins of which are adorned with the lofty Pine and Cedar tree. These prairies were completely covered with fine low grass, and decorated with beautiful flowers of various colors; and some of them are so extensive and clear of timber and brush that the eye might search in vain for an object to rest upon. I have seen beautiful and enchanting sceneries depicted by the artist, but never any thing to equal the work of rude nature in those prairies. In the spring of the year when the grass is green and the blossoms fresh, they present an appearance, which for beauty and charms, is beyond the art of man to depict.

We continued on our journey westward, up the republican fork of Kanzas river—passing through these prairies, till the 20th of June, when we happened on another tribe of Indians, called the Otoes, from whom we obtained a quantity of sweet corn and some wild turnips; we also understood from this tribe that it was much farther to the Buffaloe country than we had before anticipated, and that game in that direction, was very scarce. From thence we proceeded in a N.W. direction, up the Republican Branch—finding but very little game; and on the 21st of June we killed our last beef, which was equally divided to each mess. Here we began to feel somewhat alarmed—starvation began to stare us in the face, and some of the company became refractory and were for turning back. Stimulated, however, by the hope of reaching game in a few days, we continued in the direction of the Buffaloe country. Hunters were sent out daily in quest of game, but as often returned without any. We still continued to travel—subsisting chiefly on muscles and small fish which we caught in the river; finally the Captain ordered two of the best horses to be killed, to keep the company from starving, which was immediately done, and the carcasses equally distributed to each mess. We proceeded on our journey slowly—sending out hunters as usual, but without success; game appeared to become scarcer and scarcer, and in a few days our provision (if I may call it such) again exhausted. Finding it impossible, owing to the scarcity of game, to continue any further up the Republican, we concluded to leave it and steer for the head waters of the Missouri.* Accordingly, we changed our direction as well as our manner of travelling. Instead of travelling in a close mat as heretofore, we now scattered over a considerable range of country for the purpose of hunting, leaving ten or twelve men only to bring on the pack-mules, and at night we would collect together with our game, which generally consisted of wolves, wild cats, muscles, and some times an Antelope. In this way we continued our journey slowly, some of the company being half starved to death, for eight or ten days, eating at night what little game we caught through the day; at last we collected one evening, I think about the middle of July, in a barren prairie where we could not get wood enough to make a fire, much less any thing to cook on it—not a mouthful of game was returned that evening. This was a trying time indeed— despondency & horror was depicted in the countenance of every man, and the enquiry, "what shall we do," was passed from every lip. In this condition, without fire or food, we spent the knight. In the morning we held a consultation to decide whether to continue in that direction or turn. We finally agreed to proceed straight ahead & by night we arrived on the banks of the river Platte, a distance of about ten miles from where we had encamped the night before, where we pitched our tents for the night. Most of our hunters had collected without game, and pronounced it very scarce, and we were about to kill another of our horses, when we saw one of our hunters approaching us with unusual rapidity, without his gun or hat and his countenance indicating great excitement. I never wish to feel more

---

*The river Platte is no doubt the one here referred to, and not the Missouri—WAGNER.

pleasure than I did as he rushed into the tent exclaiming, "I have killed two big Buck Elk!" Early the next morning—refreshed with what meat we had obtained and animated and encouraged with the hope of obtaining plenty more, we set out with unusual fine spirits. We continued to travel up the river Platte for several days—passing through extensive barren prairies, the soil being too poor even to produce grass; and game exceedingly scarce. Some of us again became alarmed, and one morning when the roll was called it was discovered that two of the company had stolen two of the best horses and started back to the state of Missouri. This had a bad effect—it impaired that full confidence which had heretofore existed between the members of the company, but we continued up the river and in a few days arrived at the Buffaloe country. After encamping, on a pleasant evening, in the latter part of July, some of the company discovered two Buffaloe bulls feeding in the prairie, about half a mile from camp. Four or five of us immediately mounted our horses and started to take them; but returned in a short time without success—one of the men having got his arm broken, by falling from his horse. But the next day we happened on a large drove of these animals, and killed six or seven of them. The flesh of the Buffaloe is the wholesomest and most palatable of meat kind. The male of these animals are much the largest—weighing from 1000 to 15000 pounds, and may be seen in droves of hundreds feeding in the plains. We remained here several days feasting upon Buffaloe meat. From thence proceeded up the river; finding an abundance of game, such as Buffaloe, Elk, Deer and Antelope—and killing more or less every day. On the first day of August we arrived at the forks of the river Platte; and by means of boats made of buffaloe skins, crossed the south Fork and continued our journey up the valley. Here the soil appeared to be very poor, producing but little grass; and in some places for three or four miles we would travel over sand plains where there were scarcely a spear of grass to be seen. Immediately on the water courses the soil is better and produces good grass. As we travelled up the river, we occasionally came in contact with cliffs of rock and hard clay, from two to three hundred feet above the level of the plain. One of these cliffs is very peculiar in its appearance, and is known among the whites as "Chimney cliff," and among the natives as "Elk Peak." It is only about 150 yards in circumference at its basis, and about 25 at the summit; and projects into the air to the heighth of 300 feet. Its towering summit may be seen at the distance of 15 or 20 miles—presenting the appearance of some huge fabric that had been constructed by the art of man.

We continued to travel in a western direction—found game plenty—met with no difficulty in getting along; and on the 27th of August we arrived at the junction of the Laramies river with the river Platte*—about 12 or 1300 miles from the United States, and two or three hundred from the top of the Rocky Mountains. Here we stopped for the purpose of reconnoitering. Several scouting parties were sent out in search of Beaver signs, who returned in a few days and reported that they had found Beaver signs, &c. Capt. Gant then gave orders to make preparations for trapping. Accordingly the company was divided into parties of from 15 to 20 men in each party, with their respective captains placed over them—and directed by Captain Gant in what direction to go. Captain Washburn ascended the Timber Fork; Captain Stephens the Laramies; Captain Gant the Sweet Water—all of which empty into the river Platte near the same place. Each of these companies were directed to ascend these rivers until they found Beaver sufficiently plenty for trapping, or till the snow and cold weather compelled them to stop; at which event they were to return to the mouth of the Laramies river, to pass the winter together. While at this place [we] engaged in secreting our merchandize, which we did by digging a hole in the ground, sufficiently large to contain them, and covering them over so that the Indians might not discover them. . . .

*The route followed after reaching the Platte to the mouth of the Laramie later became a portion of the celebrated Oregon Trail, and Chimney Rock one of its most celebrated landmarks—WAGNER.

On the 4th of September, having every thing in readiness, after shaking hands all around, we separated, each party to meander the rivers that had been respectively allotted to them, with the intention, if nothing happened them, of re-assembling in the latter part of December, to spend the winter together.

Mr. Stephen's party [of twenty-one men, including the narrator] commenced their tour up the Laramies river and continued several days without any important occurrence. Found the prairies or plains in this direction very extensive—unobstructed with timber or brush—handsomely situated, with her and there a small creek passing through them, and in some places literally covered with game, such as Buffaloe, White and Black tailed Deer, Grizzly, Red, and White Bear, Elk, Prairie Dog, wild Goat, Big horned mountain Sheep, Antelope, &c.

On the 20th of Sept. we stopped on the bank of a small creek, to let our horses graze, at the junction of which we seen signs of beaver. Two hunters were sent up this stream with their traps and guns on search of beaver, who, if they should be successful in finding game, were not to return until the next day—the main body of the company to move on slowly. After travelling several miles, & hearing nothing of our hunters, we deemed it advisable to encamp for the night, which we did. About midnight we were alarmed by the report of two rifles. Supposing it to be hostile Indians, we put ourselves in an attitude of defence, as soon as possible by throwing up a fort of logs and brush, and keeping up sentinels until morning. On the next morning, about sun rise the two hunters came in, and informed us that it was the report of their guns that had alarmed us, as they had fired them off near the spot where they had expected to find the camp, with the hope of receiving some signal. They had meandered the creek till they came to beaver dams, where they set their traps and turned their horses out to pasture; and were busily engaged in constructing a camp to pass the night in, when they discovered, at a short distance off, a tremendous Grizzly Bear, rushing upon them at a furious rate.—They immediately sprang to their rifles which were standing against a tree hard-by, one of which was single and the other double triggered; unfortunately in the hurry, the one that was accustomed to the single trigger, caught up the double triggered gun, and when the bear came upon him, not having set the trigger, he could not get his gun off; and the animal approaching within a few feet of him, he was obliged to commence beating it over the head with his gun. Bruin, thinking this rather rough usage, turned his attention to the man with the single triggered gun, who, in trying to set the trigger (supposing he had the double triggered gun) had fired it off, and was also obliged to fall to beating the ferocious animal with his gun; finally, it left them without doing much injury, except tearing the sleeve off one of their coats and biting him through the hand. Four men were immediately despatched for the traps, who returned in the evening with seven or eight beaver. The Grizzly Bear is the most ferocious animal that inhabits the prairies, and are very numerous. They no sooner see you than they will make at you with open mouth. If you stand still, they will come within two or three yards of you, and stand upon their hind feet, and look you in the face, if you have fortitude enough to face them, they will turn and run off; but if you turn they will most assuredly tear you to pieces; furnishing strong proof of the fact, that no wild beast, however daring and ferocious, unless wounded, will attack the face of man.

On the morning of the 22d Sept. we again renewed our tour travelling at the rate of 8 or 10 miles a day; catching a few Beaver, as we passed along—nothing strange occurring until the 30th, when we arrived at the foot of a great mountain, through which the Laramies passes, We attempted to follow the river through the mountain, but we soon found this to be impossible, as the bluffs of huge rocks projecting several hundred feet high, closed it to the very current. We then turned down the side of the mountain, on search of a place to cross it. On the 1st day of Oct. we came to a Buffaloe trail crossing the mountain, and after ascending to near the summit, we encamped for the night. About midnight it commenced snowing, and continued to fall so fast that we were obliged to remain there until the morning of the 4th, when we again renewed our journey, and in the evening we arrived in the valley on the North or West side of the mountain. Here, finding no snow & Beaver signs plenty, we deemed it advisable to remain a few days for the purpose of trapping, and the first night we caught 20 Beaver. We remained here until the 12th, when we proceeded eight or ten miles further up the South fork of the river, and again encamped for the purpose of trapping. On the 18th, finding Beaver getting rather scarce, we proceeded a few miles further up the valley, and encamped again.

This valley is supposed to be 70 or 80 miles long, and from 10 to 15 miles wide; and is enclosed on the one side by the main chain of the Rocky Mountains, and on the other by great Piney Hills, running out from the main body of the mountain, with the river Laramies passing through the centre of it, the banks of which are covered with timber, from ¼ to ½ a mile wide. Out side of this timber, the plain is completely smooth; and on a clear morning, by taking a view with a spyglass, you can see the different kinds of game that inhabit these plains, such as Buffaloe, Bear, Deer, Elk, Antelope, Bighorn, Wolves, &c. These plains are poor, sandy and level—the grass thin and short.

Oct. 22d. The nights getting somewhat cold, and snow falling more or less every day, we began to make preparations to return to our winter quarters, at the mouth of the Laramies river; and on the 25th commenced our tour down the river. On the 28th we arrived at the mountain, that we crossed going up, but found it impossible, owing to the enormous depth of the snow to pass over it. On the morning of the 30th we started a number of men up and down the valley, on search of a place to cross the mountain, who returned the next day and reported that they had found no passing place over the mountain; when under these circumstances a majority of the company decided in favor of encamping in this valley for the winter, and when the ice melted out of the river, in the spring, commence trapping until such times as the snow melted off the mountain; when we would return to the mouth of the river, where we had secreted our goods.

On the 1st day of November we commenced travelling up the valley, on search of a suitable place to pass the winter, and on the evening of the 4th, we arrived at a large grove of Cottonwood timber, which we deemed suitable for encamping in.—Several weeks were spent in building houses, stables, &c. necessary for ourselves, and horses during the winter season.—This being done, we commenced killing Buffaloe, and hanging up the choice pieces to dry, so that if they should leave the valley we would have a sufficient quantity of meat to last us until spring. We also killed Deer, Bighorn Sheep, Elk, Antelope, &c., and dressed the hides to make moccasins. . . .

About the 1st of December finding our horses getting very poor, we thought it necessary to commence feeding them on Cottonwood bark; for which purpose each man turned out and pealed and collected a quantity of this bark, from the grove in which we were encamped for his horses; but to our utter surprise and discomfiture, on presentng it to them they would not eat it, and upon examining it by tasting, we found it to be the bitter, instead of the sweet Cottonwood. Immediately upon finding we were deceived, men were despatched up and down the valley, on search of Sweet Cottonwood, but returned without success. Several weeks were spent in fruitless exertion to obtain feed for our horses; finally we were compelled to give it up, and agreed that our horses must all starve to death. The great depth of the snow, and the extreme coldness of the weather, soon prevented our horses from getting any thing to subsist upon, & they commenced dying. It seldom happened during all our difficulties, that my sympathies were more sensibly touched, than on viewing these starving creatures. I would willingly have divided my provision with my horses, if they would have eat it.

On new-yearsday, notwithstanding our horses were nearly all dead, as being fully satisfied that the few that were yet living must die soon, we concluded to have a feast in our best style; for which purpose we made preparation by sending out four of our best hunters, to get a choice piece of meat for the occasion. These men killed ten Buffaloe, from which they selected one of the fattest humps they could find and brought in, and after roasting it handsomely before the fire, we all seated ourselves upon the ground, encircling, what we there called a splendid repast to dine upon. Feasting sumptuously, cracking a few jokes, taking a few rounds with our rifles, and wishing heartily for some liquor, having none at that place we spent the day.

On the 8th . . . we found our horses . . . well nigh defunct. Here we were in this valley, surrounded on either side by insurmountable barriers of snow, with all our merchandise and nothing to pack it upon, but two mules—all the rest of our horses being dead. For ourselves we had plenty to eat, and were growing fat and uneasy;—but how we were to extricate ourselves from this perilous situation, was a question of deep and absorbing interest to each individual. About the 10th we held a consultation, to decide what measures should be taken for our relief. Mr. Stephens, our pilot, having been at Santafee, in New Mexico, some 8 or 10 years previous, informed the company that horses in that place, were very cheap; and that he was of the opinion he could take them to it, if they saw proper to follow him. It was finally agreed upon by the company, that a part of them should start for Santafee; but not, however, without a good deal of confusion; as many were of the opinion that the snow on the mountain in the direction of Santafee, would be found to be as insurmountable, as in the direction of their merchandize, and also that the distance was too great to attempt to travel on foot, at that season of the year. It appearing from the maps to be little short of 800 miles.

On the morning of the 14th, finding every thing in readiness for our Santafee trip, we set out, each man with his bedding, rifle and nine Beaver skins, packed upon his back; leaving four men only to take care of our merchandize, and the two mules. The beaver skins we took for the purpose of trading to the inhabitants of Santafee for horses, mules, &c. We appointed from the middle of April till the middle of may, as our time for returning; and if we did not return within that time, our four men were to wait no longer, but return to the mouth of the Laramies river, to meet the rest of the company. We continued in the direction of Santafee, without any extraordinary occurrence, for several days—found game plenty and but little snow, until we arrived at the foot of a great mountain, which appeared to be totally covered with snow. Here we though it advisable to kill and jirk some buffaloe meat, to eat while crossing this mountain, after which we continued our course; finding much difficulty in travelling, owing to the stormy weather & deep snow—so much so indeed, that had it not been for a path made by the buffaloe bulls it would have been impossible to travel.

The channel of the river where it passed through these mountains is quite narrow in places and the banks very steep. In such places the beaver build their dams from bank to bank; and when they become old the beaver leave them and they break and overflow the ground, which then produces a kind of flag grass. In the fall of the year, the Buffaloe collect in such places to eat this grass, and when the snow falls too deep they retreat to the plains; and it was in these trails that we ascended the mountain.

We still continued our course along this buffaloe path, which led us to the top of the mountain; nothing occurring more than it continued to snow day and night. On the 25th we arrived on the top of the mountain, and wishing to take a view of the country, if it should cease snowing. In the morning it still continued to snow so rapidly that we were obliged to remain in camp all day, and about the middle of the day, we eat the last of our jirk, and that evening we were obliged to go to bed supperless.

On the 29th it still continued to snow, and having nothing to eat, we thought it high time to be making some move, for our preservation, or we must perish in this lonely wilderness. The question then arose, shall we return to the valley from whence we came, or continue in the direction of

Santafee. This question caused considerable disturbance. Those who were in favor of going ahead, argued that it was too far back to game—that it would be impossible to return before starving to death; while those who were for return- ing contended that it was the highth of imprudence, to proceed in the direction of Santafee. Accordingly we made preparations, and started. We travelled across the summit of the mountain, where we found a plain about a mile wide, which with great difficulty, owing the the fierceness of the wind, we succeeded in crossing; but when we attempted to go into the timber, on the opposite side from the mountain, we found it impossible, in consequence of the depth of the snow, and were obliged to turn back and re-cross the plain. As we returned by the fire we had made going over the plain the first time, we halted for the purpose of mutually deciding what to do; when it was determined by the com- pany, that we would, if possible, return to our four men & two mules. We then started on search of the buffaloe path which we had followed the top of the mountain; but owing to the strong wind, that had blew for several days, and the increased depth of the snow, it was invisible. We then attempted to travel in the snow without the path, but we found this equally as impossible, as in the direction of Santafee.

Here we were, in a desolate wilderness, uninhabited (at that season of the year) by even the hardy savage or wild beast—surrounded on either side by huge mountains of snow, without one mouthful to eat, save a few beaver skins—our eyes almost destroyed by the piercing wind, and our bodies at times almost buried by the flakes of snow which were driven before it. Oh! how heartily I wished myself at home; but wishing, such a case appeared useless—action alone could save us. We had not even leather to make snow shoes, but as good fortune would have it, some of the men had the front part of their pan- taloons lined with deer skin, and others had great coats of different kinds of skin, which we collected together to make snow shoes of. This appeared to present to us the only means of escape from starvation and death. After gathering up every thing of leather kind that could be found, we got to making snow shoes, and by morning each man was furnished with a pair. But what were we to subsist upon while crossing the mountain, was a painful question that agitated every bosom, and employed every tongue in company. Provision, we had none, of any description; having eaten every thing we had that could be eat with the exception of a few beaver skins, and, after having fasted several days, to attempt to travel the distance of the valley, without any thing to eat, appeared almost worse than useless. Thinking, however, that we might as well perish one place as another, and that it was the best to make an exertion to save ourselves; and after each man had selected two of the best beaver skins to eat as he travelled along, we hung the remainder upon a tree, and started to try our fortune with the snow shoes. Owing to the softness of the snow, and the poor construction of our snow shoes, we soon found this to be a difficult and laborious mode of travelling. The first day after we started with our snow shoes travelled but three or four miles and encamped for the night, which, for want of a good fire, we passed in the most distressing manner. Wood was plenty but we were unable to get it, and it kept one or two of the men busy to keep what little fire we had from going out as it melted the snow and sunk down. On the morning [30th Jan.] after roasting and eating some of our beaver skins, we continued our journey through the snow. In this way we continued to travel until the first day of February, in the afternoon, when we came to where the crust on the snow was sufficiently strong to carry us. Here we could travel somewhat faster, but at the best not much faster than a man could crawl on his hands and feet, as some of them from hunger and cold were almost insensible of their situation, and so weak that they could scarcely stand on their feet, much less walk at speed. As we approached the foot of the mountain the snow became softer and would not carry us. This caused the most resolute despair, as it was obviously impossible, owing to extreme weakness, for us to wade much further through the snow. As we moved down the mountain plunging and falling through the snow, we approached a large spruce or cedar tree, the drooping branches of which had prevented the snow from falling to the ground about its trunk—here we halted to rest. While collected under the sheltering bows of this tree, viewing, with horrified feelings, the wayworn, and despairing countenances of each other, a Mr. Carter, a Virginian, who was probably the nighest exhausted of any of the company, burst into tears and said, "here I must die." This made a great impression upon the remainder of the company, and they all, with the exception of a Mr. Hockday and myself, despaired of going any further. Mr. Hockday, however, after some persuasion, telling them that if they had strength to follow us we would break the road as far as possible, if not out to the valley, succeeded in getting them started once more.—Mr. Hockday was a large muscular man, as hardy as a mule and as resolute as a lion; yet kind and affectionate. He was then decidedly the stoutest man in the company, and myself, probably the next stoutest. As for our captain, Mr. Stephens, he was amongst the weakest of the company.

We resumed our journey, and continued to crawl along through the deep snow slowly till the evening of the fourth, when we arrived in the plain at the foot of the mountain. Here we found the snow so shallow that we could dispense with the use of our snow shoes; and while in the act of taking them off some of the men discovered, at the distance of 70 or 80 yards; two animals feeding in the brush, which they supposed to be buffaloe, but from blindness, caused by weakness and pine smoke, could not be positive. Mr. Hockday and I were selected to approach and kill one of the animals without regard to what they might prove to be, while the remainder of the company were to go to a neighboring grove of timber and kindle a fire. Having used our guns as walking canes in the snow, we found them much out of order, and were obliged to draw out the old loads and put in new ones, before attempting to shoot. After taking every precaution we deemed necessary to insure success, we started and crawled along on our hands and knees, until we approached within ten or fifteen steps of the animals, when Mr. Hockday prepared to shoot; but upon finding that he could not see the sight of the gun or hold it at arms length, forbore, and proposed to me to shoot. I accordingly fixed myself and pulled trigger. My gun missed fire! I never was so wrecked with agitation as at that moment. "There," said I, "our game is gone, and we are not able to follow it much further;" but as good fortune had it, the Buffaloe, (for such we had discovered them to be,) did not see nor smell us, and after raising their heads out of the snow, and looking around for a few moments for the cause of the noise, again commenced feeding. I then picked the flint of my gun, fired and broke the back of one of the Buffaloe, my ball not taking the effect within 18 inches of where I thought I aimed.—The men in the grove of timber, on hearing the report of my rifle came staggering forth to learn the result, and when they received the heart-cheering intelligence of success they raised a shout of joy. It was amusing to witness the conduct of some of the men on this occasion. Before we had caught the buffaloe they appeared scarcely able to speak—but a moment after that, were able to hollow like Indians at war. I will not describe the scene that followed here—the reader may imagine it——an account of it would be repulsive and offensive rather than agreeable. This was the ninth day since we had eaten any thing but dried beaver skins. We remained at this place four days feasting upon the carcass of this Buffaloe, during which time we recruited considerably in strength and spirits, and on the 8th we resumed our journey down the river in search of our four men and mules, and soon landed in the valley where game was plenty, and but little snow to obstruct our march. We continued our journey, killing plenty of game and living well, without any strange occurrence until the 14th, when we halted within a short distance of our old camp, and sent two or three of our worst looking men ahead to see whether they would be recognized by the four men. They were not know immediately on arriving at the camp, but no sooner engaged in conversation than they were recognized by the four men, and heartily welcomed back.

Here we remained at our old station until the 14th of March, during which period, having plenty of good buffaloe meat to eat we regained our usual health and appearance.

21

THOMAS FITZPATRICK:
A Close Call

*Thomas Fitzpatrick (c. 1799–1854) was one of the more promi-
nent of the early Western mountainmen. History has not dealt
so well with him as with his contemporaries, Jim Bridger and Kit
Carson, but in his day he was widely known and respected as a
trapper and trader. Born in County Cavan, Ireland, in about
1799, he had come to America while still in his teens and,
drifting west, had established a reputation as a trapper and
woodsman in the Rockies by the time he was twenty-five. John
C. Frémont and Stephen Kearny, in their renowned explorations of the West, esteemed him as one of the best guides. The
Cheyennes and Arapahoes, whom he served as agent and trader
from 1846 until his death, considered him "the one fair agent"
they had ever had. They called him Broken Hand or Three
Fingers because of an injury he had suffered when a rifle ex-
ploded; and his hair was said to have turned prematurely gray
from the harrowing experiences he had had on the frontier. The
most famous of his adventures, recorded by Zenas Leonard in
his* Narrative, *began in June 1832, when Fitzpatrick was out
hunting and trapping in the Oregon Country with a large party*

of men, Leonard among them. Fitzpatrick decided to try his luck on his own, promising to return to camp in a few days. When he failed to reappear, however, his comrades began to fear that he had fallen prey to the Blackfeet or to some wild animal. Rescue parties were quickly sent out and, as Leonard recalled, "diligent search was kept up for some time." Fitzpatrick "was at length found on the banks of the Pieres river . . . completely exhausted, and so much wasted in flesh, and deformed in dress, that, under other circumstances, he would not have been recognized. The poor man was reduced to a skeleton, and was almost senseless. When his deliverers spoke of taking him to camp, he scarcely seemed to comprehend their meaning." Finally, after much rest and care, Fitzpatrick was able to tell his friends what had happened. Leonard gives Fitzpatrick's story "in his own words."

For three or four days after I left the company I travelled without any difficulty, and at great speed, but the fourth and fifth, the weather being dull and cloudy, I got strayed from my course, and soon found myself in the midst of a rough hilly country, abounding with large loose rocks which some places almost prevented me from passing at all, and covered with various kinds of timber of the most magnif[i]cent description. In passing the nights in these solitudes my rest was constantly disturbed by the dismal howl of the wolf and the fierce growl of the bear—which animals were very numerous and would frequently approach within a few steps and threaten to devour me. One day after a toilsome ride, I dismounted, turned my horse loose to graze and seated myself on a rock, with the little remaining provision I had, to refresh myself. While thus seated resting my wearied limbs, and satisfying the gnawings of hunger, I was suddenly startled by a scrambling on the rocks immediately in my rear. I turned round and beheld a huge bear approaching me in double quick time. I

From *The Adventures of Zenas Leonard, Fur Trader and Trapper, 1831–1836* (1839) Reprinted by W. F. Wagner, ed. (Cleveland: 1904), pp. 103–109.

instantly sprang to my feet, for I was well acquainted with his mode of warfare. I turned and faced his lordship, when he approached within about six feet of me, rose on his hind feet and most impudently stared me right in the face, for more than a minute. After discovering that I was no ways bashful, he bowed, turned and run—I did the same, and made for my horse. Bruin was not so easy fooled; he seen my retreat & gave chase. I thought I could reach my horse and mount before the bear could reach me, but the approach of the bear frightened my beast, and just as I was going to mount he sprang loose and threw me on the broad of my back. The bear was at my heels, and I thought that all chance of escape was now gone. Instantly I was again on my feet,—and, as it were, in a fit of desperation, rushed towards the bear, which, fearing, as they do, the *face* of man, again turned and run.—Sir Bruin stopped to secure the little morsel I had been eating, and retired a few paces to devour it. While the bear was thus employed, I crept to my gun, keeping the rock between him and me, having reached it, took deliberate aim and killed him dead on the spot. Having secured my horse, I fell to work at the carcase of my vanquished foe, and, after cooking and eating a choice piece of his flesh, left the rest to feed his kindred. It being now near night, I travelled two or three miles further, and encamped for the night. The next morning appeared more favourable over head, and I made an early start. Being on the banks of a small creek, I concluded to follow it a while. After winding my way through the rocks and trees, till near the middle of the day, I came to a valley which seemed to be hemmed in on every side by huge towering hills. I had not travelled far in this valley before I found myself ushered into the presence of a hostile tribe of Indians. I halted to devise some means to effect a return without being discovered; but I soon found that it was too late. Immediately in my rear was a choice set of young warriors—in front, and on both sides by high and craggy mountains. My noble steed, than him, I would defy the whole Indian world to produce a stouter, swifter, or better, was now brought to the test. He started with the velocity of the rein deer,—boun[d]ing over ditches, stones logs and brush.—Soon I began to ascend the mountain, but found it much too steep and rough. The Indians dismounted and followed on foot. I applied the whip, but in vain. My horse was compelled to yield to exhausted nature—and I dismounted, and left my much prized animal to fall a prey to the savages. I ran up the mountain with all possible speed, but finding that I must eventually be overtaken, I secreted myself in a hole among the rocks, and closed the mouth of it with leaves and sticks. After remaining a few minutes in this subterraneous cavern, I heard the ferocious yells of triumph of my pursuers, as they captured my lamented horse. The victory was not yet complete, although the horse was the principal prize. Some of them followed on and came close to my hiding place, passed and re-passed within reach without discovering me. What a moment of intense anxiety was this! All chance of escape cut off. No prospect of mercy if taken! Hope began to die—and death inevitable seemed to be the very next incident that would occur. They continued their search until near sunset, for they knew that I had not reached the summit of the mountain. As they retired down the mountain, squads of four or five would frequently halt and hold a busy consultation—then suddenly return to complete their search, as if they feared that some hollow tree or rocky cavern might escape unexplored. Finally, they gave me up in despair, and retired into the valley, with my horse.

Now that I had escaped this scrutinizing search, I began to breathe more free and easy; but I was yet far from being out of danger. I was conscious that I had lost the course to the Columbia river, and could not tell how to regain it, even if I should succeed in escaping from my present perilous situation. I remained secreted in the rocks till long after dark, when I crawled out, and surveyed the country as well as the darkness of the night would permit, and finally started in the direction which I thought I would have the least chance of meeting the Indians. I had not travelled far, however, until I was again doomed to be disappointed, for I was on the very borders of their encampment. Happily the camp was all quiet, and I returned quietly to my hiding place on the mountain, hoping that on the morrow I would be able to make some new discovery by which to extricate myself from these savages—which I judged to be the merciless Blackfeet. Early in the morning of the next day the hunt was resumed with increased vigilance; but again returned with disappointment. After the sound of their voices no longer reached me, I crawled to the mouth of the hole from which I presently beheld them running races with the horse they had taken from me. In this sport they spent the day. This village did not appear to be their permanent residence, but was handsomely situated on the banks of a small creek, and I suppose they had came here on a sporting expedition. The second night I made another effort to save myself, and gradually descended the mountain, to the creek some distance below the camp.—This I followed, until daylight again compelled me to hide myself; which I did by crawling into the brush close to the creek, where I secreted myself till darkness again gave me an opportunity to resume my journey. During the day I seen a number of the Indians pass and repass up and down the valley, whom I supposed to be hunters. This day I again had a view of my horse under the saddle of the chief of the tribe, as I supposed; but did not attempt to rescue him. The following night I travelled a short distance down the creek when I came to where it empties into the Pieres river. Here I came to my reckoning of the country, and thought that if I could escape from hunger and beasts of prey, I could manage to elude the Indians. Supposing that the Indians were not so numerous on the opposite side of the river, I resolved to cross over— for which purpose I built a raft of old logs, laid my shot-pouch, gun, blanket, &c. on it, and pushed for the opposite shore. After getting nearly across, the current became very rapid, and I began to descend the river at a rapid rate until I struck a rock which tore my frail craft to pieces—committing myself, gun, blanket and all to the watery element. Being weak from hunger and exertion, it was with great difficulty that I succeeded in reaching the land, with the loss of my only companion, and my only

hope in this wilderness of dangers—my gun. I stood on the
bank in the midst of despair. I had no other weapon than a
butcher knife to fight my way through a country swarming
with savages and equally dangerous wild beasts. On my
knife depended all hope of preventing starvation. The loss
of my blanket was also severe, as the weather was sometimes quite cold, and I had no other clothing than a shirt
and vest—having thrown the rest away when pursued by
the Indians on the mountain. I followed the banks of this
river for two days, subsisting upon buds, roots, weeds, &c.
On the second evening whilst digging for a sweet kind of
root, in a swamp, I was alarmed by the growl of wolves,
which were descending the hill to the river, about fifty
yards distant. The only chance of escape now, was to climb
a tree, which I did immediately. Here I was compelled to
roost until daylight, in the most painful agitation. The
wolves tearing up the ground and gnawing at the tree so
that I sometimes feared they would cut it through. The third
day I travelled with great speed, not even stopping for any
thing to eat. On the fourth I happened where the wolves
had killed a buffaloe.—Here I satisfied my appetite by
collecting all the meat that was left on the bones, made a fire
by rubbing two sticks together, and cooked it. From the
gluttenous fill which I took of this meat, I was enabled to
travel three or four days, without any particular occurrence;
but I found that the further I descended the river, the
scarcer became the roots, buds, &c., on which I must de-
pend for subsistence, and I was finally obliged to turn my
attention to get something to eat, without travelling any
further. For several days I loitered about from place to place,
but could find no nourishment. My body began to grow
weaker and weaker, until I was no longer able to walk. Still
my mind held its sway, and I was well aware how desperate
was my situation. Finally loosing all prospect of getting any
thing more to eat, & no hope of being found by my companions or friendly Indians, I thought of preparing myself for
death, and committed my soul to the Almighty. I have no
recollection of any thing that occurred after this, until I
found myself in the hands of my deliverers.

22

GEORGE NIDEVER:

Pierre's Hole and the Walker Expedition

George Nidever (1802–1883) had the honor, together with Joe Meek and Zenas Leonard (see Selections 19 and 20), of being a participant in two of the more prominent episodes in the era of the mountainmen: the battle of Pierre's Hole in 1832, which was the most noted encounter between trappers and Indians: and Captain Joseph Reddeford Walker's expedition to the Pacific in 1833, which opened the overland route to California for the pioneers and the Forty-Niners. Nidever also had the good fortune, in later life, to be discovered by a California historian, who recorded his reminiscences and thereby saved the old mountainman from oblivion.

Nidever was typical of that rough and restless breed that wandered the West during the height of the fur trade: neither famous nor especially heroic, but skilled in woodcraft, a good shot, cleer, and dependable. He was the product of a restless frontier family, often on the move–in this, too, he was typical–and had been raised first in Tennessee, then in North Carolina, and later in Missouri, where his family had settled in

1816. In 1830, young George Nidever and a friend, Alexander Sinclair, joined a party bound up the Arkansas River for the trapping grounds of Colorado and New Mexico. Nidever spent the next three years in the mountains, hunting, trapping, fighting Blackfeet at Pierre's Hole, and eventually joining Captain Walker's trip to California across Nevada and the upper Sierras. Together with a few others, Nidever decided to remain in California. He married but, far from settling down, spent another twenty-five years roaming up and down the coast, fighting Indians, campaigning with John C. Fremont in the conquest of California, and hunting sea otters and grizzly bears. He remained an exellent marksman until well into his seventies. His reminiscences, excerpted here, were dictated in 1878, to a preserver of historical data, in whose archives they remained until they were published for the first time in 1937. But although Nidever's reminiscences were dictated forty-five years after the events described, and, although Nidever's memory was sometimes faulty as to dates and numbers, the events themselves must have been emblazoned on the old man's mind, for his descriptions agree well with other more contemporary accounts.

The following excerpt begins with the breakup of the 1832 summer rendezvous at Pierre's Hole, a circular valley just west of the Tetons, where hundreds of trappers—either free trappers, members of the various brigades of the Rocky Mountain and American fur companies, or, like Nidever, members of small, independent companies—had converged to await the arrival of supply trains from the States. Most of the great names of the fur trade were there, including Jim Bridger, Joe Meek, Bill Williams, William and Milton Sublette, and Thomas Fitzpatrick, who had just turned up, more dead than alive, after his harrowing escape from the Blackfeet (see previous selection).

About the beginning of Aug. [July 17, according to most accounts] the trappers began to leave for their respective

From *The Life and Adventures of George Nidever, 1801–1883,* William H. Ellison, ed. (Berkeley: University of California Press, 1937), pp. 26–34. Originally published by the University of California Press; reprinted by permission of the Regents of the University of California.

hunting grounds. Our party had decided to trap that season on the Marys [Humboldt] River, a small stream about South West of Salt Lake. We left Pierre's Hole in company with Frapp [Henry Fraeb] and Wyatt [Nathaniel J. Wyeth, a Boston merchant], our courses being the same for some distance. Frapp's company was mostly made up of Canadian French half-breeds. Our first camp was about 15 [8] miles from the rendezvous. Frapp's and Wyatt's companies camped together, while we were a short distance in their rear.

The next morning about 8 o'clock we packed up and rode along to Wyatt's and Frapp's camp, only a few hundred yards ahead, and had hardly reached it when Indians were discovered coming towards us in large numbers, and we immediately recognized them as Blackfeet. They belonged to a village of some 400 warriors or more, that with their women, children, and camp baggage were moving north. They had discovered us before we did them, no doubt, and had resolved on attacking us. They were riding down on us at full speed and barely gave us time to prepare for them. We hurriedly formed a breastwork of our packs and despatched a young boy on our fleetest horse back to Pierre's Hole for aid. We saw from their numbers that we would need help, but by holding the Indians in check for two or three hours we knew reinforcements would reach us. As soon as the Indians arrived within range they began shooting, to which we replied. Conspicuous among them was a chief dressed in a bright scarlet coat, and he rode somewhat in advance of his men, who began to scatter and surround us upon arriving within shooting distance. On came the chief and out rode one of Wyatt's men, Goddar [Godin], a Canadian half-breed, to meet him. Across his saddle Goddar carried a short rifle which the chief did not see until, when within 40 or 50 yds. of him, Goddar raised it and shot. The chief fell from his saddle dead, and before his companions could come up to him his coat was stripped off by Goddar who amidst a heavy fire reached our camp in safety with his trophy. We continued to exchange shots, with a loss to the Indians of one or two killed, and to us of several wounded, until about ten o'clock, when the Indians suddenly took shelter in the heavy narrow belt of woods that lay between us and the river. We soon discovered the cause of this unexpected movement, in the coming of our reinforcements, that began to appear in sight and a few minutes later were among us to the number of about 250. Most of them were without saddles, having lost no time in setting out as soon as our messenger reached them. A council was held and Wm. Sublette was elected as our leader. Many were opposed to attacking them as, beging posted in the heavy timber, we would find it difficult to drive them out, and our loss would be considerable. These objections were overruled by Sublette and others, who said we would have to fight them anyway and now that we had them at a disadvantage, we must profit by it.

The plan of attack was formed and the attacking party [including several hundred Flatheads and Nez Percés] got into line, and advanced, when the firing at once became general. Just after we entered the timber, our captain Alex. Sinclair was shot in the thigh [and later died of his wounds], Phelps, a man who joined us at Pierre's Hole, was wounded in about the same place, and Wm. Sublette was shot in the arm. Our attacking party did not consist of much over 100 men, the rest refusing to join us. As we advanced and drove the Indians towards the river, the wings of our line gradually turned in until they rested on its bank and we had them surrounded.

Upon penetrating into timber we found that the Blackfeet had constructed a fort of logs on the bank of the river in the form of a half moon, the rear opening towards the river. We continued to advance, dodging and crawling form tree to tree and log to log, every foot stubbornly contested by the redskins, until almost sunset. Some of our men had succeeded in getting in the rear of the fort, which, however, afforded its inmates some shelter even on the open side, as it was filled with trees. One of the trappers of Frapp's company got very near the rear of the fort, almost up to it in fact, by crawling flat on the ground and pushing and rolling a large log so as to protect his head.

Several shots struck the log but the trapper got into the [rear] position and abandoned his log for a tree without being harmed.

Another one of Frapp's men, a Canadian half-breed, tried to distinguish himself by rashly crawling up to the very wall of the fort and then peeping over the top. He paid for his temerity with his life. He had barely raised his head above the breastworks of logs when he received two bullets in his forehead. He was half drunk at the time, liquor having been distributed among the men during the early part of the fight. By sunset we had got so close to the fort that we determined to set it on fire, but before doing so it was agreed to give the Indians a chance to surrender. Accordingly, a renegade Blackfoot who was among Frapp's men was instructed to talk with them and try and induce them to surrender. They refused, however, and answered that, although they would all be killed that day, the next day it would be our turn, as they had sent word to a very large village of their nation, situated only a short distance from there, numbering some 1500 lodges.

It was well known that there was a very large village nearby, and that, should they send out all of their force after us, there would be some heavy fighting in which we would in all probability get worsted. Upon hearing the answer of the Indians, Frapp became alarmed and withdrew his men at once and this obliged the rest of us to retire, and those from Pierre's Hole having returned, we travelled on about 9 miles and went into camp with the same companies as the night previous. The next morning several of us went back to the scene of the fight. Within the fort and its immediate vicinity the ground was strewn with dead bodies mostly of women and children; but a very few warriors among them.

We counted 50 dead bodies, and inside of the fort were the bodies of 20 fine horses. Of the from 300 to 400 Indians which it was calculated the fighting men of the Blackfeet numbered, but very few escaped.

At the beginning of the engagement several got away, many of them being shot in attempting to swim the river. We afterwards learned through the Indians that when we withdrew our men only 6 Indians were left alive in the fort. The dead Indians were thrown into the river to prevent them from falling into our hands. [The Indians later admitted to twenty-six killed. The trappers lost five men killed and six wounded, the Flatheads and Nez Percés seven dead and seven wounded.]

Many of the women were shot unintentionally as in the timber it was impossible to distinguish the women from the men; the children were killed no doubt by stray shots.

The Indians make a very poor fight on foot, their usual mode of fighting being to lay [lie] in ambush or to cut off small detached parties with such numbers as to make success sure.

We lost no time in getting out of this neighborhood, pushing forward as rapidly as possible. A few days later we struck buffalo and halted to get meat. We also furnished meat to Wyatt, whose men were mostly green in these matters.

Having got a sufficient supply we continued our journey without further adventure. We parted with Wyatt's company about 100 miles from Pierre's Hole and with Frapp just north of Salt Lake. We trapped on the Marys River with fair success until Oct., when we went North intending to winter in the Green River valley where we had passed the previous winter. We found it already occupied by some of the Snake Indians, and buffalo very scarce so that we determined upon making no permenent quarters but [to] move about from place to place. We visited the head waters of the Red [Colorado] Yellowstone rivers and trapped a few beavers between the Green and Platte rivers. The cold was very severe. When up near the head waters of the Yellowstone we had several horses stolen by the Indians, and knowing with almost a certainty that the Crow were the thieves, we visited their villages in the hopes of recovering our property, but unsuccessfully offered them a reward to return them.

A white man by the name of Ballard was living among the Crow Indians and served as interpreter. It was rumored that he was a fugitive from justice. During the same winter we met a party of 40 Crow Indians. Their number emboldened them, so that they acted very saucily. One of them, a large powerful fellow, took a fancy to my powder horn. He made signs for me to give it to him, and upon being refused he took out his knife and was about to cut the string with which it was hung from my shoulder and take it. I had my hand on the handle of my knife and was determined to kill him the moment he cut the string; at the same time I called out to our men to look out for themselves. Our Captain spoke some Crow tongue and warned the Indian, who immediately desisted from his design, all of our men having at that time laid hold of their rifles. The Indians saw that we meant to fight them if necessary and they wisely let us alone.

This nation is one of the most thieving nations of all those that live in the mountains. We lost several horses by them and were never able to find any of them.

In April of the following year we went into the waters of the North Fork of the Platte. Here we encamped and had our horses picketed a few hundred yards away. One morning, having gone out with a companion to bring in horses, we discovered a band of something like 80 Rees [Arikara] Indians, riding down on us. We had barely time to get back to camp before the Indians reached the stock, which they immediately drove off. Here a man by the name of Gillum was, it was supposed, killed by these Indians. He had a very fine horse picketed out in another direction and, contrary to all advice, persisted in going for it. We never found him again. This mishap obliged us to travel over 300 miles on foot back to the Green River valley, the place appointed for the rendezvous the next year. We did not winter in the valley, however, but wandered about from place to place as we had done the previous winter. The cold this season was very severe; at times even at midday it was very uncomfortable.

This winter's experience decided me, as also some others of our company, to seek a warmer climate, and having heard many wonderful stories of California, we settled upon coming here. In the spring, there were a large number of trappers gathered at the rendezvous in Green River valley and among them Captain Walker and Company, bound for California.* We joined him, making a party in all of 36. [Leonard put the number at 58.] Upon the breaking up of the rendezvous we started southward, intending to trap a short time on the Marys River. The Indians troubled us so much, however, that we found it impossible to remain; they stole our traps and made it necessary to be continually on our guard to prevent an attack. They became very bold and at last offered to let us go through their country unmolested if we would give them our horses and meat. They spoke the Snake tongue, a language which most of our men were familiar with. [These were Paiutes, also called Diggers.] We continued to travel along and they followed us, gathering additional force, as they proceeded, from other villages. Just before we gave up trapping entirely, they shot at one of our men, by name of Frazier, while he was setting his traps, and it was only by the veriest chance that he escaped them. From this time on, we doubled our guards and our precautions, making detours from the trail when necessary to avoid passing through narrow defiles, thickly wooded places and all other places favorable for an ambuscade. A few days before reaching the Sierra Nevada mountains we found that our trail passed through a large, thick body of willows, and, as we had seen the Indians around the day before, we determined to avoid the willows by making a detour in the adjoining plain. This precaution saved some lives if not those of the whole party. Hardly had the trail been left when the Indians, to the number of 400 to 500, emerged from the thicket; they formed in several distinct bodies or companies, representing no doubt the respective villages to which they belonged.

We halted and prepared for a fight. Thirty-four of the Indians advanced in a body, and 15 of our men, myself among the number, were ordered out to meet them. From

*Walker was the chief lieutenant in the fur company of Captain Benjamin L. E. Bonneville, who sent him to California to search out new trapping grounds.—ED.

50 to 60 yds. from our company, we halted and awaited the Indians. We allowed them to get quite close before opening fire, but when we did shoot it was with such telling effect that but *one* of the 34 escaped. This appeared to completely disenhearten our enemies for they permitted us to pass without further opposition. After entering the mountains, I went ahead one day with the Captain and another of our men to select a camping place for water; we became somewhat separated in our search, and upon entering the timber I discovered fresh sings of Indians. This alarmed me somewhat as I feared for the Captain and our companion, who, like myself, had probably each taken a different course. I had just begun to look about for more signs when, glancing back in the direction I had come, I saw two Indians, with head down and at a trot coming along my trail. I supposed that they were following my tracks, so I lost no time in getting behind a tree and preparing for them. It took them some few minutes to reach me and in the meantime they would stop every few yards and look back, and listen as if pursued. I saw that they had not see me or discovered my tracks, as they passed within a few feet of me, jabbering as they went along. I at first had a notion to let them go but the death of my brother, so treacherously murdered by these red devils, was too fresh in my mind. The Indians were travelling in single file, and watching my chance, just before they would have to turn around a small point of rocks, I fired, shooting both of them dead at the first shot. I took their blankets, the only articles they had worth taking, as they were armed with bows, and returned to the company. This was the last of the Indians. In June of 1834 we crossed the Sierra Nevada mountains and came down through a valley between the Merced and Tuolemi [Tuolumne] rivers, into the San Joaquin Valley. Here we found an abundance of elk, deer, and bear. In Nov. following, we arrived at Gilroy's Ranch and went into camp close by, where we remained about a month.

While here the men employed themselves in hunting deer for the pelts. Leaving our camp at Gilroy's, we proceeded to Monterey, where we arrived about the middle of

Dec. Here we spent Christmas. Shortly after, Captain Walker returned to the mountains with some 20 men. He was one of the best leaders I have ever met, a good hunter and trapper, thoroughly versed in Indian signs and possessed of good knowledge of the mountains. He could find water quicker than any man I ever met.

Later he returned to Cal. on his second trip. I remained in Monterey with a few others of our company.

23

KIT CARSON:
The Making of a Myth

The fame of Kit Carson (1809–1868) as the foremost scout and Indian fighter of his generation was due as much to the skill of his publicists as to his own native abilities. When he first met John C. Frémont in 1842 and agreed to become his guide, Carson was well known only among the mountain men. But Fremont's reports of his exploring expeditions in the West dramatized the prowess of "clear steady blue-eyed" Carson and made him a national hero. His deeds were related on the floor of the Senate, in the press, and in dime novels, and with each telling Carson's image was magnified in the public imagination. A young army lieutenant who later rode with Carson recalled that he had expected to find a man "over six feet high—a sort of modern Hercules in his build—with an enormous beard, and a voice like a roused lion." What he found instead was "a plain, simple, unostentatious man; rather below the medium height, with brown curling hair, little or no beard, and a voice as soft and gentle as a woman's."

The first public mention of Carson was not at all auspicious.

In October 1826 a notice appeared in a Missouri newspaper promising one cent reward for the return of a runaway saddler's apprentice, "Christopher Carson, a boy about 16 years old, small of his age, but thick-set." By the time the notice appeared, however, the boy was long gone, having joined a trading expedition bound for Taos and Santa Fe. But Carson's real education began in 1829, when he signed on as a cook for a long trapping tour of the Southwest. On the trek across the Arizona and California deserts to the San Joaquin Valley, he encountered every wilderness hazard imaginable, from thirst and starvation to Indian attacks and grizzly bears. The trip was his high school and university, and from it he emerged an experienced trapper and Indian fighter. During the next ten years, traveling sometimes with Jim Bridger and Tom Fitzpatrick (see Selections 21 and 25), but more often with parties of his own, Carson ranged over the whole of the West. He later recalled that "the happiest days of my life were spent trapping." When at last he joined Frémont, who was about to begin exploring the West for the government, Carson could report without exaggeration "that I had been some time in the mountains and could guide him to any point he wished to go." Carson was hired and so began his new career as pathfinder to "The Pathfinder." Frémont's report of the expedition to the South Pass in 1842, and to Salt Lake, the Columbia, and California a year later, made both men famous. On a third trip, in 1845–1846, they became embroiled in the conquest of California, during which Carson's deeds added to his legend of courage and daring. Riding East in March 1847 with news of events in California, Carson found himself greeted as a popular hero, and appointed a lieutenant in the Mounted Riflemen by President Polk.

Carson spent his later years near Taos, serving as Indian agent and attempting for a time to run a farm. As a military leader he campaigned against the Navajos, Apaches, Kiowas, and Comanches, and during the Civil War he organized New Mexican troops for the Union. Brevetted a brigadier general in 1865, he died three years later in Fort Lyon. The following excerpts from his autobiography, probably written with the aid of a friend in 1856 (and lost for almost seventy years), describe events from Carson's early years as a trapper. Incidents from

this period–including some related here–provided his biog-
raphers, fictional and otherwise, with some of their best
material.

In the fall of 1830 (1831) I joined the party under Fitzpatrick [see Chapter 21] for the Rocky Mountain on a trapping
expedition. We traveled north till we struck the Platte river
and then took up the Sweet Water, a branch of the Platte.
We trapped to the head of the Sweet Water and then on to
Green River, and then on to Jackson's Hole, a fork of the
Columbia River, and from there on to the head of Salmon
River. Then we came to the camp of a part of our band that
we had been hunting, then we went into winter quarters on
the head of Salmon River. During winter we lost some four
or five men when out hunting Buffalo. They have been
killed by the Blackfeet Indians.

In April 1831, (1832) we commenced our hunt again. We
trapped back to the Bear River, the principal stream that
empties into the Great Salt Lake, then on to the Green
River. We then found a party of trappers under charge of
Mr. Sinclair. They left Taos shortly after we had. They had
wintered on little Bear River, a branch of Green. They told
me that Captain Gaunt was in New Park [at the headwaters
of the North Platte, in the area of Jackson County,
Colorado], that he and party had wintered near the
Laramie. I wished to join his party. Four of us left the party
and struck out in search of Gaunt. In ten days, we found
him and party at the New Park.

We remained trapping in the Park for some time, and
then through the plains of Laramie and on to the south fork
of the Platte, then to the Arkansas. On our arrival on the
Arkansas, Gaunt took the beaver we had caught to Taos.
The party remained on the Arkansas trapping. The beaver
was disposed of, the necessaries for our camp were purchased and, in the course of two months, Gaunt joined (us).

From *Kit Carson's Own Story of His Life*, Blanche C. Grant, ed. (Taos, New Mexico, 1926), pp. 20–26, 31–37.

We trapped on the waters of the Arkansas until the river began to freeze, and then went into winter quarters on the main stream. During the winter we passed a pleasant time. The snow was very deep and we had no difficulty in procuring as much buffalo meat as we required.

In January (1833) a party of men had been out hunting and returned about dark. Their horses were very poor, having been fed during the winter on cottonwood bark; they turned them out to gather such nourishment as they could. That night a party of about fifty Crow Indians came to our camp and stole nine of the horses that were loose. In the morning we discovered sign of the Indians and twelve of us took the trail of the Indians and horses. We traveled some forty miles. It was getting late. Our animals were fatigued for the course over which we came (was difficult) The snow was deep, and many herds of buffaloes having passed during the day, was the cause of our having a great deal of difficulty, keeping the trail.

We saw, at a distance of two or three miles, a grove of timber. Taking into consideration the condition of our animals, we concluded to make for the timber and camp for the night. On our arrival, we saw fires some four miles ahead of us. We tied our animals to trees, and as soon as it became dark, took a circuitous route for the Indian Camp.

We were to come on the Indians from the direction in which they were traveling. It took us some time to get close enough to the camp to discover their strength, as we had to crawl, and used all means that we were aware of, to elude detection. After considerable crawling, etc. we came within about one hundred yards of their camp. The Indians were in two forts of equal strength. They were dancing and singing, and passing the night jovially in honor of the robbery committed by them on the whites. We saw our horses, they were tied at the entrance of the fort. Let come what would we were bound to get our horses. We remained concealed in the brush until they laid down to sleep, suffering from the cold.

When we thought they were all asleep, six of us crawled towards the animals. (The) remainder was to remain where they were as a reserve for us to fall back on in case of not meeting with success. By hiding behind logs and crawling silently towards the fort, the snow being of great service to us for when crawling we were not liable to make any noise.

We finally reached the horses, cut the ropes, and by throwing snow balls at them drove them to where was stationed our reserve. We then held council taking the views of each in regard to what had best be done. Some were in favor of retiring; having recovered their property and received no damage, they would be willing to return to camp. Not so with those that had lost no animals. They wanted satisfaction for the trouble and hardships they had gone through while in pursuit of the thieves. Myself and two more were the ones that had not lost horses and we were determined to have satisfaction, let the consequences be ever so fatal. The peace party could not get a convert to their side. Seeing us so determined to fight (there is always a brotherly affection existing among the trappers and the side of danger always being their choice) we were not long before all agreed to join us in our perilous enterprise.

We started the horses that were retaken to the place where we tied our other animals, with three men as escort.

We then marched direct for the fort from which we got our horses. When within a few paces of the fort, a dog discovered us and commenced barking. The Indians were alarmed and commenced getting up. We opened a deadly fire, each ball taking its victim. We killed nearly every Indian in the fort. The few that remained were wounded and made their escape to the other fort, the Indians of which commenced firing on us; but without any effect, we, keeping concealed behind trees and only firing when we were sure of our object. It was now near day, the Indians could see our forces, as it being so weak, they concluded to charge on us. We received them and when very close, fired on them, killing five and the balance returned to the fort. After some deliberation among the Indians, they finally made another attempt which met with greater success to them. We had to retreat. But there being much timber in the vicinity, we had but little difficulty in making our camp, and then, being reinforced by the three men with the horses, we awaited the approach of the enemy. They did not attack us. We started for our main camp and arrived in the evening.

During our pursuit for the lost animals we suffered considerably but, in the success of having recovered our horses, and sending many a red skin to his long home, our sufferings were soon forgotten. We remained in our camp without any further molestation until Spring (1833). We then started for Laramie on another trapping expedition.

. . . We passed the summer trapping on the head of Laramie and its tributaries, keeping to the mountains, our party being too weak to venture on the plains.

One evening, when we were on the route to join Bridger's party I had selected the camp for the night, I gave my horse to one of the men and started on foot for the purpose of killing something for supper, not having a particle of anything eatable on hand. I had gone about a mile and discovered some elk. I was on the side of a ridge. I shot one and immediately after the discharge of my gun, I heard in my rear a noise. I turned around and saw two very large grizzly bears making for me. My gun was unloaded and I could not possibly reload it in time to fire. There were some trees at a short distance. I made for them, the bears after me. As I got to one of the trees, I had to drop my gun, the bears rushing for me I had to make all haste to ascend the tree. I got up some ten or fifteen feet and then had to remain till the bears would find it convenient to leave. One remained but a short time, the other remained for some time and with his paws would nearly uproot the small aspen trees that were around the one which I had ascended. He made several attempts at the one in which I was, but could do no damage. He finally concluded to leave, of which I was heartily pleased, never having been so scared in my life. I remained in the tree for some time, and, when I considered the bears far enough off, I descended and made for my camp in as great haste as possible. It was dark when I arrived and (I) could not send for the elk which I had killed, so we had to pass the night without anything to eat. During the night we caught beaver, so we had something for breakfast.

We remained in this place (head of the Laramie) some ten or fifteen days when Bridger came making his way for summer rende(z)vous (1834). We joined him and went to Green River (the place of rendezvous). Here was two camps of us. I think that there was two hundred trappers encamped.* Then, till our supplies came from St. Louis, we disposed of our beaver to procure supplies. Coffee and sugar were two dollars a pint, powder the same, lead one dollar a bar and common blankets from fifteen to twenty five dollars apiece.

We remained in rende(z)vous during August (1834) and in September camp was broken up and we divided into parties of convenient size and started on our fall hunt. In the party of which I was a member then, (there) were fifty men.

We set out for the country of the Blackfeet Indians, on the head waters of the Missouri. We made a very poor hunt as the Indians were very bad. Five of our men were killed. A trapper could hardly go a mile without being fired on. As we found that we could do but little in their country, so we started for winter quarters.

In November (1834) we got to Big Snake River, where we camped. We remained here till February, 1833 (1835). Nothing of moment having transpired till February, (when) the Blackfeet came and stole eighteen horses. Twelve of us followed them and caught up in about fifty miles. They had travelled as far as they could on account of the snow. We endeavored to get the horses (some shots had been fired) but could not approach near enough to the Indians to do any damage. They had snow shoes, we had none, they could travel over the snow without any difficulty, we would sink in the snow to our waists.

The horses were on the side of a hill where there was but little snow. Our only object now as to get the horses. We wished a parley. The Indians agreed. One man for each

*Among them was Zenas Leonard (see Selection 20), just returned from California.

(side) was to proceed halfway the diatance between us and have a talk.

It was done. We talked some; the Indians saying that they thought we were Snake Indians (and that they) did not wish to steal from the Whites. We informed them that if they were friendly why did they not lay down their arms and have a friendly talk and smoke. They agreed and laid down their arms. We done the same. One man to guard the arms. We then met at the place where the two first were talking (and) talked and smoked.

The Indians were thirty strong. They sent for the horses, (but) only returned with five of the worst. They said (they) would not give any more. We broke for our arms, they for theirs. Then the fight commenced. I and Markhead* was in the advance, approaching two Indians that were remaining in the rear concealed behind two trees. I approaching one and Markhead the other. Markhead was not paying sufficient attention to the Indian who, I noticed, him raise his gun to fire. I forgot entirely the danger in which I was myself and neglected my Indian for the one of Markhead's. As the Indian was ready to fire on Markhead, I raised my gun and took sight. The Indian saw it and endeavored to conceal himself. I fired and he fell. The moment I fired I thought of the Indian that I was after. I noticed him. He was sighting for my breast. I could not load in time so I commenced dodging as well as I could. He fired, the ball grazed my neck and passed through my shoulder.

We then drew off about a mile and encamped for the night. It was very cold (and we) could not make any fires for fear the Indians might approach and fire on us. We had no covering but our saddle blankets. I passed a miserable night from the pain of the wound, (it having bled freely) which was frozen.

In the morning the Indians were in the same place. We were not strong enough to attack, so we started for camp. Bridger with thirty men then started for the place where we

---

*Markhead also appears in Ruxton's portrait of "Old Bill" Williams (see Chapter 18).—ED.

had left the Indians, but when they arrived the Indians had gone to the plains and of the stolen animals we had only recovered the five which they had given us.

In a few days we set (out) on our spring hunt, trapped the waters of the Snake and Green Rivers, made a very good hunt and then went into Summer quarters on Green River (1835).

Shortly after making rendezvous our equipment arrived, then we disposed of our beaver to the traders that came up with our equipments. We remained in summer quarters till September.

There was in the party of Captain Drips* a large Frenchman, one of those overbearing kind and very strong. He made a practice of whipping every man that he was displeased with,—and that was nearly all. One day, after he had beaten two or three men, he said, that for the Frenchmen he had no trouble to flog and, as for the Americans, the would take a switch and switch them.

I did not like such talk from any man, so I told him that I was the worst American in camp. Many could trash (thrash) him only (they didn't) on account of being afraid and that if he made use of any more such expressions, I would rip his guts.

He said nothing but started for his rifle, mounted his horse and made his appearance in front of the camp. As soon as I saw him, I mounted my horse and took the first arms I could get hold of, which was a pistol, galloped up to him and demanded if I was the one which he intended to shoot. Our horses (were) touching. He said no, but at the same time drawing his gun so he could have a fair shot at me. I was prepared and allowed him to draw his gun. We both fired at the same time; all present saying that but one report was heard. I shot him through the arm and his ball passed my head, cutting my hair and the powder burning my eye, the muzzle of his gun being near my head when he fired. During our stay in camp we had no more bother with this bully (of a) Frenchman.

*Captain Andrew Drips, a member of The American Fur Company and a noted mountain guide.—GRANT.

24

OSBORNE RUSSELL:

Winter Quarters and a Summer Rendezvous

Better than anywhere else the color and flavor of the mountainman's life is preserved by Osborne Russell (1814–1892) in his journal of his nine years as a trapper in the Rocky Mountains. Russell's wit, his keen eye for detail, and his obvious relish for the life he was living make his account a marvelously graphic picture of a world that was already beginning to fade. Furthermore, unlike most trappers, whose only care for the country around them was the wealth that it could bring them, Russell was deeply sensitive to the beauties of the landscape. His descriptions of the wonders of the Yellowstone area are among the finest to be found, and he was not above spending a freezing night on a mountaintop just so he could watch the sunrise.

Russell was born in 1814 in a small village on the Kennebec estuary in Maine, where, though he received little schooling, he developed into a studious and inquisitive young man. He ran away to sea at sixteen but deserted his ship at New York and spent the next three years in the service of a fur company in

*Wisconsin and Minnesota. In the spring of 1834, at Indepen-
dence, Missouri, he joined at trading expedition lead by
Nathaniel J. Wyeth and bound for the Rockies and the mouth of
the Columbia. That summer he helped build Fort Hall in Idaho,
soon to become a key outpost on the Oregon Trail.*

*Russell trapped and hunted in the mountains for the next six
or seven years, first as an employee of Wyeth's Columbia River
Fishing and Trading Company, than as part of Jim Bridger's
brigade. Later he struck out on his own as a free trapper
operating out of Fort Hall, covering wide expanses of territory
and experiencing a fair share of mishaps and adventures. In
1842, ready for a quieter life, he joined an immigrant party
bound for Oregon, where he bought a piece of land, joined a
church, read a good deal, and became a prominent figure in local
politics. Drawn to California by the Gold Rush in 1848, he tried
mining for a time, and had some success as a merchant and
operator of a boarding house in Placerville.*

*It was while he was living in Oregon that Russell read James
Ohio Pattie's narrative (see Selection 15) and was inspired to
compile his own account of life in the mountains, using his
journal notes. He sent the manuscript to New York for publication, but it did not appear until 1914, at Boise, Idaho. The
following excerpts begin with Russell's account of some of the
day-to-day doings of the trapper: cooking buffalo meat and
keeping winter quarters. He also gives perhaps the best contemporary description of the social highlight of the trapper's year,
the summer rendezvous, a wilderness fair attended by hundreds
of Indians and mountainmen come to exchange stories, to drink,
and to trade their peltries for another year's supply of
provisions.*

The time for which myself and all of Mr. Wyeth's men
were engaged had recently expired, so that now I was
independent of the world and no longer to be termed a
"greenhorn." . . .

From *The Journal of A Trapper, or, Nine Years in the Rocky Mountains, 1834–1843*, L. A.
York, ed. (Boise, Idaho: Syms-York, Co., Inc., 1914, 1921), pp. 42–45, 55, 62–64, 85.

December 20th [1835] I bid adieu to the "Columbia River Fishing and Trading Company" and started, in company with fifteen of my old messmates, to pass the winter at a place called "Mutton Hill," on Portneuf, about forty miles southeast from Fort Hall. . . . We lived on fat mutton until the snow drove us from the mountains in February. Our party then dispersing, I joined Mr. Bridger's company, who were passing the winter on Blackfoot Creek, about fifteen miles from the fort, where we staid until the latter part of March. Mr. Bridger's men lived very poor and it was their own fault, for the valley was covered with fat cows when they arrived in November, but instead of approaching and killing their meat for the winter they began to kill by running on horseback, which had driven the buffalo all over the mountain to the head of the Missouri, and the snow falling deep, they could not return during the winter. They killed plenty of bulls, but they were so poor that their meat was perfectly blue, yet this was their only article of food, as bread and vegetables were out of the question in the Rocky Mountains, except a few kinds of roots of spontaneous growth, which the Indians dig and prepare for food. It would doubtless be amusing to a disinterested spectator to witness the process of cooking poor bull meat as practiced by this camp during the winter of 1835–6. On going through the camp at any time in the day heaps of ashes might be seen with the fire burning on the summit and an independent looking individual, who is termed a camp kicker, sitting with a "two-year-old club" in his hand watching the pile with as much seeming impatience as Philoctele did the burning of Hercules. At length, poking over the ashes with his club [to work loose a great mass of meat, which, on his hitting it with his club, bounded] five or six feet from the ground like a huge ball of gum elastic. This operation, frequently repeated, divests the ashes adhering to it and prepares it for carving. He then drops his club and draws his butcher knife calling to his comrades, "Come Major, Judge, Squire, Dollar, Pike, Cotton and Gabe, won't you take a lunch of Simon?" each of whom acts according to the dictates of his appetite in accepting or refusing the invitation. I have often witnessed these philosophical and independent dignitaries collected round a bull's ham just torn from a pile of embers, good-humoredly observing as they hacked the huge slices from the lean mass that this was tough eating but that it was tougher where there was none, and consoling themselves with a promise to make the fat cows suffer before the year rolled around. . . .

We passed away the time very agreeably, our only employment being to feed our horses, kill buffalo and eat, that is to say, the trappers. The camp keepers' business in winter quarters is to guard the horses, cook and keep fires. We all had snug lodges made of dressed buffalo skins, in the center of which we built a fire and generally comprised about six men to the lodge. The long winter evenings were passed away by collecting in some of the most spacious lodges and entering into debates, arguments or spinning long yarns until midnight, in perfect good humor, and I for one will cheerfully confess that I have derived no little benefit from the frequent arguments and debates held in what we termed "The Rocky Mountain College," and I doubt not but some of my comrades who considered themselves classical scholars have had some little added to their wisdom in the assemblies, however rude they might appear. . . . [Describing the 1837 summer rendezvous, which took place near the headwaters of Green River, in what is now western Wyoming, Russell is easily distracted by the chance to tell of a skirmish with a party of Indians.]

[At Green River] we found the hunting parties all assembled waiting for the arrival of supplies from the States. Here presented what might be termed a mixed multitude. The whites were chiefly Americans and Canadian French, with some Dutch, Scotch, Irish, English, half-breed and fullblood Indians of nearly every tribe in the Rocky Mountains. Some were gambling at cards, some playing the Indian game of "hand" and others horse racing, while here and there could be seen small groups collected under shady trees relating the events of the past year, all in good spirits and health, for sickness is a stranger seldom met with in these regions. Sheep, elk, deer, buffalo and bear skins mostly supply the mountaineers with clothing, lodges and bedding, while the meat of the same animals supply them with food. They have not the misfortune to get any of the luxuries from the civilized world but once a year, and then in such small quantities that they last but a few days.

We had not remained in this quiet manner long before something new arose for our amusement. The Bannock Indians had for several years lived with the whites on terms partly hostile, frequently stealing horses and traps, and in one instance killed two white trappers. They had taken some horses and traps from a party of French trappers who were hunting Bear River in April previous, and they were now impudent enough to come with the village of sixty lodges and encamp within three miles of us in order to trade with the whites as usual, still having the stolen property in their possession and refusing to give it up. On the 15th of June four or five whites and two Nez Perce Indians went to their village and took the stolen horses (whilst the men were out hunting buffalo) and returned with them to our camp. About three o'clock p.m. of the same day thirty Bannocks came riding at full gallop up to the camp, armed with their war weapons. They rode into the midst and demanded the horses which the Nez Perces had taken saying they did not wish to fight with the whites. But the Nez Perces, who were only six in number, gave the horses to the whites for protection, which we were bound to give, as they were numbered among our trappers and far from their own tribe. Some of the Bannocks, on seeing this, started to leave the camp. One of them as he passed me observed that he did not come to fight the whites; but another, a fierce looking savage, who still stopped behind, called out to the others, saying, "We came to get our horses or blood and let us do it." I was standing near the speaker and understood what he said. I immediately gave the whites warning to be in readiness for an attack. Nearly all the men in camp were under arms. Mr. Bridger was holding one of the stolen horses by the bridle when one of the Bannocks rushed through the crowd, seized the bridle and attempted to drag it from Mr. Bridger by force, without heeding the cocked rifles that surrounded him any more than if they had been so many reeds in the hands of children. He was a brave Indian, but his bravery proved fatal to himself, for the moment he seized the bridle two rifle balls whistled through his body. The others wheeled to run, but twelve of them were shot from their horses before they were out of reach of rifle. We then mounted horses and pursued them, destroyed and plundered their village, and followed and fought them three days, when they begged us to let them go and promised to be good Indians in future. We granted their request and returned to our camp, satisfied that the best way to negotiate and settle disputes with hostile Indians is with the rifle, for that is the only pen that can write a treaty which they will not forget. Two days after we left them three white trappers, ignorant of what had taken place, went into their village and were treated in the most friendly manner. The Indians said, however, they had been fighting with the Blackfeet.

July 5th a party arrived from the States with supplies. The cavalcade consisted of forty-five men and twenty carts drawn by mules, under the direction of Mr. Thomas Fitzpatrick, accompanied by Captain William Stewart on another tour of the Rocky Mountains.

Joy now beamed in every countenance. Some received letters from their friends and relations; some received the public papers and news of the day; others consoled themselves with the idea of getting a blanket, a cotton shirt or a few pints of coffee and sugar to sweeten it just by way of a treat, gratis, that is to say, by paying 2,000 per cent on the first cost by way of communication. For instance, sugar $2 per pint, coffee the same, blankets $20 each, tobacco $2 per pound, alcohol $4 per pint, and common cotton shirts $5 each, etc. And in return paid $4 or $5 per pound for beaver. In a few days the bustle began to subside. The furs were done up in packs ready for transportation to the States and parties were formed for the hunting the ensuing year. One party, consisting of 110 men, was destined for the Blackfoot country, under the direction of L. B. Fontanelle as commander and James Bridger as pilot. I started, with five others to hunt the headwaters of the Yellowstone, Missouri and Big Horn Rivers, a portion of the country I was particularly fond of hunting.

. . . A trapper's equipment in such cases is generally one animal upon which is placed one or two epishemores, a riding saddle and bridle, a sack containing six beaver traps, a blanket with an extra pair of moccasins, his powder horn and bullet pouch, with a belt to which is attached a butcher knife, a wooden box containing bait for beaver, a tobacco sack with a pipe and implements for making fire, with sometimes a hatchet fastened to the pommel of his saddle. His personal dress is a flannel or cotton shirt (if he is fortunate enough to obtain one, if not antelope skin answers the purpose of over and undershirt), a pair of leather breeches with blanket or smoked buffalo skin leggings, a coat made of blanket or buffalo robe, a hat or cap of wool, buffalo or otter skin, his hose are pieces of blanket wrapped around his feet, which are covered with a pair of moccasins made of dressed deer, elk or buffalo skins, with his long hair falling loosely over his shoulders, completes his uniform. He then mounts and places his rifle before him on his saddle. Such was the dress equipage of the party, myself included, now ready to start. After getting the necessary information from Mr. Bridger concerning the route he intended to take with the camp, we all started in a gallop in a westerly direction and traveled to the Big Horn and there commenced separating by twos and threes in different directions. . . .

25

JAMES BRIDGER:

"Old Gabe" Leads the Way

James Bridger (1804–1881) who was known to his fellow trappers as "Old Gabe," was one of the most prominent figures in the era of the mountainmen, and although he neither wrote nor dictated his memoirs, stories about him appear, it seems, in practically every diary, journal, and chronicle of the early West. Virginia-born and Missouri-raised, Bridger was one of William Ashley's 100 "enterprising young men" that set out in 1822 to trap among the head waters of the Missouri River. He lived in the wilderness so long that at one time, he said, he had not tasted bread for seventeen years. He knew the West better than any of his contemporaries, and he was one of the first Anglo-Americans to see the cliff dwellings at Mesa Verde, and probably the first to see the Great Salt Lake (in the fall of 1824). He remembered everything he saw and so, in later years, proved an invaluable guide to emigrants, explorers, and military expeditions. "With a buffalo skin and a piece of charcoal," wrote one army officer, "he will map out any portion of this immense region, and delineate mountains, streams, and . . . valleys . . .

with wonderful accuracy." Meantime, the fort that Bridger built in 1843 in southwestern Wyoming became an important way-station on the Oregon Trail, where travelers stopped for supplies and information about the road ahead. Gradually the legends grew about the crusty old trapper, tall and keen-eyed, who loved hearing Shakespeare and who walked around for years with a three-inch Indian arrowhead imbedded in his back. And Bridger, with his mountainman's love of tall tales and his mountainman's impatience with greenhorns, helped perpetuate the myths. He pretended, for instance, that he could see the smoke from an Indian campfire from fifty miles away, and he claimed that at Yellowstone "I'll show you peetrified trees a-growing, with peetrified birds on 'em a-singing peetrified songs."

The accounts that follow show Bridger at his best: scouting and yarn-spinning on two army expeditions. The first account was written by Captain Howard Stansbury, for whom Bridger acted as guide in the fall of 1850 on an expedition in search of an overland route that would be easier and more direct than the traditional Platte–Sweetwater–South Pass route to Fort Bridger. The route they explored lead directly eastward from Fort Bridger across southern Wyoming, and eventually became the general route of the Overland Stage, the Pony Express, the Union Pacific railroad, and, more recently, Interstate Highway 80. Arriving at Fort Bridger on September 5, 1850, Stansbury reported that "Major Bridger, although at a considerable sacrifice of his own interest, with great spirit, offered his services as guide, he being well acquainted with the ground over which it was my desire to pass. The offer was most cheerfully accepted." Setting out on September 10, the party crossed the Bitter Creek–Little Snake divide a week later.

[September 18:] We are now upon the war-ground of several hostile tribes, who make this region the field of

From *An Expedition to the Valley of the Great Salt Lake of Utah,* by Captain Howard Stansbury (Philadelphia, 1852), pp. 239–240, 252–254; and from *The History of the Powder River Indian expedition of 1865,* by Captain H. E. Palmer (Lincoln, Nebraska, 1887), quoted in *A Biographical Sketch of James Bridger,* by Grenville M. Dodge (New York, 1905), pp. 19–21.

mutual encounter, and increased vigilance is consequently necessary to guard against a surprise—an occurrence which, as one of its least unpleasant consequences, might leave us on foot in the midst of the wilderness. All firing of guns, without express permission, except in case of the most urgent necessity, has been strictly forbidden, and every man slept with his arms by his side.

As we were reposing our weary limbs before the camp-fire, regaling ourselves with a pipe, now our only luxury, Major Bridger entertained up with one of those trappers' legends which abound as much among these adventurous men as the "yarns" so long famous among their counter-part, the sailors, on a rival element. A partner of his, Mr. Henry Frappe [Fraeb], had a party of what, in the language of the country, are called "free men," that is, indepndent traders, who, some nine years before, were encamped about two miles from where we then were, with their squaw partners and a party of Indians. Most of the men being absent hunting buffalo, a band of five hundred Sioux, Cheyennes, and Arapahoes suddenly charged upon their camp, killed a white man, an Indian, and two women, drove off a hundred and sixty head of cattle, and, chasing the hunters, killed several of them in their flight, the res-idue escaping only by abandoning their horses and hiding in the bushes. Intelligence of this onslaught reached Major Bridger, then occupied in erecting a trading-post on Green River; he sent Frappe advice to abandon his post at once, for fear of worse consequences. The advice, however, was neglected, when, about ten days after, as his party was on their way to join his partner, they were again suddenly attacked by another large party of the savage allies. He had but forty men; but they instantly "forted" in the corral attached to the trading-post, and stood on their defence. The assault lasted from noon until sundown, the Indians charging the pickets several times with great bravery; but they were finally repulsed with the loss of forty men. Frappe himself was killed, with seven or eight of his peo-ple.

I give this as a sample of the perilous adventurers in which these rude and daring men, almost as wild as their savage foes, were engaged, as things of course, and which they related around their camp-fires with a relish quite professional. . . .

[Crossing—and naming—Bridger's Pass, near what is now Rawlins, Wyoming, the party passed around Medicine Bow mountain, over the Laramie plains, and across the Laramie River, where Stansbury made camp in a grove of cottonwoods.]

. . . In the mean time, Indian scouts made their appearance upon the surrounding hills, reconnoitring us, and seemed to be as uncertain of our character and intentions as we were of theirs. Having completed our little field-work, the United States flag was displayed, and we sat down to lunch, having eaten nothing since sunrise. Finding the Indians only hovered around at a distance, Major Bridger, shouldering his rifle, walked out toward them, and made various signs to an advance party that came out to meet him. We soon perceived that they had recognised him; when, finding that we were white men, and not a hostile band of Indians as they had supposed, they commenced a perfect race for our camp, and in a few minutes a stream of Indians galloped up, holding out their hands to shake with any and every body they met. They proved to be a large band of Ogallalahs, (one of the numerous bands of Sioux,) who had discovered us early in the morning, and had been anxiously watching our movements all the day, having mistaken us for a war-party of Crows. As soon as they saw the flag displayed, they knew at once that we were whites, but had hesitated to approach us, through fear of the small-pox, which they represented as raging below and in the neighbourhood of Fort Laramie. They had fled hither to avoid it, and were much alarmed lest we should have it among us. Being assured to the contrary, they poured in upon us from all quarters, and our camp was soon crowded with them. Several of the chiefs and head men had certificates from the commanding officer at Fort Laramie, and from different emigrant companies, as to their friendly character, which they handed to me with an *empressement* which showed the great importance they attached to them.

Some coffee, flour, and sugar were served out to them, together with all the tobacco I could spare; and after a plentiful repast, they departed for their village on the Laramie, about two miles below, with every demonstration of good-will. The head chief, who rejoiced in the very original title of "Buffalo Dung," gave me a warm invitation to pay him a visit in the morning; which I promised to do. . . .

Among the Sioux was one solitary, dignified old Cheyenne chief, who figured in the undress frock of a major of artillery, buttoned closely up to his throat, and of which he seemed not a little vain. To my surprise, I found that he did not understand the Sioux tongue at all, and communicated with those of that tribe wholly by signs. The Sioux chief with the unpronounceable name, the translation of which has already been given, was a noble-looking old man, and very much disposed to be sociable. He explained to me that he was greatly afflicted with sore eyes, and begged for something to cure them. I had nothing but an old pair of goggles, with very dark green glasses, which I gave him, and with which he was very much delighted, mounting them with great complacency, although it was then very nearly dark. With a spy-glass, also, they were very much pleased, and through it watched the erection of their lodges with great wonder and interest. A Colt's revolver, when explained to them, excited many remarks, and evidently increased their respect for the strength of our little party.

There was one circumstance, however, that attracted my attention in this interview with these untutored sons of the forest more than any other; and that was the perfection and precision to which they appear to have reduced a system of purely arbitrary and conventional signs, by which, all over this vast region, intercourse, though of a limited character, may be held between tribes who are perfect strangers to each other's tongue. After partaking of such food as could be hastily prepared for them, the principal men seated themselves on the ground, in a circle around the camp-fire in front of the tent, and the pipe of peace was filled and duly circulated in regular succession. Our esteemed friend and experienced mountaineer, Major Bridger, who was personally known to many of our visitors, and to all of them by the repute of his numerous exploits, was seated among us. Although intimately acquainted with the languages of the Crows, Blackfeet, and most of the tribes west and north-west of the Rocky Mountain chain, he was unable to speak to either the Sioux or Cheyennes in their own tongue, or that of any tribe which they could understand. Notwithstanding this, he held the whole circle, for more than an hour, perfectly enchained and evidently most deeply interested in a conversation and narrative, the whole of which was carried on without the utterance of a single word. The simultaneous exclamations of surprise or interest, and the occasional bursts of hearty laughter, showed that the whole party perfectly understood not only the theme, but the minutiae of the pantomime exhibited before them. I looked on with close attention, but the signs to me where for the most part altogether unintelligible. Upon after inquiry, I found that this language of signs is universally understood by all the tribes.

[The following account was written by an officer in an army expedition sent against the Powder River Indians in 1865, for which the sixty-one-year-old Bridger acted as a guide and scout.]

Left Piney Fork at 6.45 a. m. [August 26]. Traveled north over a beautiful country until about 8 a. m., when our advance reached the top of the ridge dividing the waters of the Powder from that of the Tongue River. I was riding in the extreme advance in company with Major Bridger. We were 2,000 yards at least ahead of the General [P. E. Conner] and his staff; our Pawnee scouts were on each flank and a little in advance; at that time there was no advance guard immediately in front. As the Major and myself reached the top of the hill we voluntarily halted our steeds. I raised my field glass to my eyes and took in the grandest view that I had ever seen. I could see the north end of the Big Horn range, and away beyond the faint outline of the mountains beyond the Yellowstone. Away to the northeast the Wolf

Mountain range was distinctly visible. Immediately before us lay the valley of Peneau creek, now called Prairie Dog creek, and beyond the Little Goose, Big Goose and Tongue River valleys, and many other tributary streams. The morning was clear and bright, with not a breath of air stirring. The old Major, sitting upon his horse with his eyes shaded with his hands, had been telling me for an hour or more about his Indian life—his forty years experience on the plains, telling me how to trail Indians and distinguish the tracks of different tribes; how every spear of grass, every tree and shrub and stone was a compass to the experienced trapper and hunter—a subject that I had discussed with him nearly every day. During the winter of 1863 I had contributed to help Mrs. Bridger and the rest of the family, all of which facts the Major had been acquainted with, which induced him to treat me as an old time friend.

As I lowered my glass the Major said; "Do you see those ere columns of smoke over yonder?" I replied: "Where, Major?" to which he answered: "Over there by that ere saddle," meaning a depression in the hills not unlike the shape of a saddle, pointing at the same time to a point nearly fifty miles away. I again raised my glasses to my eyes and took a long, earnest look, and for the life of me could not see any column of smoke, even with a strong field glass. The Major was looking without any artificial help. The atmosphere seemed to be slightly hazy in the long distance like smoke, but there was no distinct columns of smoke in sight. As soon as the General and his staff arrived I called his attention to Major Bridger's discovery. The General raised his field glass and scanned the horizon closely. After a long look, he remarked that there were no columns of smoke to be seen. The Major quietly mounted his horse and rode on. I asked the General to look again as the Major was very confident that he could see columns of smoke, which of course indicated an Indian village. The General made another examination and again asserted that there was no column of smoke. However, to satisfy curiosity and to give our guides no chance to claim that they had shown us an Indian village and we would not attack it, he suggested to

Captain Frank North, who was riding with his staff, that he go with seven of his Indians in the direction indicated to reconnoitre and report to us at Peneau Creek or Tongue River, down which we were to march. I galloped on and overtook the Major, and as I came up to him overheard him remark about "these damn paper collar soldiers" telling him there was no columns of smoke. The old man was very indignant at our doubting his ability to outsee us, with the aid of field glasses even. . . . Just after sunset on August 27 two of the Pawnees who went out with Captain North towards Bridger's column of smoke two days previous came into camp with the information that Captain North had discovered an Indian village.

26

GRIZZLY ADAMS:

The Wild Yankee of the Sierras

The fame of Grizzly Adams (1812–1866), the bushy-bearded California mountainman, rests on his unique propensity for making friends with grizzly bears—the most ferocious beasts in the mountains and the most feared by western frontiersmen. Adams kept grizzlies for pets. He trained them to hunt, to carry his pack, and to snuggle up to him on cold nights.

Born in Medway, Massachusetts, Adams a member of the New England Adams clan, was a shoemaker by trade. As a young man he worked briefly for a wild animal company, collecting wild beasts in the forests of Maine, New Hampshire, and Vermont. One day he was badly mauled while trying to tame a Bengal tiger for his employers, and the experience kept him at the cobbler's bench for the next fifteen years. But he grew bored with village life and, "being of a roving and adventurous disposition," he joined the California gold rush in 1849, leaving his wife and family to fend for themselves.

Adams had little success in the gold fields, and even less at trading, farming, and ranching. What he didn't lose to robbers and swindlers he lost by his own recklessness. Finally, "disgusted with my fellow men and their hypocrisy, their betrayal of confidence, their treachery and fraud," Adams headed for the Sierras, where he found that he had lost none of his talent or appetite for capturing wild beasts. Grizzlies were his greatest challenge, and his encounters with Ursus horribilis often left Adams torn and bloody. But he refused to be intimidated. Eventually he collected a whole menagerie—brown bears, grizzlies, wolves, elks, pumas—which he exhibited in San Francisco. P. T. Barnum brought Adams' show to New York in 1860, and in the same year Adams' autobiography, as told to a San Francisco newspaperman, was published in Boston.

Adams died in a few months after arriving in New York, having had his head split open by a blow from one of his grizzlies; but for a short time his book and his menagerie made him a celebrity, and helped to inspire the founding of the Central Park Zoo in New York and the Fleishhacker Zoo in San Francisco. Though a recent biographer has pointed out that Adams seldom let facts stand in the way of a good story, his skill at hunting and training grizzlies was real enough. In the following excerpt Adams recounts his capture of one of his favorite pets, Ben Franklin.

As the spring of 1854 approached, and the snow line moved higher and higher towards the summits of the mountains, and the grass began to spring upon slope and shelf, and the game to follow, and the hunters to come up, we had occasional visits from the rovers of the countries below. One of these was Mr. Solon, of Sonora, who stopped on his way to the famous Yosemite Valley, that most sublime region of California, and perhaps of the world. He came, he told me, having heard of my hunting, to persuade me to go upon a general hunt in the great valley; and it was not long before we projected a trip, which was to last about a month. The agreement between us was, that, in consider-

From The Adventures of James Capen Adams, Mountaineer and Grizzly Bear Hunter of California, by Theodore H. Hittle (Boston: 1861), pp. 196–221.

ation of my furnishing a horse, two mules, and the assistance of Tuolumne, I was to receive two thirds of the prizes and profits of the expedition. We immediately proceeded to make arrangements for the hunt; and, at the end of a few days, after bringing up the mules from Howard's, and laying in a stock of provisions for the subsistence of Stanislaus during our absence, we started off over the mountains southeastward, taking with us, besides the horse and mules, my bear Lady Washington, and a greyhound which I had purchased on my last visit to Howard's, and brought up with me.

Our road was rough and difficult; but, after travelling three days, we arrived upon the brink of the great valley. The first view of this sublime scenery was so impressive that we were delayed a long time, as if spellbound, looking down from the mountain upon the magnificent landscape far below. It is vain to attempt to convey the effect produced by those giant and picturesque cliffs three thousand feet high, that romantic valley-bottom with its green carpet and silvery stream, and those groves of trees, which are formed and placed as if a skilful artist had disposed them to portray the essence of romance. It is vain to attempt with words alone, to convey the impressions produced upon the mind by such an enchanting sight; magnitude may be imagined, beauty may be conceived, but the breadth and scope of these rocks, the tempered tints of these distances, the influence of the sublime forms, inclosing within their compass lawns and groves and grassy banks, presenting at every turn new and unimagined spendors,—all these must be seen and felt, to be fully comprehended.

But, however grand the valley looked from above, it was not until the next day, when we descended into it and looked upward, that we obtained the grandest views; just as, at Niagara, the most awe-inspiring sight is from the foot of the falls, looking up at the waters, pouring, as it were, out of heaven. There is a fall here, too, thousands instead of hundreds of feet in height; but it was not the fall, so much as the scenery below and around, that ravished my eyes, and produced impressions upon my mind that are ineffaceable. Who could ever forget those stupendous cliffs, with their fit associates, the tapering evergreens? or the greenswards, and oak and cotton-wood groves of the valley, with such surroundings?—and Flora adorns the carpet underneath, as brightly as the rainbows paint the spray above. We spent the entire day visiting every interesting point, and searching out the varied beauties of this inexhaustible valley.

The next morning, we moved about ten miles above the falls, and pitched our camp in a grassy glen, where for several days we hunted with great success, slaying deer, antelopes, and bears. In this camp, the greyhound unexpectedly presented me with a litter of puppies, one of which grew up to be Rambler, the companion of Ben, and, as such companion, a sharer in my affection for that noble animal.

My next adventure, and the most fortunate of all my career, was the capture of Ben Franklin, the flower of his race, my firmest friend, the boon companion of my afteryears. Upon reviewing the adventure now, it seems that an inexplicable influence was at work within me, foreshadowing the singular good-fortune in store, and attracting me, with an irresistible impulse, to brave the dangers and fatigues of beseiging, day after day, and night after night, the stronghold of his ferocious dam, slaying her in the very portals of her den, and seizing her offspring by fighting my way over her body.

We had moved to the head waters of the Mariposa River. On the first hunt there, I discovered a grizzly's den, and no sooner had my eyes fallen upon it, than I forgot all other hunting; I thought and dreamed of nothing else than how to take it; this, at once, became all my ambition. Deer, antelopes, panthers, wolves, and other bears there were, in plenty, about me; it seemed, too, that they crossed my path more frequently than ever; but they were unheeded; all my mind was taken up with the one sole idea of what proved to be the greatest of my achievements. Fired with this single thought, I determined to separate from my companions, leaving them to employ themselves as their inclinations pleased; as for myself, I had chosen my post, and would station myself at it, to succeed in my undertaking or die in the attempt.

Having thus resolved, I cleaned my rifle and pistol, sharpened my knives, prepared muzzles and strings, furnished myself with provisions, and, packing my blankets upon a mule, started off for the scene of my labors. It was a cañon-like ravine between two hills, densely covered with thickets of chaparral, with here and there a bunch of juniper bushes, a scrubby pine, or a cedar. A heap of fresh dirt in the thicket on one side, indicated the site of the den. It resembled the earth which a miner wheels out and dumps at the opening of a tunnel; and in size was as much as about fifty cart-loads. The chaparral about it contained some thorn bushes, but could still be penetrated. Like almost all the Californian chaparral, it was thornier than that found in Washington; but not so much so as that of Mexico, which cannot be safely entered, unless a man be clothed in leather.

In a short time after arriving, which was late in the afternoon, I climbed a tree, and reconnoitred the entire ravine. From that position, I observed and chose a spot for concealment in a bunch of junipers, on the opposite side of the cañon, and about a hundred yards distant from the den; and, upon cautiously crawling up, found, as I had anticipated, that it afforded a fair view of its mouth at the same time that it screened me entirely from observation. Though it was impossible to see far into the den, I soon ascertained its character to be similar to that usually dug by the California grizzly;—in form something like an oven, having an entrance three or four feet in diameter and six or ten feet long, with a larger space, or den proper, rounded out a the extremity, intended for the lying-in place of the dam and the bedding of the cubs. A number of such dens I had seen in the Sierra, varying only according to their position and the quality of the ground in which they were excavated. The ravine here was rugged and narrow; and the den penetrated its steep, bushy side, about fifty feet above the bed of the stream, at this time dry, which formed the bottom of the cañon.

After making these observations, and satisfying myself that my position was the most judicious possible, being convinced that there were cubs in the place, I went back to the mule, built up a little fire for her protection, and then, leaving her to herself, I took my blankets, returned to my post in the juniper bushes, and commenced my watch, which I kept up unremittingly till morning. It was an uncomfortable vigil; the ground was so steep that there was no level place to lie down, and the night was very cold. I thought several times in the course of it that I could hear the barking of cubs in the direction of the den; but, with this exception, every thing in the ravine was silent and dreary. Other wild beasts had evidently been driven away from the region by the fear of the savage tenant, who made all a desert in her neighborhood; so that even the lugubrious howls of the wolf and coyote, which custom had made music to my ears, were inaudible; and for the very want of melancholy noises, I was more than usually melancholy.

As the light of dawn began to peep, the thought struck me to discharge my rifle for two reasons: first, to see what effect it would have; and, again, to put in a fresh charge. Upon doing so, the report echoed off among the hills, as if they were playing with the unaccustomed sound. It had barely died away, when there seemed to be a snuffing underground, very faint at first, but growing louder and louder, until there was no mistaking it for the growl of a bear. I climbed a small tree, and looked and listened attentively, in hopes of seeing her; but the sound died away in a few minutes, and again all was silent. Descending to my place in the bushes, I continued to watch, now peeping into the den, and then looking at the vultures and buzzards sailing high overhead, till the sun rose, which, in that narrow gorge, was not until nearly noon. I then returned to the mule, moved her to a new pasture, and provided myself with a meal of dried venison, which I ate with excessive relish, and washed down with water from a spring at the foot of the ravine. After satisfying myself, feeling much refreshed, I cautiously returned to the juniper bushes, resumed my watch, and sat most of the afternoon with my arms ready for action;—but there were no signs of bears, and no noises save the chirping of a few birds among the chaparral. Shortly after mid-day I got a short nap, and in the evening went back and built a fire near the mule; but before dark I was at my post again, and there I remained, shivering, till morning.

About daybreak there was again a noise in the den, and I thought the old bear might be stirring, and prepared for her reception; but it was a vain expectation; for in a short time all was quiet, and it seemed as if she never would show herself. As the morning advanced, however, I discharged my rifle again, and was gratified, not only with a snuff in the den, but also with the sight of the occupant's head and paws, as she came to the mouth of her stronghold; but the most grateful circumstance was the yelping of the cubs, which could now be distinctly heard. Being thus convinced, beyond the possibility of a doubt, of the presence of what I sought, I directly made arrangements for an encounter with the dam.

For an attack, my position, chosen for an outlook, was too far distant; and, besides, a rugged, deep hollow intervened; so that, even had a ball wounded the animal, I would not be near enough to improve the advantage. Accordingly, after attending to the wants of my mule and eating my lonely meal, I moved my position across the ravine to a point about forty yards above the den, from which I could easily see the bank of excavated dirt, though not the entrance. To reach this point, I had to move through the bushes very circumspectly, and, therefore, slowly; in many places it was necessary to use my knife in cutting my way; and much noise would inevitably have brought the ferocious brute upon me, while unprepared. Upon reaching the position at last, there appeared to be nothing to disturb my view, except several twigs which stuck up a few yards in front; these I found it necessary to remove; and, for this purpose, laying aside my rifle for the first time in two days, and crawling forwards under the brush, I rose, cut the twigs with my knife, laid them aside, and, creeping back to my position, as cautiously as if in an Indian ambush, again felt safe in the companionship of my rifle.

As the third evening approached, I visited the mule as

before, but neglected to make a fire; and, hurriedly returning, took up my post for the night. Up to this time excitement had kept me wakeful, but tired nature now called for rest; and, as I sat with my blankets drawn closely round me, and my rifle between my knees, I unwittingly fell asleep, and for many hours was totally unconscious of my purposes in that wild and savage glen, and the dangers which surrounded me. It was nearly morning when I was suddenly aroused and dreadfully started by the screech of a panther on the hill above me. For a moment my very bones quaked with terror; but I soon reasoned myself calm. What a fool, thought I, to be thus started by the cry of a panther, a cowardly brute, which dare not stand face to face and fight with a man; while here I am, inviting a combat with a grizzly bear, the savagest beast that ranges the forest! With this comfortable reflection, it worked up my courage, and, being greatly refreshed with my sleep, felt bold enough to face almost any odds—but the panther did not approach; and in less than twenty minutes a distant scream notified me that he was already far beyond my reach.

Daylight came, but the bear still remained housed, and I began to think she would not make her appearance. My watching was now becoming very irksome, and, feeling much like bringing the adventure to an issue, I determined to rouse her. There was some danger in this; for my plan would probably atrract her directly to me, and, as sure as she should see me, I knew she would give no time to draw an aim. Before putting my plan in execution, therefore, I stuck my cap full of green twigs, and stationed myself in such a manner in the bushes that it would take a nice eye to discern my form, even though looking directly towards me. Having thus disposed myself, cocking and drawing my rifle, I uttered one of those terrific yells with which I have so often started the grizzly to his feet. It echoed like the roar of a lion up the cañon; and in a moment afterwards there was a booming in the den like the puffing and snorting of an engine in a tunnel, and the enraged animal rushed out, growling and snuffing, as if she could belch forth the fire of a volcano. She rose upon her hind feet, and exhibited a monster form,—limbs of terrible strength. She looked around in every direction; but in a few moments, seeing nothing to attack, she sat down upon her haunches, with her back towards me and her face towards the opposite side of the cañon, as if her enemy were there.

During these few minutes I stood as motionless as a statue, hardly breathing, waiting and watching an opportunity to fire. Had I met such an animal unawares, in an unexpected place, her ferocity would have made me tremble; but after my long watch I was anxious to commence the attack, and felt as steady as a piece of ordnance upon a battery. As I watched, I saw her turn her head towards the den; and, fearing she would retire, I gave a low, sharp whistle, which brought her to her feet again, with her breast fronting directly towards me. It was then, having my rifle already drawn, that I fired; and in an instant, dropping the rifle, I drew my pistol in one hand and my knife in the other. The bear, as the ball slapped loudly in the fat of her breast, staggered and fell backwards, and began pawing and biting the ground,—a sure sign of a deadly hurt. Copious streams of crimson blood also gushed from her breast, and I knew that they came from the fountainhead. The work was, indeed, nearly done; but so anxious was I to complete it at once, that I commenced leaping over the bushes to plunge my knife in her dying heart; when, gathering her savage strength, she rose, and, with one last, desperate effort, sprang towards me. The distance between us was only thirty feet, but, fortunately, full of brush, and she soon weakened with the prodigious energy requisite to tear her way through it. I discharged the six shots of my revolver, the last of which struck under the left ear, and laid her still for a moment; when, leaping forwards, I plunged my knife to her vitals. Again she endeavored to rise, but was so cloaked with blood that she could not. I drew my knife across her throat, and after a few convulsive struggles she expired.

My feelings, as she thus lay dead at my feet, it would be difficult to describe. I looked at the hills around, to see if any eye had beheld my success; but all was silence. I looked to the heavens; but all was quiet, only a vulture was circling like a speck in the distant ether. I was alone in the gorge, and, as I looked upon the dead monster, felt like Alexander sated with victory, and wishing another foe to engage, worthy of my prowess.

It is with pleasure that I dwell upon this part of my story, and I would fain distinguish it with living words. In all the after-course of my career, I could look back upon it with peculiar satisfaction; and rarely, in the following years, did I pat the shaggy coat of my noble Ben, but I recurred to my fatiguing and solitary vigils in the Mariposa cañon, my combat with the monster grizzly, my entry in her den, and seizure of her offspring. The whole adventure is impressed upon my memory, as if it had occurred but yesterday.

No sooner was the dam dead, than I turned towards the den, and determined to enter it without delay. Approaching its mouth, accordingly, I knelt, and tried to peer in; but all was dark, silent, and ominous. What dangers might lurk in that mysterious gloom, it was impossible to tell; nor was it without a tremor that I prepared to explore its depths. I trembled for a moment at the thought of another old bear in the den; but on second thought I assured myself of the folly of such an idea; for an occurrence of this kind would have been against all experience. But in such a situation, a man imagines many things, and fears much at which he afterwards laughs; and therefore, though there was really no difficulty to anticipate, I carefully loaded my rifle and pistol, and carried my arms as if, the next instant, I was to be called upon to fight for life, Being thus prepared, I took from my pocket a small torch made of pine splinters, lighted it, and, placing my rifle in the mouth of the den, with the torch in my left and the pistol in my right hand, I dropped upon my knees and began to crawl in.

The entrance consisted of a rough hole, three feet wide and four feet high. It extended inwards nearly horizontally, and almost without a turn, for six feet, where there was a chamber, six or eight feet in diameter and five feet high, giving me room to rise upon my knees, but not to stand up;—and its entire floor was thickly carpeted with leaves

and grass. On the first look, I could see no animals, and felt
grievously disappointed; but, as I crawled around, there
was a rustling in the leaves; and, bending down with my
torch, I discovered two beautiful little cubs, which could
not have been over a week old, as their eyes, which open in
eight or ten days, were still closed. I took the little sprawl-
ers, one after the other, by the nape of the neck, lifted them
up the light, and found them very lively. They were both
males; a circumstance which gave me reason to presume
there might be a third cub, for it is frequent that a litter
consists of three, and I looked carefully; but no other was to
be found. I concluded, therefore, that if there had been a
third, the dam had devoured it,—a thing she often, and, if a
cub dies, or be deformed, she always, does. Satisfying
myself that there were no others, I took the two, and,
placing them in my bosom, between my buckskin and
woollen shirt, once more emerged into daylight.

The possession of the prizes delighted me so much that I
almost danced my way down through the bushes and over
the uneven ground to the spot where my mule had been
left; but, upon arriving there, it gave me great concern to
find that she was gone. At first I thought surely she had
been stolen; but, as my bag of dried venison remained
undisturbed upon the tree, and much more as the tracks of
a panther were to be seen in the neighborhood, I became
convinced that she had been attacked by my disturber of
the previous night, and had broken away. Indeed, upon
further examination, I found her track, leading off through
the chapparral; and, following it over a hill and through
another cañon, at length found her grazing in a grassy
valley. She seemed much frightened at first upon seeing
me, but when I called her "Betz," she stopped, turned
around, looked, and then came up, apparently glad to meet
me again. Her haunches bore several deep and fresh
scratches, which were still more convincing evidences to
my mind that the panther had sprung upon her, but that
she had broken loose and escaped.

Mounting the mule, I returned to the dead bear, and,
cutting her up, packed a portion of her meat; the remainder
I left in the mouth of the den; and, turning my face out of the

ravine, I proceeded in excellent spirits, bearing the cubs still in my bosom, towards the camp of my companions. Upon reaching there, shortly after dark, I showed Solon what I had accomplished; and, placing the cubs before him, chose one for my own and presented him with the other. He thought that this was more than his share; but I insisted upon his receiving it, and he did so with a thankful heart. He asked me the story of the capture, and I told it, from the moment of my leaving camp to my return. He wondered much at my patient watching in the juniper bushes, and said he would not have done it, but still he wished he had been with me;—and thus we went on talking, till the dying embers admonished us of the lateness of the hour. Before retiring, Solon christened his cub General Jackson; I remarked that General Jackson was a great man in his way, but I would call my bear Ben Franklin,—a greater name. Such was the manner that, in one and the same day, I captured and christened my noble Ben.

The next morning, Solon expressed a desire to see the den, and we hunted in that direction. Upon arriving at the spot, we found that the bear-meat, which I had left at its mouth the previous day, was torn to pieces and almost entirely eaten. What had done this we did not know, and conjectured vultures; but, as our supply of meat was already ample, the loss gave us no concern, and we thought nothing more of the matter; and, as we had brought with us several torches, I told Solon to light one if he wished to examine the den, and go in. He, however, seemed backward about venturing, and finally I seized the torch myself, and prepared to lead the way. As I did so, the leaves in the den rustled in a singular manner, and, upon getting in nearly to the chamber, I heard a jump and a growl. This startled me for a moment; but, having my pistol in my hand, I kept my ground, and, holding the torch over my head and looking keenly before me, soon perceived the dark outlines of a wolf, sitting upon his haunches close up against the further side of the den, and grinning at me with a most ferocious expression.

The wolf, notwithstanding his cowardly disposition, is an ugly fellow to deal with in close quarters, and many men in this situation would have been very willing to leave him alone; but I determined to give him fight, and called to Solon to stand ready, provided he should get past me. Then, sticking my torch in the ground, and drawing my knife in my left hand, having my revolver in my right, I fired at the growling brute, and would directly have fired a second shot, but, without giving me time to do so, the beast bounded past, in the endeavor to escape. As he did so, I seized his tail and struck with my knife; but this did not stay his progress, and he would have certainly escaped, but, fortunately, Solon was well prepared, and gave a blow which laid him cold, as he emerged.

Having thus cleared the den a second time, I handed the torch to Solon, and he stooped down and started in. He had crawled but a few feet, however, when, in a spirit of mischief, I cried out to him to beware of the other wolf;—and he suddenly backed out, so terribly frightened that I was sorry for him. He would have become angry about the matter, but I laughed the humor out of him, and after a while he entered the den. I followed; and after viewing the place to our complete satisfaction, we came out and returned to camp.

Having thus caught our cubs, it next became a matter of difficulty, which troubled me several days, how to feed them. In the morning, I had given them a mixture of water, flour, and sugar, which was the nearest approach to milk I could think of; but this substitute would hardly answer for any length of time. While thinking over the matter, however, an idea struck me; and, on being put in execution, it worked much better than could have been anticipated. This was no less than making the greyhound suckle them. To make room, we destroyed all the greyhound's litter except one, and foisted the cubs in their places. As was to be expected, the hound was at first a little ugly towards these strange foster-children, and would snap and bite them; but by degrees she admitted them freely, and would even lap and fondle them,—so that, in fine, they at last shared in her affection with her own offspring. To prevent the scratching of their paws, we made little buckskin mittens; and these were put on every time they sucked,—which continued for about three or four weeks. They were only a little heavier and clumsier than the puppy at first; but they grew fast, seeming to thrive well on the milk; and by degrees we taught them to eat bruised meat, and finally, entirely weaned them.

Meanwhile we continued our hunting; and on several occasions, while in the region, Solon made trips down the mountains to the nearest mines, taking with him the horse and mules, packed with fresh and dried meat, which sold readily to the miners, and for a good profit. During these trips, Tuolumne and I, upon our excursions, took with us Lady Washington in place of a pack-animal; for, by this time, she had become so well trained that she answered every purpose. I had made a kind of saddle of green hide, resembling a Mexican *aparejo;* and with this we could pack upon her loads of two hundred pounds' weight, which she would cheerfully carry.

Our success in hunting exceeded our expectations, and various were the adventures we met with. One day I left camp with the Lady, and travelled over a large extent of country without meeting anything worthy of notice. In the evening, I came into the midst of a region of large cliffs and shelving rocks, full of holes and caves, and with many large cedar and pine trees. It was too far distant to think of reaching camp that night, and I therefore determined to spend the night there; and, searching out a safe spot near a spring of water, took up my station, having the Lady lying at my side. I had not been sitting long, when a gray wolf, with two fine pups about a month old, approached; and as it was not yet dark, I easily killed her.

The cubs gave me greater difficulty, having run into a cleft in the rocks, from which it was only with smoke that they could be dislodged. As they came out, I seized them; but, catching the last by the tail instead of the neck, it turned and bit my hand severely; however, I kept my hold and secured him. I then built up a fire near the spring, and threw myself upon the grass, waiting for whatever might come. In the course of half an hour, a band of deer approached, and it was not long before I saw half a dozen pairs of glistening eyes looking curiously at the fire. They presented a beautiful sight, and it was almost with sorrow that I fired at the foremost one, which fell; but the rest scampered off. The remainder of the night, having first roasted and eaten a bit of fresh venison, I endeavored to sleep, but was much disturbed by wolves and panthers, which kept up a dreadful howling and shrieking. In the morning very early I mounted the cliffs, and reached a very rough and barren region, higher up in the mountains than I usually went. Looking around, I soon discovered a flock of mountain sheep, in every respect similar to Rocky Mountain big-horns. I crept forward among the rocks very cautiously, till within sixty yards of the flock, but could procure aim only at an old ram which had a broken horn. I waited a considerable length of time, in hopes of seeing a better head; but at last, getting out of patience, fired at what there was. As the ball struck, the ram bounded, like a piece of India-rubber, high into the air, and fell dead, flat upon the rock; but the remainder of the flock ran up the cliffs, and before I could reload, had entirely disappeared. The ram, which weighed about seventy-five pounds, and the deer killed in the night, I packed upon the Lady, and, taking the wolf pups in a bag, travelled back to camp.

On another occasion, Solon and I started out very early; and, coming to a spot where two ravines came together, he started up one and I the other. I had not gone more than a quarter of a mile before I heard Solon cry out for help. I bounded up the ridge which separated us, and, upon reaching the top, saw him lying under a large tree in the other ravine, and a panther on top of him, apparently gnawing into his neck. I shouted to him to lie still, and, drawing my rifle, fired at the beast; but, in my anxiety to shoot wide of my comrade, I did not strike the panther fair, and he bounded off into the bushes, and escaped.

In answer to my inquiries in relation to this singular adventure, Solon told me that as he was walking up the ravine, looking only forward, and paying no attention to the trees overhead, the beast suddenly leaped upon his back and struck him to the ground. In the same moment that he fell, he cried out for me, and pulled the cape of his buckskin coat over his neck—and this evidently saved his life. How he came to have such forethought was strange; some others might have done so, but most men would never have thought of it; I, for one, would have sooner drawn my knife and fought. I asked why he did not fight; he replied that he was afraid to move, supposing that it would only infuriate the animal. Such a caution, said I, would have been good in case of a bear; but the panther is made of different stuff. By nature a coward and a sneak, he has the cruelty of cowardice, daring the combat only when he has a sure advantage, and wreaking a bloodthirsty ferocity most upon an unresisting victim. A determined stroke with a knife, though it might not have killed, would have terrified and put him to flight.

In the meanwhile, I stripped the coat from Solon's back, and found his shoulders severely scratched by the panther's claws. His neck, also, was badly bitten, but not dangerously; for the buckskin had fortunately saved it. Still the wounds were serious enough to require the best of my surgical skill, and I at once placed them under treatment. I led the patient directly to a spring which was not far distant; and, making him bend over it, with a piece of hollowed bark I poured water over his wounds, until he complained bitterly of the cold. I then put on his shirt, saturated with water, and over that, his coat; and, drawing off my own coat, put that, also, upon him. This was an easy matter, as my shoulders were much broader than his, and, besides, my clothing was always worn very loose, so as to give me perfect freedom of action.

A further article of prescription was, that he should drink as much water as possible; but he replied that he was not thirsty, and wished to know why he should do so. I explained the reason, by saying that he would soon become warm; the water would, more readily, induce perspiration, and that would ease his pains. He then followed the direction; and, as we returned to camp, though he started stiff, in a short time, by warming up and perspiring, he felt well, and travelled as comfortably as ever. My surgery, however, did not end here; for, upon reaching head-quarters, and examining the wounds closely, I found there were two, more serious than anticipated, in the back of Solon's head, where the marks of the panther's teeth were plainly visible. To reach them, it was necessary to shave the hair; and, as my bowie-knife was the nearest approach to a razor in the camp, it was not without wailing and gnashing of teeth that the tonsorial operation was accomplished. Indeed, before it was half done, the patient cried that I was worse than the panther. I excused myself by the wretchedness of my razor, and hacked away again; when he refused to submit any longer to what he called my horrible butchery. Like an expert doctor, however, I had Tuolumne holding his head; and, though he gritted his teeth and shouted with pain, I went on, with apparently the most unfeeling coolness, with my work, until the hair was as short as the nap of velvet; after which I bandaged the wounds with wet rags, and put my patient to bed.

Solon passed a good night, and the next morning, seeing he could get along alone, I determined to hunt up the panther; and, taking Tuolumne, proceeded at once to the ravine where the accident had occurred. We soon found the trail, here and there marked with spots of blood, and followed it for more than a mile over a hill into a deep canon. We at last came to a very rugged and brushy place, where it was necessary to creep; and, crawling along, we were suddenly startled by a low growl, and, looking low under the bushes, beheld the beast glaring upon us from a cleft in the rocks. At her side lay five kittens; but there was blood upon them and upon her, giving evidence that my shot the day previous had not been harmless. Indeed, had it not been for the shot, I doubt whether the panther would have allowed us to approach so near her den, without either attacking or fleeing.

Our situation, under any circumstances, was not without its danger; but so used to perils had I become, that not a moment did my judgment desert me. It had always been my practice, when out with Tuolumne, upon getting into danger like this, to give him the first fire. He was a good marksman; and, if he killed, it would be a great encouragement to him; if he did not, it would require a degree of coolness, which he did not possess, to fire an effective second shot. Accordingly, at my beck now, he discharged his rifle. He struck her, but not to kill, and the coward brute turned to fly; but, as she exposed her side, I bored her through the middle with my shot, and she dropped in her tracks. We immediately rushed up and secured the kittens, which were about a week old. We afterwards examined the dead body, and found, besides the wounds in the breast and groin which she had received, that my ball, the previous day, had struck her shoulder, and buried itself in her neck. We then drew our knives and whipped off her skin, preserving the head and claws, and, taking it and the cubs, set out upon our return. On arriving at camp again, Solon complained of lonesomeness; but when I presented him with the skin of the panther, he grew cheerful, and enjoyed the story of our adventure with great relish; but he would have wished, he said, to have been in Tuolumne's place, and have had the first fire at the beast.

For three or four days after this, we continued our hunting, and, on several occasions, made efforts to kill mountain sheep. These wary animals inhabit the rockiest and most inaccessible heights of the mountains. Wherever there is a high, rugged, jaggy, treeless waste, with only here and there a stunted bush, a clump of bushes or scanty bunches of grass, there may they be looked for, lurking in the clefts and nooks of the cliffs. It requires a good hunter to approach them; he must keep himself out of sight; he must allow no breath of wind to carry notice of his vicinity to their keen nostrils; he must be a sure marksman, for no second shot can be hoped for. In an instant's alarm, the shaggy flock, as if gifted with wings, fly up the precipices, and only the eagle can follow them.

Upon breaking up camp, to return to our general headquarters on the Merced River, we had, besides numerous bales of dried meat and hides, quite a family of young animals, consisting of two bear cubs, two wolf pups, five panther kittens and two fawns, which we caught upon one of our excursions. These young animals we packed in boxes or baskets, and placed on top of the bags and bales carried by the horse and mules. Lady Washington also, on the journey homeward, was required to bear her proportion, which she obediently did, till the panthers, which consti-tuted a portion of her burden, began to whine; and she then became so uneasy that I was compelled to lead her until they were quieted.

We travelled back over the mountains by slow and easy stages until we arrived at our old camp, and were welcomed by our faithful Stanislaus, who, during our absence, had protected our interests with remarkable ability. It was with satisfaction, therefore, that I presented him, as well as Tuolumne, with a new bowie-knife, a new suit of clothes, and new blankets, which Solon, in one of his trips to the mines, had purchased at my direction. Both lads, upon receiving their presents, repeated to me their assurances of devotion, and willingness to continue in my service; to which I replied that the Rocky Mountains was the next mark of my ambition; and they answered that I should lead on, they were ready to follow.

27

WILLIAM F. CODY:
"Buffalo Bill" Gets His Start

The appearance of "Buffalo Bill" Cody (1846–1917) and his Wild West Show in the exhibition halls of America and Europe in the 1880s and 1890s symbolized better than anything else the transformation of the frontier from a hard reality into a glamorous fiction. Trained buffaloes, carefully orchestrated Indian battles, heroes brave and true, and Cody himself, strutting and posing in his buckskins and fancy boots, a shock of white hair cascading over his shoulders, presented America with a colorful and romantic vision of its frontier heritage that was far removed from the dangers and hardships, the dirt and brutality and tedious, backbreaking labor that prevailed in the wilderness.

But William F. Cody was no stranger to the realities of frontier life. Born on a farm in Iowa, he was working at age eleven as a "cavvy boy," tending horses and cattle on an overland supply train. By the time he was fourteen he had tried fur trapping and gold prospecting, and in 1860 he was riding the pony express. By then he was an experienced plainsman, and during the 1860s he worked as a scout and guide for the Army in its operations against the Plains Indians. An officer who rode with him later recalled that Cody's eyes were better than a pair of field glasses, that he was an expert at following a trail, and a perfect judge of distance and the lay of the land. It was at this time, too, that Cody, though barely twenty, acquired a reputation—and a nickname—as the best buffalo hunter on the plains, having been hired to supply meat for the construction camps of the Kansas Pacific railroad.

The appearance early in the 1870s of dime novels and a play, The Scout of the Plains, *which glorified his adventures, brought Cody to national attention. Reveling in his new-found role of popular hero, Cody took to the stage himself, beginning a new career as a show business personality and entrepreneur. Although he again served as an army scout in the Sioux War of 1875–1876, performing some of his most spectacular feats, his later years were largely divided between his ranching operations in Nebraska and Wyoming, and his immensely successful Wild West Show. But his true fame rested on his early years as a scout, buffalo hunter, and Pony Express rider, and it was mostly these exploits that he recounted in his* Autobiography, *which appeared in 1879 and which was as colorful, often as preposterous, and as wonderfully entertaining as his Wild West Show.*

I was now in my fifteenth year and possessed of a growing appetite for adventure. . . .

I was not long in finding it. In April, 1860, the firm of Russell, Majors & Waddell organized the wonderful "Pony Express," the most picturesque messenger-service that this country has ever seen. The route was from St. Joseph, Missouri, to Sacramento, California, a distance of two thousand miles, across the Plains, over a dreary stretch of sagebrush and alkali desert, and through two great mountain ranges.

The system was really a relay race against time. Stations were built at intervals averaging fifteen miles apart. A

From *Buffalo Bill's Life Story; An Autobiography*, by William F. Cody (New York: Cosmopolitan Book Corporation, 1920), pp. 44–48, 112–114, 117–118, 122–126.

rider's route covered three stations, with an exchange of horses at each, so that he was expected at the beginning to cover close to forty-five miles—a good ride when one must average fifteen miles an hour.

The firm undertaking the enterprise had been busy for some time picking the best ponies to be had for money, and the lightest, most wiry and most experienced riders. This was a life that appealed to me, and I struck for a job. I was pretty young in years, but I had already earned a reputation for coming safe out of perilous adventures, and I was hired.

Naturally our equipment was the very lightest. The messages which we carried were written on the thinnest paper to be found. These we carried in a waterproof pouch, slung under our arms. We wore only such clothing as was absolutely necessary.

The first trip of the Pony Express was made in ten days—an average of two hundred miles a day. But we soon began stretching our riders and making better time. Soon we shortened the time to eight days. President Buchanan's last Presidential message in December, 1860, was carried in eight days. President Lincoln's inaugural, the following March, took only seven days and seventeen hours for the journey between St. Joseph and Sacramento.

We soon got used to the work. When it became apparent to the men in charge that the boys could do better than forty-five miles a day the stretches were lengthened. The pay of the rider was from $100 to $125 a month. It was announced that the further a man rode the better would be his pay. That put speed and endurance into all of us.

Stern necessity often compelled us to lengthen our day's work even beyond our desires. In the hostile Indian country, riders were frequently shot. In such an event the man whose relief had been killed had to ride on to the next station, doing two men's ride. Road-agents were another menace, and often they proved as deadly as the Indians.

In stretching my own route I found myself getting further and further west. Finally I was riding well into the foothills of the Rockies. Still further west my route was pushed. Soon I rode from Red Buttes to Sweetwater, a distance of seventy-six miles. Road-agents and Indians infested this country. I never was quite sure when I started out when I should reach my destination, or whether I should never reach it at all.

One day I galloped into the station at Three Crossings to find that my relief had been killed in a drunken row the night before. There was no one to take his place. His route was eighty-five miles across country to the west. I had no time to think it over. Selecting a good pony out of the stables I was soon on my way.

I arrived at Rocky Ridge, the end of the new route, on schedule time, and turning back came on to Red Buttes, my starting-place. The round trip was 320 miles, and I made it in twenty-one hours and forty minutes.

Excitement was plentiful during my two years' service as a Pony Express rider. One day as I was leaving Horse Creek, a party of fifteen Indians jammed me in a sand ravine eight miles west of the station. They fired at me repeatedly, but my luck held, and I went unscathed. My mount was a California roan pony, the fastest in the stables. I dug the spurs into his sides, and, lying flat on his back, I kept straight on for Sweetwater Bridge eleven miles distant. A turn back to Horse Creek might have brought me more speedily to shelter, but I did not dare risk it.

The Indians came on behind, riding with all the speed they could put into their horses, but my pony drew rapidly ahead. I had a lead of two miles when I reached the station. There I found I could get no new pony. The stock-tender had been killed by the Indians during the night. All his ponies had been stolen and driven off. I kept on, therefore, to Plonts Station, twelve miles further along, riding the same pony—a ride of twenty-four miles on one mount. At Plonts I told the people what had happened at Sweetwater Bridge. Then, with a fresh horse, I finished my route without further adventure.

[One day in 1867, near Fort Hays, Kansas], news came that buffaloes were coming over the hill. There had been none in the vicinity for some time. As a consequence, meat was scarce.

I took the [work] harness from Brigham, mounted him bareback and started after the game, being armed with my new buffalo killer which I had named "Lucretia Borgia," an improved breech-loading needle-gun which I had obtained from the Government.

As I was riding toward the buffaloes I observed five men coming from the fort. They, too, had seen the herd and had come to join the chase. As I neared them I saw that they were officers, newly arrived at the fort, a captain and four lieutenants.

"Hello, my friend!" sang out the captain as they came up. "I see you are after the same game we are."

"Yes, sir," I returned. "I saw those buffaloes coming. We are out of fresh meat, so I thought I would get some."

The captain eyed my cheap-looking outfit closely. Brigham, though the best buffalo horse in the West, was decidedly unprepossessing in appearance.

"Do you expect to catch any buffaloes on that Gothic steed?" asked the captain, with a laugh.

"I hope so."

"You'll never catch them in the world, my fine fellow. It requires a fast horse to overtake those animals."

"Does it?" I asked innocently.

"Yes. But come along with us. We're going to kill them more for the sport than anything else. After we take the tongues and a piece of the tenderloin, you may have what is left."

Eleven animals were in the herd, which was about a mile distant. I noticed they were making toward the creek for water. I knew buffalo nature, and was aware that it would be difficult to turn them from their course. I therefore started toward the creek to head them off, while the officers dashed madly up behind them.

The herd came rushing past me, not a hundred yards distant, while their pursuers followed, three hundred yards in the rear.

"Now," thought I, "is the time to get in my work." I

pulled the blind bridle from Brigham, who knew as well as I did what was expected of him. The moment he was free of the bridle he set out at top speed, running in ahead of the officers. In a few jumps he brought me alongside the rear buffalo. Raising old "Lucretia Borgia," I killed the animal with one shot. On went Brigham to the next buffalo, ten feet farther along, and another was disposed of. As fast as one animal would fall, Brigham would pass to the next, getting so close that I could almost touch it with my gun. In this fashion I killed seven buffaloes with twelve shots.

As the last one dropped my horse stopped. I jumped to the ground. Turning round to the astonished officers, who had by this time caught up, I said:

"Now, gentlemen, allow me to present you with all the tongues and tenderloins from these animals that you want."

Captain Graham, who, I soon learned, was the senior officer, gasped. "Well, I never saw the like before! Who are you, anyway?"

"My name is Cody," I said.

Lieutenant Thompson, one of the party, who had met me at Fort Harker, cried out: "Why, that is Bill Cody, our old scout." He introduced me to his comrades, Captain Graham and Lieutenants Reed, Emmick, and Ezekial.

Graham, something of a horseman himself, greatly admired Brigham. "That horse of yours has running points," he admitted.

The officers were a little sore at not getting a single shot; but the way I had killed the buffaloes, they said, amply repaid them for their disappointment. It was the first time they had ever seen or heard of a white man running buffaloes without either saddle or bridle.

I told them Brigham knew nearly as much about the business as I did. He was a wonderful horse. If the buffalo did not fall at the first shot he would stop to give me a second chance; but if, on the second shot, I did not kill the game, he would go on impatiently as if to say: "I can't fool away my time by giving you more than two shots!" . . .

The western end of the Kansas Pacific was at this time in

the heart of the buffalo country. Twelve hundred men were employed in the construction of the road. The Indians were very troublesome, and it was difficult to obtain fresh meat for the hands. The company therefore concluded to engage expert hunters to kill buffaloes.

Having heard of my experience and success as a buffalo hunter, Goddard Brothers, who had the contract for feeding the men, made me a good offer to become their hunter. They said they would require about twelve buffaloes a day—twenty-four hams and twelve humps, as only the humps and hindquarters of each animal were utilized. The work was dangerous. Indians were riding all over that section of the country, and my duties would require me to journey from five to ten miles from the railroad every day in order to secure the game, accompanied by only one man with a light wagon to haul the meat back to camp. I demanded a large salary, which they could well afford to pay, as the meat itself would cost them nothing. Under the terms of the contract which I signed with them, I was to receive five hundred dollars a month, agreeing on my part to supply them with all the meat they wanted.

Leaving Rose to complete our grading contract, I at once began my career as a buffalo hunter for the Kansas Pacific. It was not long before I acquired a considerable reputation, and it was at this time that the title "Buffalo Bill" was conferred upon me by the railroad hands. Of this title, which has stuck to me through life, I have never been ashamed.

During my engagement as hunter for the company, which covered a period of eighteen months, I killed 4,280 buffaloes and had many exciting adventures with the Indians, including a number of hairbreadth escapes . . .

[While thus employed] I had my celebrated buffalo shooting contest with Billy Comstock, a well-known guide, scout, and interpreter. Comstock, who was chief of scouts at Fort Wallace, had a reputation of being a successful buffalo hunter, and his friends at the fort—the officers in particular—were anxious to back him against me.

It was arranged that I should shoot a match with him,

and the preliminaries were easily and satisfactorily arranged. We were to hunt one day of eight hours, beginning at eight o'clock in the morning. The wager was five hundred dollars a side, and the man who should kill the greater number of buffaloes from horseback was to be declared the winner. Incidentally my title of "Buffalo Bill" was at stake.

The hunt took place twenty miles east of Sheridan. It had been well advertised, and there was a big "gallery." An excursion party, whose members came chiefly from St. Louis and numbered nearly a hundred ladies and gentlemen, came on a special train to view the sport. Among them was my wife and my little daughter Arta, who had come to visit me for a time.

Buffaloes were plentiful. It had been agreed that we should go into the herd at the same time and make our "runs," each man killing as many animals as possible. A referee followed each of us, horseback, and counted the buffaloes killed by each man. The excursionists and other spectators rode out to the hunting-grounds in wagons and on horseback, keeping well out of sight of the buffaloes, so as not to frighten them until the time came for us to dash into the herd. They were permitted to approach closely enough to see what was going on.

For the first "run" we were fortunate in getting good ground. Comstock was mounted on his favorite horse. I rode old Brigham. I felt confident that I had the advantage in two things: first, I had the best buffalo horse in the country; second, I was using what was known at the time as a needle-gun, a breech-loading Springfield rifle, caliber .50. This was "Lucretia," the weapon of which I have already told you. Comstock's Henry rifle, though it could fire more rapidly than mine, did not, I felt certain, carry powder and lead enough to equal my weapon in execution.

When the time came to go into the herd, Comstock and I dashed forward, followed by the referees. The animals separated. Comstock took the left bunch, I the right. My great forte in killing buffaloes was to get them circling by riding my horse at the head of the herd and shooting their leaders. Thus the brutes behind were crowded to the left, so that they were soon going round and round.

The particular morning the animals were very accommodating. I soon had them running in a beautiful circle. I dropped them thick and fast till I had killed thirty-eight, which finished my "run."

Comstock began shooting at the rear of the buffaloes he was chasing, and they kept on in a straight line. He succeeded in killing twenty-three, but they were scattered over a distance of three miles. The animals I had shot lay close together.

Our St. Louis friends sent out champagne when the result of the first run was announced. It proved a good drink on a Kansas prairie, and a buffalo hunter proved an excellent man to dispose of it.

While we were resting we espied another herd approaching. It was a small drove, but we prepared to make it serve our purpose. The buffaloes were cows and calves, quicker in their movements than the bulls. We charged in among them, and I got eighteen to Comstock's fourteen.

Again the spectators approached, and once more the champagne went round. After a luncheon we resumed the hunt. Three miles distant we saw another herd. I was so far ahead of my competitor now that I thought I could afford to give an exhibition of my skill. Leaving my saddle and bridle behind, I rode, with my competitor, to windward of the buffaloes.

I soon had thirteen down, the last one of which I had driven close to the wagons, where the ladies were watching the contest. It frightened some of the tender creatures to see a buffalo coming at full speed directly toward them, but I dropped him in his tracks before he had got within fifty yards of the wagon. This finished my "run" with a score of sixty-nine buffaloes for the day. Comstock had killed forty-six.

It was now late in the afternoon. Comstock and his backers gave up the idea of beating me. The referee declared me the winner of the match, and the champion buffalo hunter of the Plains.

On our return to camp we brought with us the best bits of meat, as well as the biggest and best buffalo heads. The heads I always turned over to the company, which found a very good use for them. They were mounted in the finest possible manner and sent to the principal cities along the road, as well as to the railroad centers of the country. Here they were prominently placed at the leading hotels and in the stations, where they made an excellent advertisement for the road. Today they attract the attention of travelers almost everywhere. Often, while touring the country, I see one of them, and feel reasonably certain that I brought down the animal it once ornamented. Many a wild and exciting hunt is thus called to my mind.